This superb collection of poetry, fiction and drama, culled from its pages published over many years, *Art & Understanding: Literature from the First Twenty Years of A&U* is a worthy, artistic, and important literary achievement, reminding us that the fight against AIDS is winnable but not over.

—Stanley Bennett Clay, author of *In Search of Pretty Young Black Men* and *Armstrong's Kid*

D1244971

I admire and respect the work *A&U* has done for the AIDS pandemic through it's literary crusade, providing insight and perspective through personal stories to illustrate the reality of the disease.

—Nick Adams, actor and AIDS advocate

A&U provides education, entertainment, and enlightenment for all ages; it's hard to combine all three under one banner, and it's especially hard to do it continually for 20 years. Here's to a job well done and to their continued success at doing so.

—Keir Gilchrist, actor

art&understanding

Literature from the First Twenty Years of A&U

Edited by Chael Needle and Diane Goettel

With a Foreword by David Waggoner

Black
Lawrence
Press

Black Lawrence Press

www.blacklawrence.com

Executive Editor: Diane Goettel
Interior Design: Rebecca Maslen

ISBN: 978-1-936873-12-8

Published 2014 by Black Lawrence Press
Printed in the United States

Some of the pieces in this anthology may be slightly different than they
were when they were originally published in the magazine.

CONTENTS

2001–2005

2006–2011

FOREWORD

Looking back and remembering when the first issue of *Art &
Understanding* came off the presses, I didn't think that twenty-
three years later, there would still be a magazine publishing
fiction, plays, essays, poetry, and creative nonfiction about the
AIDS crisis. In fact, I didn't think there would still be AIDS,
or at the very least, AIDS discrimination.

What you have before you are the first twenty years of *Art &
Understanding*, now commonly known as *A&U*; it's been a
microcosm of the publishing history of the AIDS pandemic for
two decades and counting. Young voices and older voices, unpublished fiction writers and bestselling poets alike, have been
published in *A&U*. Some have likened *A&U* to a literary Quilt,
featuring writers of all acumens. Some still in high school,
some Pulitzer prize winners, all of *A&U*'s writers share the
common thread that AIDS has affected their lives—and that
they have chosen to write about it.

Although *A&U* features writers whose first language is English, there have been many instances where their work is
known outside the United States. But in total, this book is truly
American. It has, in a sense, a unique place in contemporary
literature, for it doesn't pretend to be the best of AIDS writing; rather, it claims—and I think rightly so—a different kind
of "best of" status. It is a book about the American imagination and how the realities of AIDS were written by those we
have lost, and by those we are still fortunate to have writing
about them. This book is a sampler of the variety of voices
united against AIDS. The artistic vision of the hundreds, if not
thousands, of Americans who have put aside their day-to-day
literary activities and, with fortitude, have clearly spoken of
the pain, the sorrow, and the insult that a virus has made of the
bodies of millions.

This virus that causes AIDS is a muse of sorts. This wicked biological entity shared by so many in either their blood or in their familial relations, this destroyer of families and communities has united all of us to speak the truth, and not simply mourn through elegies for those who have fallen. Americans, through their literature, have always confronted the darkness, the untamed wilderness, the unknown but not unbearable. American writers are still writing against the failing light; against the sun that rises in the east on one shore, and sets in the west on the other.

Likewise, AIDS has extinguished many literary lives—the numbers are staggering and too long to list in this foreword— but take my word for it, the losses are remembered here by both *A&U*'s collected authors and the readers they address. For any publishing enterprise requires an audience, and without one, it is surely a vain enterprise. What makes *Art & Understanding: Literature from the First Twenty Years of A&U* so expressive of this community of pain but also relief is that we continue to this very day to recognize that the literary community cannot be obliterated by a single virus. The virus has too many foes. And it has too many words pitched against it. Like some sort of mythological monster, AIDS is the Medusa and the writers in this anthology are its fearless Perseus. Not afraid to look at the virus in all its ugliness—through reflection rather than blinded by fear—*A&U*'s writers are not just about vanquishing a disease that continues to ravage entire continents. Rather, *A&U*'s mission has always been to preserve for future generations what it was like to live through the age of AIDS: *A&U* is a literary time capsule. Not an ancient relic that you have to dig out of the ground fifty years hence, but something that reads as fresh as it did when the first voices—some of them published here for the first time—were brought forth.

Sure, there has been a diminishing of the AIDS press, as it once was called, but there are still hundreds of important American writers who still create important AIDS-themed literature. We've all noticed a gradual lessening of the HIV/AIDS crisis in America. More men, women, and children are thriving due to the direct effect of antiretrovirals. Although universal access is still a dream and not a reality, there has been a sharp decline in AIDS deaths here and abroad. A magazine built out of a crisis, or rather as a response to a crisis, *Art & Understanding* (*A&U*) has brought together disparate voices, both young and old, poor and wealthy; but all sharing a common goal: to destigmatize the disease, make it less foreign and more familiar to the hundreds of thousands of the magazine's readers, both afflicted by the disease or impacted by its destruction. Today, twenty years after the first issue hit the stands, many of the same readers are still with us—due in part to the success of their medications and due in part, I hope, to the talents of the poets, essayists, fiction writers, and dramatists that continue to write for *A&U*.

Herein is collected in this, an anthology of twenty years of *Art & Understanding*, the remembrance of the early years of an epidemic as well as the ongoing aspirations of newer voices who will, I hope, inspire a new generation of literary AIDS activists (and readers) to continue to write against AIDS. If anything, this anthology is proof that Writing=Life, and that those writers we have lost are best remembered by those who are following in their footsteps, one word at a time.

—David Waggoner

INTRODUCTION

Around 1991

"No one writes about the dead anymore./The fear of infection and loss isn't so dramatic now," writes Raymond Luczak in his backward-glancing poem, "Two Decades and then Some," included in this anthology.

Twenty-three years ago, when *A&U* was launched, AIDS was a decade old in the public consciousness, and yet attention to the disease was waning even then. News reports dwindled and fell into their still-current cadence of "event" coverage—new discoveries, new statistics, new pledges of funding, new strategies, new appeals. This archiving is only one kind of history, however—linear, chronological, big-picture. It helps us make sense of broad shifts, but it also tries to shoehorn AIDS into a narrative of progress.

Yet AIDS does not fit into a narrative of progress, unless one looks at the pandemic from a great distance, like a series of snapshots from Google Earth. Health rebounds; health falters. Vaccine trials fail. Prevalence rates go down, and then up. A once-suppressed virus develops resistance. Stigma abates and then is just as quickly reactivated. The pandemic continuously uncovers anew the systemic forces that persist—poverty, racism, gender oppression, homophobia, ableism—and exacerbate our life chances in the age of AIDS. So, writing a history demands closer attention to the synapses of everyday life, their sparks and pulses, their sputterings and breakdowns, minding the gap from here—to there.

How does one mark time when our clocks run differently?

A timeline runs through the anthology, noting who and what over the first twenty years have shaped the collective impact of HIV/AIDS on our lives: scientific discoveries, protests, advances in treatment, the deaths of public figures from AIDS-related complications, advocates who have stepped forward, organizations that have been formed, major works of art. Interwoven with this is another kind of timeline. The poetry, plays, fiction and nonfiction that make up the anthology—call it the history of how and why we care. It accounts for unscheduled emotions and unscripted thoughts. It's the record of our realities that nobody asked for—hearts burdened with others' disaffection; minds busied with processing stigma and discrimination and alienation; bodies avoided or banned or untreated; but, also, speaking out against untruths and injustices; making positive changes that benefit the lives of others; fashioning a path to wellness.

Against fear

Our society still wants to see AIDS through the lens of isolated individuals buffered by fear. Fear encourages us to close ourselves off to others. Fear encourages us to worry about our own survival, and not the survival of others. But survival is never an independent feat. We need others. We forge relationships, ones not sanctioned by the flows of capital or the pressures of patriarchy. Literature, like AIDS, lays bare the open secret of our interconnectedness. Here is the network by which all of our bloodlines are connected. Here are the genealogies of our affection.

Although the anthology is organized chronologically, taking five-year strides at a time to cover the first twenty years of *A&U*, it also showcases themes and issues that recur.

Against fear, we offer humor. In "Pouf Positive", a one-act-play by Robert Patrick, we meet Robin, a man whose body fails where his dignity and wit do not.

Against fear, we offer activism. Paula Martinac's heroine, Meg, honors a dear friend by participating in civil disobedience. She demands, "Money for AIDS!" in Senate chambers, a photograph of her friend pinned to her chest.

Against fear, we offer empowerment. See "Property Values" by Aldo Alvarez, which features a couple able to stand up to prejudice with the support of their family.

Against fear, we offer compassion. In "The Clay Ring" by Angela Lam Turpin, ex-lovers eke out enough time for tenderness.

Each piece of writing in this collection is an offering, a memory, an elegy, and a guide for the living.

Names project

The intent of the magazine was to archive cultural responses to AIDS—to become a meeting place of sorts for likeminded writers, artists, and readers. The loss of lives in the arts community was devastating. By 1991, in the literary arts alone, we had already lost Sam D'Allesandro, Allen Barnett, Joseph Beam, Bruce Chatwin, Nicholas Dante, Tim Dlugos, Robert Ferro, John Fox, Hervé Guibert, Michael Grumley, Michael Lynch, Peter McGehee, Cookie Mueller, and Manuel Ramos Otero, among many others. We would soon lose Steve Abbott, Isaac Asimov, Harold Brodkey, William Dickey, Melvin Dixon, David B. Feinberg, Essex Hemphill, James Merrill, Paul Monette, John Preston, Assotto Saint, George Whitmore, David Wojnarowicz, and Donald Woods. The loss did not stop there. Yet writers kept finding places to meet and share words with others. These poems, stories, plays, and essays are some of those meeting places.

In an essay adapted from a keynote speech at OutWrite '92, an LGBT writers conference, Melvin Dixon writes about how we can preserve the future of gay and lesbian publishing in the face of generational loss, "*[l]*esbians lost to various cancers, gay men lost to AIDS,"[1] in the face of his own death. He asks: "What kind of witness will you bear? What truthtelling are you brave enough to utter and endure the consequences of your unpopular message?"[2] And though he was speaking about gay and lesbian literature, he was also, in effect, speaking about AIDS literature:

> "…As for me…I may not be well enough or alive next year to attend the lesbian and gay writers conference, but I'll be somewhere listening for my name.
>
> I may not be around to celebrate with you the publication of gay literary history. But I'll be somewhere listening for my name.
>
> If I don't make it to Tea Dance in Provincetown or the Pines, I'll be somewhere listening for my name.
>
> You, then, are charged by the possibility of your good health, by the broadness of your vision, to remember us."[3]

The literature collected here carries the torch of Dixon's provocative challenge…

—Chael Needle & Diane Goettel

---

1   Dixon, Melvin. "I'll Be Somewhere Listening for My Name." *Love's Instruments.* Chicago: Tia Chua Press, 1995. Print 73–79.
2   Ibid.
3   Ibid.

art&understanding

Literature from the First Twenty Years of A&U

1991–1995

1991 The Red Ribbon becomes the international symbol of AIDS awareness thanks to the work of Visual AIDS two years earlier. • "Magic" Johnson announces he has HIV. • Queen's Freddie Mercury and movie star Brad Davis die. • *Art & Understanding* (later called *A&U*) becomes America's first nationally distributed HIV/AIDS lifestyle magazine.

1992 CDC expands the definition of AIDS to include women. • Tennis star Arthur Ashe discloses he has AIDS. • Actor Anthony Perkins, actor Robert Reed, artist David Wojnarowicz, writer and scholar Melvin Dixon, and sci-fi writer Isaac Asimov die. • Disclosing she is HIV-positive in a speech, Mary Fisher advocates for AIDS at the 1992 Republican National Convention.

1993 AZT is found to prevent the transmission of the virus from mother to child. • U.S. Congress and President Bill Clinton approve an immigration ban for HIV-positive people from entering the United States. • Tony Kushner's AIDS opus *Angels in America* opens on Broadway. • Derek Jarman releases the film *Blue*. • Holly Johnson, lead singer of Frankie Goes to Hollywood, divulges he is HIV-positive. • Singer Héctor Lavoe dies.

1994 Tom Hanks wins the Oscar for best actor for his role as a PWA in the hit film *Philadelphia*. • Pedro Zamora, a gay HIV-positive Cuban American, joins the nascent reality show *The Real World* on MTV. • Bill T. Jones debuts *Still/Here* to rave reviews. • Filmmaker and writer Marlon Riggs and poet Assotto Saint die. • David B. Feinberg publishes *Queer and Loathing: Rants and Raves of a Raging AIDS Clone* shortly before his death. • E. Lynn Harris's *Invisible Life* becomes a best-seller.

1995 FDA approves HAART—highly active antiretroviral therapy—a cocktail of drugs that slows the progression to AIDS in HIV-positive patients. • Olympic medalist and swimming star Greg Louganis announces he has HIV. • June 27 is declared the first annual National HIV Testing Day. • Record producer David Geffen donates $4 million to GMHC and New York's God's Love We Deliver, making it the largest single cash donation to the AIDS cause to date. • Rap star Eric "Eazy-E" Wright dies. • Mark Doty publishes *Atlantis*.

David Bergman
The Care and Treatment of Pain
In memory of Allen Barnett

I came to learn what the well can learn
from the dying and the gravely sick:
the fine art of living with the quick
unknitting of flesh. Tired and gaunt,
he faced me across the small banquette
and spoke as rare and welcomed rains
steamed up, like smoke from a cigarette,
the dark windows of a restaurant.

"See these bubbles rising from my head,
purple cancers 'winking at the brim'
which nothing's stopped, not even a grim
experiment with interferon
shot straight into my tumorous scalp.
So far the only result has been
I can find how far the lesions spread
by counting the needles going in.

Yet by the eighth I seem to lose track,
and at the tenth, I begin to curse
and not to myself. Meanwhile the nurse
continuing to work without pause,
reserves her comments until she's through:
'This wasn't so bad. It hardly hurt.
You need a positive attitude.'
Then leaves me listening to her skirt

rustle down the antiseptic hall.
I'm free to go. I gather my things,
coat and hat and a lampshade I brought
for a friend even sicker than I
who can't get out and lives nearby.
But on the street when I feel the sting
of the wind pushing me to the wall,
I allow myself the chance to cry,

this once to luxuriate in pain,
to bathe myself in the swirling tide
of the purest grief and then to ride
our agony so that I can reach
what has always stood on the other side:
a hopelessness that is not despair,
but a truth meant to bring me no where
except to myself and to this time.

And there I am in the busy street
surrounded by those who do not care
whether I'm to live, or how, or where
as long as I ask nothing of them.
They turn as I stagger on my feet,
a joke that can't even force a groan,
a drunken reveller who stands alone,
his humorless lampshade in his hand.

If now it seems I have only pain
to remind me that my life is real,
I mention it not as an appeal
for sympathy or understanding,
rather from a wish to make it plain
that it's earned a certain tender love
that I used to give to other things
which now I have no desire of."

He smiles at me—the lesson done,
and grabbed the tab and rose from his seat,
"Next time," he said, "it'll be your treat,
that is if there'll be another one."
He took from the rack his coat and hat,
a half-read book and a hand-carved cane,
and throwing a kiss to where I sat,
he walked through the cool Manhattan rain.

Easter Sunday, 1991

Mark O'Donnell
Pandora Then Heard a Small Voice
a friend has been diagnosed with AIDS

"Don't despair yet. I am Hope, Pandora!
Not a part of the mere world
—now overcast with pox,
roiling, many-fingered evils
and flying carnivorous fauna and flora—
but here, safely curled
in your tiny, infinite box,
exempt from the blackened air's upheavals.

I am Hope, the unspendable coin—
because to remain yours
I must remain virgin mystery.
The escaped and inescapable ills
I'm too frail to join
on their flight to colonize all shores.
I will recline, glinting, hinting while history
spins caterwauling over the hills."

Michael Lassell
Brady Street, San Francisco
for Roberto Muñoz

The apartment
is still standing, still about to fall.
It's circled now in Technicolors of
competing graffiti
more artful than we were to
stay in love.
Our names in cement are long gone.
It's my first time back since the news.

From the street
nothing seems to have changed.
My mind too has trapped the action in mid-flight:
how I hid in the closet (naked) the
first morning your family descended unannounced
and told your father we'd had
balls for breakfast when my Spanish slipped on
eggs. You shot your
one-note nasal laugh and spun on your heel,
but I'd cracked the shell of tension.
Your mother sat on the couch—
a miniature goddess of plenty, her feet
not touching the floor—and adopted me
in her knowing smile.

Here's a junk drawer more of memories:
an orange cat that lived through an airshaft fall;
the Twin Peaks fog from our bedroom window bay;
snacking on Stevie Wonder and your skin;
the double mattress we had to carry home
on our backs because
it cost every cent we'd saved.

After the first fight over nothing you
slammed into the street. I screamed
from the third floor into the dark I'd
die if
you didn't love me; you cried and
crept back up the stairs creak by
indolent creak.
We stayed together.
That time.
And when the loving was over—
three years, two apartments,
and a continent later—
no one died. Not
altogether. At least not
right away.

We left behind the odor of queers in the carpet,
the grease from our last
cooked meal,
a hole I punched in the plaster with my anger
and covered with the Desiderata so
the landlord wouldn't howl.

You see, it only takes a score of years
to make the bitter memories sweet,
like lemons in a sugar glaze.
I'd eat an orchard of them for you now
if you could be alive again to see me try.

Tim Dlugos
Signs of Madness

Recognizing strings
of coincidence as having
baleful or hermetic meaning,
e.g. the fact that each
of Ronald Wilson
Reagan's three names has
six letters, Mark of
the Apocalyptic Beast,
languorous and toothless
though it would have to be
to fit that application.
Smelling burning flesh
of sulphur, or a sweet
antibiotic sweat that
leaches into sheets
and pillows, like the smell
my mother had when she was
dying, or the one I suddenly
developed in the weeks before
I came down with AIDS.
Muttering at motorists
in other cars, hearing
one's voice pronounce
unspoken imprecation.
Wanting to impose Islamic
law for lapses of behavior
or taste within the city limits.
Limiting one's television
fare to programs one recalls
from childhood. Wanting
to call childhood friends
and ask them how they're doing,
how their lives have changed
since junior high. Memorizing
names of senators, bishops

of the church, or nominees for
Vice President from major
parties, and reciting them
at night to get to sleep.
Listing signs that all
may be no more right
in one's mind than is right
in the world, and feeling
less anxiety from identifying
symptoms in one's thinking and
behavior than comfort
in the list's existence
and delight at having
called it forth.

Virginia Pye
What World

It's best to begin with some conceit. Some way of summing up. It's elusive, her meaning, that's why she's sure she must begin with a phrase, a string of words like clues. There has to be an image to show this much sadness and confusion and understanding. To show the costs. The costs are crucial. But she's stuck still on that first phrase. She's sure she'll never get it right and then the phone rings.

What she remembers is that we each thought of one another as our long lost love. The mom we never had. The dad we deserved. The woman who would set things right. The man. That was fine at the time, she thinks, although it shortened the life of things considerably.

The answering machine picks up and she listens to one of June's miserable messages. Chipper: "Busy as bees over here. Call, why don't you?" Then, in a truer voice, "Mags, I'm just wondering. You OK?" Maggie flicks down the volume. Presses erase before June's even hung up.

Don came from Ohio. He once said he grew up in one of those districts of warehouses and packing sheds, sections of town Maggie made the mistake of saying people only drove through. He was trying to let her know he was a man of the people. Liar. At the funeral, she saw his family's large brick home. His grandfather started the copper mill in town. Old thorny Congregationalist outlived his eldest grandson. Donald Stone Sr. had an eccentric grand uncle who broke free from the church in town to form his own congregation. Freer, less under the hand of the state, the shadow of England, a church of equals, that was his intention. Maggie remembers this now because she never did get to talk to Don about the ancient minster's dreams. Turns out the older Stone had a partner in building his church: Maggie's own great, great grand uncle or some such distant ancestor. In a family genealogy she had found a photo of the two men arm in arm in 1879. A pair of idealists and free-thinkers, one with his sleeves rolled, the other topped by a bowler. The shot didn't identify which man was which. She wished she had shown it to Don, so together they could have guessed whose was whose.

"Look at us, my love," she would have said, "Inheritors of America."

Maggie wonders now if it would've bothered Don, not knowing who was who in that picture. He was a scientist searching for facts. Only practicing scientist she had ever known. Doctors she could almost understand, but that was about it. You could wait a good thirty seconds for the end of one of Don's sentences. Keith was the one who connected that to Don being a groundwater hydrologist. Keith said Don's eloquence was his precision. Or did he say it the other way around?

People said so many things about Don in those last months. No one had mentioned how he looped his rock climbing rope in perfect concentric rings, stacked his papers just so. No one stood up at the memorial service and said he folded his napkin at the end of every meal. When his hair was long, years before when they were in their twenties, Maggie can't remember ever seeing it out of its ponytail. She slept beside the man and doesn't think she ever saw his hair outspread on the pillow.

Precise then, clear in all things. Maybe she'll being with that. She will want to say early on that he died of AIDS. Otherwise people will search for it. She can almost make out the tops of the trees in Central Park. She can definitely make out the garbage men blocking traffic, dragging, scraping the overflowing cans out into the street at rush hour. The sound of horns rise, echoing off the buildings almost like music.

Don would ask her, did she catch his meaning? Did she understand the difference, say, between feeling tired and feeling sleepy? He wasn't serious. It was his idea of a joke. But he would ask her, could she see the distinction? He was always trying to pin things down. He never could imagine how she wrote for a living. He agonized over words. Perhaps he was the writer amongst them, caring as he did about meaning.

But now, she thinks, he's nothing but mystery. That enormous conceit, complete unknowing, death. You can't begin with that, she thinks. Too obvious and heavy-handed. She reminds herself this piece is only for the alumni bulletin, but after keeping silent at the memorial this is what she has to offer. She presses her fingers to the chilly windowpane and wonders if she ever knew the man, which has to be part and parcel of the longing, being in the midst of so much desire, such desperate hopefulness. Goes without saying they were much younger then.

Two weeks before, Maggie had gotten the phone call from Carolyn saying Don was finally dying. Maggie thought for a moment, then apologized for the silence. We had all known he was dying for the previous two years. There were fits of wellness, but only brief ones. The phone call had to come. Maggie wondered anyway, what do you say to a dying man three thousand miles away that you haven't been able to say to him as he lies sleeping beside you in the morning years before? You say what you said then, Maggie thinks, only you mean it more.

She had taken out a photo of him and looked hard. Don and a younger Maggie together eight years before. That shot he took by holding the camera in his out-stretched arms, their two heads huddled close as the fisheye lens bent them into the frame. Don's chipped tooth had never looked so large. His chapped lips. Maggie's hair crossed her eyes. She wished she could brush it aside and see her younger self more clearly. A shy girl, pressing her cheek against his.

She remembers the thought: this is what he'll have of me. He was moving to California that week. She had tried to look as if she couldn't have cared less. He was forever out of reach and she was more in love than she ever admitted, even now. In the photo, she tried not to show the double vision that made her aware already of the memory of the moment before the moment had even passed.

She returns to her desk and turns on the light. Richard will be home soon. "It's likely that the entire time we knew Don, he was HIV Positive," she jots down. "We just didn't know it until two years ago when he became ill. He may, or may not, have sensed it sooner." Her mind wanders. She's written nothing she'll keep. There's nothing more crucial to write about, she thinks, and yet her mind's off again: what to make for dinner, June's phone message, Richard's list of chores they must do together that weekend before winter sets in. How else could death be with us, she wonders, if not in a list demanding we caulk the windows and take out the air con- ditioner? Moth balls. Remember moth balls.

Carolyn must be hovering about her home like this, too, Maggie imagines, cleaning cabinets and straightening closets. Wondering what she'll do with his clothes and those books none of us understood except him. They met playing softball. Don had told Maggie about it long distance. Carolyn was tough. She slid into second, taking a good gouge out of his shin with her cleats. Just the kind of thing Don would fall for. Their love making was tough, he had said. She was getting over a long relationship with a woman. Also just Don's speed. Someone who could understand his tastes, he said, making Maggie cringe. She always felt too conventional. They weren't committed, Carolyn and Don. He didn't believe in that sort of thing, a single lover for the rest of one's life. How absurd.

Maggie thought he was right, in theory, still it made her face flush, even over the phone. She had been married to Richard for six months and was just beginning to make sense of the idea. That's why, as he told Maggie about Carolyn, he added that he'd never been with anyone who ignited him the way she did. His syntax was uncharacteristically ambiguous; somehow his precision had failed. Maggie couldn't tell if he meant her or Carolyn. "Which one of us?" she wanted to shout. "Who?" Only she didn't dare. She was with Richard now and always. And, of course, she never did ask Don about the men.

Maggie chooses to remember instead the touch of his hand on her thigh the last night before he moved away. They dragged themselves up the stairs to her apartment past the cigar smoke from 1A, the cat piss outside 3C, the bike on the landing. His fingers traced a line up the back of her bare leg. Then, hours later, after making love and Maggie's surprisingly ferocious tears, Don walked off under streetlight in the rain. It rained for weeks. For weeks, she thinks now, I lived in rain.

Carolyn was there with him when he died. "You can rest now, honey," she said and he shut his eyes and finally did. It's what anyone would have said, any of us: Maggie or Keith or Sebastian or Rachel or June or even Richard. But Carolyn, Don's newest love, had been the one. When Don told Maggie he had gotten married to Carolyn up in Reno, grabbing the certificate from the Justice of the Peace and then dashing across the snowy street to the Two Doves or the Silver Bells, he had put it all as a question, as if to ask, was it ok with her that he had done so.

She said she was happy for him. Don pressed her over the phone. Did it make her feel the way he had felt when she told him she'd decided to marry Richard? No, Maggie said, honestly and not honestly. She was happy for him. That was it. That simple.

By then she'd had plenty of time to get accustomed to the notion of him dying. Maggie understands now how easy it is to love a dying man. To finally let him have his life. To stop meddling and mucking about with each other's hearts. To wish him the best. To let him go.

And somehow in all that to forget to ask, to let it just slip your mind, the things you had meant to know. That great grand uncle, for example, to ask about him, about history and time. And more. Years of knowing taken from her, taken, really, from him. His is the sad story, she reminds herself now. His is the story that has come to an end.

Just the same, it bothers her. Don, she would ask if she could, what world is it you continue to see without me?

Arthur Nersesian
Milk and Bananas

When he told me he had been "diagnosed"
astonishment destroyed the naïve order
in which I expected people to die—
the old as barriers for the young.
He explained it would be wise
to kiss each other
every time we said goodbye.
He went over the posthumous routine:
drain the bank account,
exhume the death certificate,
file the insurance claims.
Was there anything overlooked?
The luggage of a life time
had to be packed into a briefcase:
How could I anticipate
who I would be at thirty, forty, or fifty?
Some sour like milk,
others sweeten like bananas.
When I shrugged, he answered,
"Find someone quiet, learned,
but arrogant and bitter.
Someone who gets angry quickly, forgives quickly,
who has never been loved by those he pursued,
only by those who pursued him.
Someone who feels he could've been great,
but never had the guts.
On the whole someone who feels
he got a rotten deal
—he'll tell you
whatever it is you want of me now."

Craig G. Harris
State of Grace
for Lawrence Washington

More bother than help
my nephew, just fourteen,
stands in the kitchen doorsill
watching me carve turkey and ham,
scoop up collard/mustard/turnip greens,
heat macaroni, yams, and corn puddin',
all the foods of family tradition.

Picking and nibbling
he notices the pink and black sticker on my phone
and asks the meaning of "silence equals death."
I stop to tell him of Audre Lorde's axiom:
"our silence will not protect us…,"
and the work of the
AIDS Coalition To Unleash Power,
explain to him that our
federal/state/local government officials
watch corpses pile high
with callous professionalism,
and that the survival of oppressed peoples
rests in our determination to continue to speak out
calling attention to ignorance and injustice.

He has known for some time
that his uncle is a "gay activist,"
the meaning of which becomes clearer
with each adolescent
calculation.

He wants to know more about my life
about my losses,
my special love for my brothers.
We share a secret smile
and agree we must spend more time together.

Understanding comes
with time and sharing
and feeling, I explain.

Later,
I bless the food.
the three generations assembled,
and those who have gone before
adding to the names of my biological family
those of the extended—my adodi
in my mind there is no distinction.
With palms upstretched and eyes fixed on faith
I list the ancestors upon whose shoulders we stand:
James, Bayard, Bruce,
Calu Lester, Fred Garnett, Eddie King,
Joe Beam,
Mel Boozer,
and on and on and on
until I hear myself utter your name
through tears of grief and anger
and frustration and fear
and I realize the tradition I know best
is the celebration of homegoing.

I feel my nephew's hand
comforting my shoulder
remembering that understanding
comes with time and sharing and feeling
and the passing of traditions of hope and struggle
from generation to generation.

Janet Howey
Still

He's in the late stages of AIDS.
Everything hurts;
light on his eyes,
food in his bowels,
sheet on his skin.

And he's an addict on methadone.
All day he shakes,
speaks in hoarse whispers.
Yesterday at dinner
he fell on the wall.
A long unstitched cut
curves over his eye.

He vomits his food,
soaks in his sweat,
claws for his breath,
soils his pants.

Still,
last night when he told me
he'd have to wait
'til Junkie Pride Day
to be in a parade,
he laughed like church bells
at the end of a war,
so I laughed too.

Rane Arroyo
The Amateur Matador

I.   *Before AIDS*

I was found naked in a neighbor's field.
Probation forced me into Junior College.
I chose for my major: scarecrow psychology.
I scared myself, selves.
I had the undergraduate dream of being an
    underwear model.
I was no one's heartbreak.
I was like Prometheus, the first atomic scientist
    punished for selling his secrets to the masses.
La misa was like a picnic with God.
My bed was ground zero.
It's not accidental that the atomic bomb's cloud
    takes on the shape of a man's cock.
Or that semen and stars are the same color.
Abuela warned me that Satan was hung.
I looked in many a bed for the true Cross and
    that's why I want to die in Vera Cruz.

II.   *After AIDS*

He is too young to be buried
with an interesting face or sin.
Flowers without roots blossom
atop his coffin, isle of fecundity.
The father and mother can't recall
the night the son was conceived.
Their old, nasty wound is closing up,
disappearing from this dirty earth.

Jameson Currier
Ribbons

For years Janet had trained to be an actress, taken classes in movement and speech, paid vocal coaches to help her with audition material, had photographs and resumes printed and reprinted. She had toured the country in a nonunion production of a revue of Rodgers and Hammerstein's music, then gotten her Equity card with an off-Broadway play that had subsequently closed in one night. Now, near forty, she was just growing into the types of character roles she had waited years to be able to perform. Her best friends were in the theater, wanted to be actors and designers and composers and writers; she met them in all parts of Manhattan for dinner and rehearsals, gossiped with them about new plays and musicals and backstage affairs. One evening, Janet went to a theater in the East Village to see her friend Allen perform Bertram in *All's Well That Ends Well*, and, afterwards, in the lobby of the theater, a young man presented small loops of red ribbons to theater patrons to wear pinned on their clothing to promote an awareness of AIDS.

Janet took a ribbon, her first, and pinned it proudly to her jacket. She had lost friends since the early days of the epidemic, had sung at more memorial services than she liked to remember, had volunteered at booths and benefits for Broadway Cares and Equity Fights AIDS. Now she was relieved that there was finally a way to show her support, silently, without having to constantly say, I'm sorry. Friends were always confiding in her about someone who was sick or leaving a show; now, at last, there was a way to express her compassion.

The next day, Janet auditioned for a role in a touring production of *The Sound of Music*, and, as she was singing the final phrase of "Climb Ev'ry Mountain," her tooth, a capped one, flew out of her mouth. Embarrassed, Janet lisped her apologies to the musical director and retreated to the lobby where she commiserated with her friends. Billy, a friend Janet had met from a production of *A Funny Thing Happened on the Way to the Forum*, told Janet that a mutual friend of theirs, Reb, had died the day before. Stunned, Janet did not know how to respond, and she took another ribbon from a young man who was distributing them outside the rehearsal studio.

That day, Janet and Billy decided to go for lunch at a diner in Times Square, a place where they always went after auditions. There, Janet described to Billy an audition she had had the previous week where she forgot part of her monologue from *The Glass Menagerie* and began to ramble into a speech from *Annie Hall*. After their meals, Janet accidentally spilled a cup of coffee and stained her new blouse. Upset, Janet became annoyed when the waitress, a new one, could not bring her more napkins quick enough to wipe up the mess. When the waitress reappeared Janet asked where Sam, the regular waiter, was. Flustered, the waitress said she had heard he had been ill for a few weeks. At the cash register Janet took another red ribbon from a box on the counter and placed it inside her purse.

Sometimes Janet hated wearing her ribbon; to her it was neither a fashion statement nor a political act, but something she just had to do. Sometimes it made her feel shallow and insensitive; she always noticed the color was wrong and it threw off her hair, it clashed with every outfit she owned, but she continued to wear it to demonstrate her feelings, human feelings, feelings that she, too, was worried—

worried not only for herself (she knew she was not immune to this virus) but also worried for her friends—friends who were defined as living in a high risk category.

Janet began noticing more and more ribbons, ribbons worn at auditions, at the theater, in bookstores and at the movies, on the subways and buses: satin, grosgrain, pavé, and rubied ones; even ribbons silkscreened onto clothing. At first Janet would study the faces of the other wearers, looking for some sort of sign as to how she should act: serious, solemn or proud, but then she reached a point where she never noticed faces, just ribbons in the distance: approaching, turning, following, retreating.

Days would pass between Janet's auditions; her luck at the temporary typing or receptionist jobs she found to help pay her bills was not much better than what she found as an actress. She had answered phones in abandoned buildings, flooded offices, and at lopsided desks; she had typed phone books, police reports, and TV listings, and had even taken dictation, phonetically, in languages she could not speak. One of the worst jobs she ever had was the day she spent eight hours in a small, overheated room typing license plate numbers into a computer that kept shutting off and losing everything she had done; by the end of the day Janet had stored up so much anger and frustration that she stopped to complain to her supervisor on her way out. But Janet's supervisor, a woman not much older than Janet, noticed the red ribbon pinned on Janet's jacket and before Janet could even open her mouth to protest about the working conditions, the woman had pressed her hand lightly against the twirl of the fabric, and said she had lost her brother over two years ago. On her way home that evening, Janet stopped at a drug store and bought a spool of red ribbon and a box of safety pins.

Janet was aware that her ribbon would not feed anyone, would not end discrimination, provide funds or leadership or research for a cure for AIDS. But the things she saw, the words she could not speak, forced her to acknowledge her own emotions and fears. She cut a ribbon after reading the obituary of one of her favorite soap opera actors, cut another after noticing a homeless man with a sign that read he was ill, cut more when she passed a crowd of demonstrators protesting the rising price of medications. All these ribbons she began to keep in her purse; she could never give them out to other people. They were her ribbons. At one point, Janet joked there must be hundreds in her purse by now. Sometimes, when reaching inside, she hoped she might prick herself on one of the pins—a way of keeping her anxiety and sympathy tangible with pain. In the evenings she began cutting more and more ribbons, the radio announced that almost one-third of the African population was infected, another reporter said Asia was destined to become a wasteland, infected immigrants were now being banned entry into her own country. And her purse, now a large bag, really, became crowded with more and more ribbons. When Allen told her one afternoon that his buddy had died, a young man who had moved from Memphis to Manhattan to be a comic and whom Allen had taken care of for over seven months, Janet could no longer cut just one ribbon—Allen had also confided that he, too, was now infected.

And then one day Janet landed a role in a television commercial; she had been through three callbacks for a casting agent who was looking for a large woman who could tap dance in high heels. Janet was convinced that this was her opportunity, her chance, her moment to shine—really shine—as a performer. She arrived in Times

Square, where filming was to take place, early one blustery spring morning. The wind was so irritating and chilly that morning that Janet huddled close to the archway of a building; garbage flew through the streets as fast as taxis. Janet waited for over an hour for the production crew to arrive, but when no one showed up, she went to a pay phone and called her answering service, only to find out that the director had died the evening before.

Wordless once again, Janet slammed the phone down, turned and walked toward the street, when the heel of her shoe missed the curb and she stumbled to the ground. Her purse, falling, slipped open and the wind lifted a river of red ribbons skyward like a startled flock of birds. Janet can still recall her frightened scream then—her anger and bitterness and hurt and frustration—all tossed into the sky with an anguish for deliverance.

Years later, when I met her at an audition, Janet told me she still searched the ledges of buildings for signs of her lost ribbons, fluttering in the wind like heartbeats.

Christopher Hewitt
All I Know To Do

Now even the numbers
have no meaning for me
metaphors like stars
snuff out   Oh I care
but I repeat myself
the chanting   the banners
the riotous passions
of the war against the ones
who look the other way

My friend dies
inch by inch
beneath the skin
His forehead tightens
shines
skull shield
the first sign
He works still
has friends
eats less
takes the necessary
drugs
shrugs off
side effects
says he's fine

On days off
he helps the kids
with AIDS
die as safely
as they can
and seeing his own death
in them
he mourns himself
I know

but I do not pry
do not infringe
I will probably outlive him
damnit
Damn the disease

I hold him so tightly
as if holding him
could cure him
as if one hug
could fend off
the attack
It's all I know to do
I smell his cologne
on my beard
the scent of wild gardenia
of dogwood in evening
his essence
his sweet silence
his manhood's tender courage
that I love so
that I love so

Janell Moon
Going Fishing

The day came when you couldn't walk
not even leaning on your cane
the wood too hard
pressed through your shallow skin
your bones too raw from illness.

The chill set in one November day
and it stayed
no matter what we did
we couldn't collect you back
not all of you anyway.

In the evenings we took turns
reading poetry to you
your love of language shining

one Wednesday, we carried you
to your white painted chair
the one with red flowers
so you could sit and watch
the meandering river you loved

brought fresh juices
wrapped you in warm blankets
covered your bald head with a soft felt hat
with your buttons pinned
STOP THE BAN and WE ARE EVERYWHERE

watched your eyes follow the current to the bend
you cleared your throat then
the strain showing in your neck

tell everyone I'm going now
say good-by for me
see the curve where the river narrows
I think I'll go there fishing
back to the quiet waters
the place beneath all cares...

Paula Martinac
Unusual People, Extraordinary Times

On Tuesday morning, Meg borrows a dress from her roommate India. India works as a paralegal and has several dresses, as well as a skirt or two. Meg's job at the all-night quick print has no dress code, and Meg wears the same pair of blue jeans all week. The dress hangs a little too long on Meg, but India cinches it up with a belt.

Meg's best shoes are a pair of heavy black oxfords, and when she tries these on with India's dress, India can't stop laughing. At first Meg thinks it's funny, too, then she panics when she remembers this is serious business. India's feet are a couple of sizes bigger than Meg's, and Meg yells at India, "Why can't you have normal feet?" So India calls up her lover, who takes something closer to Meg's size, and she comes to the rescue with a pair of cordovan flats.

"They don't really make it with the dress," says India, who seems to forget for a moment that this is not about fashion, "but the coat will cover the dress up."

"I could skip the dress," Meg considers, "and go naked under the coat, with Jim's picture taped over my chest."

"Girl, you'll be in enough trouble," India reminds her, "without adding 'indecent exposure' to the list."

This seems like good advice. Meg has never been arrested before, and she is not completely sure she is ready for it now. Her ex-lover Eva has been arrested for every cause from abortion rights to nuclear disarmament. She is trained in civil disobedience and goes to demonstrations just to get hauled off in a paddy wagon. She considers it one of her functions in life. "Certain people," she says, "are unusually good at civil disobedience, and they have a responsibility to do it." Meg is thinking now that, unlike Eva, she has never considered herself an unusual person, and maybe that is why their relationship didn't work.

India brings out the coat, a long tan trench coat with a thick buckle that, with the shoes and dress, makes Meg look like a business school reject. But she does not say this to India, who wears these clothes every day and probably thinks they make her look successful. On Meg, who is too short and slight to carry them off, they just look dumb.

"It's okay," India assures her, seeming to read her mind. "You're supposed to be a tourist, remember? From some podunk town. You don't have to look great."

"I just don't want to look comical," Meg says, "like it's a joke. We have to be serious about this. It won't work if any of us look silly. We won't pull it off."

Then India says something comforting like, "You look terrific. Go get 'em," and it is time for Meg to go.

She could walk, but she decides to take the bus because the shoes are just a hint too tight and they are already biting her where they cross her toes. She will have blisters tonight. But maybe she will be spending the night in jail, so blisters will be the least of her worries.

The bus cuts onto State Street and Meg thinks to herself, "Only four more blocks," and wonders if she should forget the whole thing. Her friend Jim was no activist. He bragged about not reading the newspaper. He missed most of the big things going on in the world. Whenever she said something to him about the reunification of Germany or Robert Mapplethorpe, he'd shrug his shoulders and give her a quizzical look. He was just a quiet guy with glasses and an enormous nose who worked the night shift with her at the quick print. When Meg and Eva broke up, Jim stuck with her for twenty-four hours because she couldn't stand the idea of being alone. After work that night, they stayed up and played gin rummy and ate do-nuts till it was time to work again. Jim was always falling in love with the wrong man and not getting what he wanted out of the re-lationship. "Just once," he said, "I wish some hunk would send me flowers." On his thirtieth birthday, Meg sent him a bouquet that cost a chunk of her paycheck. The card read, "I'm not a hunk, but some girls think I'm cute. Have a terrific day."

Now she has a picture of him pinned to the dress under her coat. It is a Polaroid from one night at the quick print when there was a snowstorm but their boss made them stay open anyway. They had no customers all night, and Meg and Jim made Xerox paper hats in different colors for everyone there and they turned up the radio and danced. Another guy had a pint of Jack Daniels. The picture of Jim shows him with a big smile on his face, the biggest Meg had ever seen. He has his arm around Meg, who is smiling up at him. The flash of the Polaroid makes their faces very bright, and Jim's nose prominent, while the shop behind them fades into shadow. It is the only picture she has of Jim, and she has mounted it on a piece of Xerox paper with the words, "Jim Gruba, 1959–1990," beneath it.

The bus jerks to a stop, and Meg gets off. Waiting on the corner are six other people, each dressed in his or her own conception of tourist's clothes. Bart, her friend who asked her to take part in this and whose idea it was, has thought to hang an Instamatic camera from his neck. Meg knows the others by name only. She met them two nights ago, when they convened at Bart's for a rehearsal and briefing.

She knows she is to pretend to be married to Donald, who is Bart's lover. He has brought cheap silver wedding bands and they slip them onto their fingers now on the street corner, watching each other as they do. Donald whispers, "This feels like a ceremony," and Meg nods. She knows that Donald and Bart and the others all have photographs inside their coats, too, but it is not the time or place to reveal them. She slips a hand through Donald's arm as Bart announces, "Okay, let's go."

Meg has lived in this city for all of her adult life, but she has never been inside the state capitol building. Her understanding of representative government at the state level is a little shaky. For today only, she has learned the name of her state senator, but in the moment when they pass through the doors of the capitol, she wonders how many senators there are altogether. Why didn't she look this up, or ask Bart? She turns to question Donald on this, but his brow is furrowed and she decides not to bother him. Besides, she reasons, they will learn this on their tour.

They have an eleven o'clock appointment in the rotunda with a woman in a dark suit and a nametag that reads, "Mrs. Vance." She has never been to Pottersville, she says—is it very far away? How long will they be staying, and are they enjoying their trip?

Bart answers all the questions along with Jackie, who is his wife for a day. They are the oldest and most responsible looking. Bart's hair is graying at the temples in a way that causes young men to swoon. Jackie has been active in the local feminist community for as long as anyone can remember.

Meg tries to listen to Mrs. Vance, but her eyes keep wandering off and with them, her thoughts. The rotunda is a dizzying height. There are a lot of security guards, each with a fat revolver on his hip. They have round young faces, and Meg wonders if they have ever held another job. Once she read a recruitment notice in the post office for police officers and was horrified to learn that sixteen-and-a-half-year-olds were eligible to take the test. Now what is running through her mind is "Young boys with guns." She finds she cannot release Donald's arm.

They follow Mrs. Vance through a corridor lined with paintings of men with white beards and faces and the chains of pocket watches gleaming on their dark suit coats. None of the faces are friendly, and they all look amazingly the same. Governors all, Mrs. Vance explains. Meg thinks of the current governor, a short and uninspiring man whom no one seems to recall electing. She wonders if his portrait will take on the same look as all of these.

The corridor leads into a lobby with three sets of massive mahogany double doors. Donald pats her hand on his arm. He has been to the Capitol before and must know where they are.

"The Senate chambers," Mrs. Vance announces proudly, but Meg has already figured it out. "Unfortunately, I can't take you in today. As you may know, the Senate is in session, debating the Governor's proposed budget."

Mrs. Vance says something else that Meg cannot hear over the pounding of her own heart. As Mrs. Vance rounds the corner to escort them down another hallway, Bart and Jackie turn to the rest of them and nod once, firmly. Meg puts herself into automatic drive.

And then it is happening, just like they rehearsed. On cue, Bart and Jackie burst through the doors of the Senate chambers with the rest of them close behind. In front of them, Meg discerns a sea of white men's faces turned in alarm toward the doors. They all seem to be wearing identical gray suits. Someone at the front of the hall shouts hoarsely, "What the fuck!" At Bart's signal, he and his companions throw open their coats to show the photos of their friends pinned to their chests, their voices mingling in one echoing refrain, "Money for AIDS! Money for AIDS!" Bart and Jackie quickly produce two rolls of bright red plastic tape and they begin taping themselves and the others to the mahogany doors. As she watches the tape criss-crossing her chest, binding her to this building she doesn't know, Meg feels for a moment like it is happening in a dream. She has let go of Donald's arm, but now they are taped together, and his loud voice booming over hers presses her to yell out the words. "Cut the red tape! Money for AIDS!" Then it is no dream.

What seems like longer is really only seconds. The security guards are on them, some with guns drawn. Mrs. Vance stands to the side, whining to a man with a walkie-talkie. "Oh, I didn't know," she says. "They seemed so real."

As they have planned, they do not resist arrest, but neither do they cooperate. When the police reinforcements come, dozens of them, far too many for so few, they will not walk to the paddy wagon. They have practiced this, and Meg watches as Jackie becomes dead weight, a rag doll that four police officers have to carry out. "Money for AIDS!" Jackie cries triumphantly as they struggle with her weight and disappear down the corridor.

Then they are untaping Meg and Donald. "You have the right to remain silent," a baby-faced officer says as he fumbles with the tape through plastic-gloved hands, ripping Jim's picture. She almost says, "No, not the picture!" but then remembers why she is doing this. "Money for AIDS!" she shouts into the policeman's face, then collapses into her rehearsed heap.

And then they take her out, back down the corridor, while she concentrates on being heavy. She tries not to think about the pain in her wrists where they have cuffed her, or the possibility that at any moment a gun could fire. Instead, she focuses on how hard the young officer she shouted at is breathing; it echoes in these ponderous halls. This time down the corridor, the faces of the governors look different to Meg, startled almost. Through her fear she smiles, and behind her, trailing down the hall, she hears Donald's fervent cry, "Cut the red tape! Money for AIDS!"

Outside in the sunshine and the cool air, a crowd has gathered, including news reporters who snap her picture and ask what she wants. "Money for AIDS!" she shouts again, and someone takes another shot. Over the voices of the press and the police, she hears another sound, the united chant of "Act up! Fight back! Fight AIDS!" from a group of supporters she cannot see. All she can see is the clear sky over her head, over the policeman's caps. It is a shade of blue she hasn't noticed in a long time, and the puffy white clouds form pictures against it. In one of them, she can almost see the profile of Jim's incredible nose.

Assotto Saint
Vital Signs
for David Frechette

medical absurdities multiply in necessity
stripping all dignity
low rate

there is this masked ball
nurses waltz out their delirium of blood
cold black hands; this hour, friends are few
how could six months elapse without a vanity mirror
our brother, our brother: how it was
to be alive

unearth
from a pillow of sorrow
the logic of illusions—just that, only that—
wrapped with fungi, your tongue sprouts no more metaphors
but the will endures like eucalyptus
oasis of fear

every minute or so
your red traffic-light eyes glare
& ward off the ghost who like a crow
looms to swallow your guts
numb your body into
a corpse

Robert Patrick
Pouf Positive
a one-act play
Dedicated to Robin Wood

> "Not marble, nor the gilded monuments
> Of princes, shall outlive this powerful rhyme…"
> William Shakespeare, *Sonnet 55*

Time & Place: The setting is Robin's apartment on an upper floor of a building in New York's Greenwich Village. It features everything a retentive queen would have acquired living in New York from 1967 through 1987. Posters are layered on the walls. The earliest are vivid old movie posters, then pop art, some Beardsley, some personality posters of Kennedy and Che, some psychedelic rock and religion, some gay power, some gay theater, Evita and Annie, disco stars, opera, est, Dolly Parton, and finally flyers for AIDS benefits. In every layer are photos torn from increasingly explicit male porn magazines. A clothes rack holds garments ranging from fluffy sweaters and chinos to jeans and ponchos, gowns and boas, glittered jump suits, rhinestoned T-shirts, yellow rain slickers covered in graffiti, military uniforms, djellebas, and finally a few conservative business suits. A revolving wire paperback rack holds hundreds of volumes. A shelf holds a complex stereo system and innumerable records and tapes. Many dead plants hang from the ceiling, along with a dusty crepe-paper piñata in the shape of Miss Piggy, and a mobile, whose dangling elements are a star, a dollar sign, a peace sign, a hypodermic, a gold record, a muscle man, a Rolls Royce, a computer, and Tinker Bell. Propped up in a wicker peacock chair is **ROBIN**, an emaciated man of about forty. He wears pajamas and has a coverlet over his lap. Beside him is a table covered with sickroom paraphernalia, flowers in a vase, condolence cards, a telephone, and an unactivated answering machine. Through a window beside him, we see a church steeple and an early morning sky. At rise, **ROBIN** is writing something on a pad across his knees.

ROBIN *[WITH A FINAL PENCIL FLOURISH]*
There! That just about says it! *[He tears it off, weakly, folds it, and looks for a place to put it, deciding finally on his pajama pocket.]* Now. Let's see if we can still manage a limerick. *[He speaks as he writes]* There once was a Manhattan queen—*[Phone rings. He ignores it.]*—With nothing that she hadn't seen *[Phone rings]*—Til they said, "No charades." *[Phone rings. He grows annoyed.]* "You're a person with AIDS." *[Phone rings]* "Abandon all plans for the screen?" *[Phone rings]* "You'd better put down that marine?" *[Phone rings]* "Don't subscribe to a new magazine?" *[Phone rings]* Mom didn't turn on your machine. *[Answers phone]* Okay, I can't make little songs out of my great sorrows; I may as well talk to you. But be advised: If you're calling to tell me you've got it, save both our breaths. Just say, "ditto," And leave me to my beads. Oh, Bob! Of course you haven't got it; Who'd give it to you? Except a good-hearted U.S.O. girl like me? And we were 'way back in the sixties, When the word "AIDS" was generally preceded by the words "American Military." How am I? Well, when I think of what I've got, I feel like shit, But when I think of how I got it, I can't complain. How are you? I know you've called. I hate those "Twilight Zone" episodes where people install phones in their coffins, so I haven't been answering mine. This exception is not because I still love you, but because I've written some hilarious last words and I want someone literate listening, just in case I croak while Mom and Sis are out at morning mass. They're here to identify the body—which millions could do in the dark— and to pray for the soul, the mind being unknown to them. You, I presume, have called to glean piquant detail on what it's like to die as I have lived, a sociosexualogical statistic. I know you writers, you're life's hungry men. Well, here's a fairly poignant paradox for your next play: I came home from a rally for gay rights only to learn I have the great gay wrong. Wait, that isn't a paradox, is it? It's an irony. It's an irony; it's one of life's little ironies, like Anita Bryant turning out to be right. Bob, don't bother to answer back. Anything said to me at this point Might as well be written on a decomposing squash. The brain goes first, you know—except for the portions dedicated to pain, which are apparently immune. "Do I need anything?" Oh, how droll. Wait, I may have just enough strength for a comeback to that: No, I don't need anything. I

already have cancer, pneumonia, and my mother at my side—all the things that make life worth leaving. How's that? Come over? Be serious! I look like Mia Farrow, halfway through *Rosemary's Baby*. I want you to remember me as the Botticelli flower child I once was. God! I was the prettiest queen that ever paraded for peace. And now I'm something that needs to be burnt after death. I *was* pretty, wasn't I? . . . Bob? All right, smart ass, you can answer that one, but think before you speak. *[A chime rings.]* Well, saved by the cliché; aren't you the lucky one! That's the church bell. One stroke means it's seven-thirty. At eight o'clock it's a David O. Selznick production up here. And Mom and Sis will come crawling upstairs on their knees, muttering rosaries. So I'm yours 'til eight o'clock or the end of time, whichever comes first. Oh, wait; what's that couplet by old A. E. Houseman: "And he shall hear the stroke of eight and not the stroke of nine." About the condemned man in his cell? Hah! Condemned for not being condomed! The wit and wisdom of the living dead. Like it? I leave it to you. Want anything else? Records? Tapes? The history of Western music from Mahalia to Michael Jackson? I want to give it all away before some fool plays disco at my funeral and the record gets stuck and nobody can tell and the service lasts forever! But I'm being negative. Wanna hear some positive funeral plans? I want to be freeze-dried and cut in half and made into ballerina plaques. No, actually, I insist on being cremated; it's my last chance to get my ashes hauled. No, actually, I want to be mixed with greasepaint and used as blackface for Diana Ross drags. Then I want my MasterCard and all my I.D. clipped together and flung to the cutest kid in Sheridan Square! And I don't want you reading any of your crappy monologues, or mine. I already cremated all of my so-called works. Oh, shut up. I was not a real writer. Which you, of course, are; I apologize for that base canard. All I ever had was a knack for cute coffee-table metaphors, like: "Joan Collins is as vulgar as Christmas in Mexico!" Or remember I called that nervous friend of yours, "As delicate as *The Glass Menagerie* in Braille." And then there was the noteworthy occasion when you said some skunk you were fucking instead of me was "like, a fun guy," and I was sufficiently coordinated to riposte, "Isn't fungi the plural?" Thanks. Wait, those aren't metaphors; they're similes. That's me: Simile Dickinson. Forgive the low level of repartee at this end. I haven't been reading anything except condolence cards. A pixieish fellow P.W.A. sent one that says, "What can you give the man who already has everything?" I'm designing one to be sent by well-meaning, helpless friends like you. It shows a quadruple amputee, saying, "I'm behind you one hundred percent." And, of course, Mom has been reading to me. Oh, Shirley MacLaine's latest volume, what else? Shirley claims we pay in each next life for our sins in the last one. Well, Shirl, girl, we've streamlined the process this time. Your up-to-date pervert is dying in the fast lane. No, I'm not going back into the hospital. I abhor the term, "legally alive." God, think of the great men who have nibbled on me, and now I'm nothing but a snack for a virus: something that can't even decide if it's an animal or a plant. Let me tell you, it's no picnic being one. Bob, there's nothing medical science can do: AIDS is the gift that keeps on giving. Once the perfect name for a gay bar would have been "Universal Screw and Bolt." Now it should be changed to "Tool and Die." You love that? It's almost worth talking to a fool like you. Who else would laugh at that? Nobody else gets a bipartite wisecrack in an age when plot is routinely interrupted by commercials. My luck: I got this sweet Indian doctor, who kept folding and unfolding his eyeglasses like a Rubik's Cube. He asked very shyly if he could take blood, urine, snot, stool, semen, and saliva specimens. I said, "Sure; then can we do what *I* like?" Oh, and I used one of your lines on the poor, sweet sap. He very delicately informed me there was a lot less chance of getting it if one had been "Wot dey call a 'topman.'" I couldn't resist it. I said, "Doc, I've always been a topman; you can get it further up you that way!" Then when the diagnosis came up "Bingo!", he warned me to watch out for the depression that sometimes accompanies a diagnosis of AIDS. So I said, with a show of great relief: "AIDS! Oh, doctor, thank God; I thought you said, 'Age!'" You know my motto: brighten the coroner where you are. I tried to make up by offering to be a subject for any cute tricks that science might want to try. And he said, "Mister Wood, we cannot use you as an experimental animal," and I told him, "Doc, I'm an effeminate queer; I've never been used as anything else!" Except by you, Bob, yes, we know that, you and I were truly in love. That *was* love, wasn't it? No wonder it went out of style. No, no, I'm sorry, what you said is true: when you fucked me over that tenement banister with the

Day-Glo peace signs flaking off the walls, it truly *was* the balcony scene of the sixties. Christ, I used to be so clever; now I'm reduced to quoting *you*! I *was* clever. When I was just a little girl in East Bay, California, I noticed that "East Bay" was pig Latin for "beast." But I knew I had found my niche when I realized that "Alice Faye" was pig Latin for "phallus." Yes, isn't that good? You think we can interest the virus in 1930s musicals and it'll turn queer and stop reproducing? Scratch that; you have to be born to royalty. That's how that lovely old 1940s closet queen who brought me out used to put it: "Born to royalty?" He'd spot some hunky number and lean over to me and whisper, "Do you think he was born to royalty?" Meaning was he a queen. "Born to royalty." Sigh. God knows *I* was. Twelve years old, I rummaged through the biggest country-western record barn in Central California and came up with the only Marlene Dietrich album on the West Coast. You have to be born with that instinct. And all by my little lone-some I discovered Walt Whitman, and Aubrey Beardsley, and dying my bangs with lemon juice, and ordering everything a size small, and outlining my eyes with ball-point pen so that when the boys made me cry, they wouldn't see anything running. When my age became the socially-conscious "We Generation," I had to fight my own side for my right to riot at Berkeley in pink high-heels. And when we o.d.'d on politics and became the "Me Generation," I drove to New York behind a half-naked black bodybuilder on a lavender motorcycle after using my last sunshine acid to spike the communion wine! No. I *should* have. I could have been Jimmy Jones. I could have been a contender. Instead of a drab example of the "De-Generation," turned into a serving of sushi for a flock of plankton! But let's not talk about me when I'm gone. Where was I, anyway? Oh, yes: We're-born-that-way, we're-part-of-nature's-plan. That riff. Well, it's trite but it's true. Where would the world be without its fairies? Well, we may be about to find out, mayn't we now? And you, you've been too ugly for a decade for anyone to fuck with, you'll live to see it: A world without fairies. Sigh. Bloomingdale's, of course, will have to close. There will be no girl singers to speak of and speak of and speak of. Whole strains of ferns and poodles will die out. Plaid shirts will be marked down to three ninety-five in memoriam. Of course, fairies have *been* dying out ever since the seventies Marlboro-macho movement. If I live 'til noon, I'll never understand the clones, trying to look like the bullies that beat us up in the schoolyard. They're living proof—wherever that term still applies—you don't have to learn to be gay; you have to learn to act straight—which may be the origin of the verb "to ape"! Thank you! Why, if it hadn't been for a few effeminate holdouts like me, The color beige might have vanished from the face of the earth! Ah, God! Ah, God! Ah, God! *[He grips his abdomen in pain, breathes hard, finally speaks.]* Well, give yourself a gold star; you noticed. Yes, Bob, I'm tiring myself out. I'm not having an experience I care to prolong. Remember those fantasies of attending your own funeral? It isn't as much fun as we thought it would be. Stay on the line; those snappy last words may be imminent. Hah! It's my party and I'll die if I want to! I'm sorry. I'm being disproportionately cruel. What a way to go. Look, you're okay, I'm not okay, okay? Okay. I'm dying. Everybody dies except for two unconfirmed reports from Bethlehem and Transylvania. Why does this take my generation by such surprise? Did they think we were all just going to go into reruns? Wouldn't you think a queen would be glad to learn she's about to lose all her weight, forever? Must one go through the five official stages? Wait, what are those five stages again? "Anger, denial, bargaining, depression, and acceptance." Well, back up: here comes my acceptance speech. "I am now and I have always been a flaming faggot, responsible for style in its every manifestation. I have my own five steps: flippancy, sentimentality, sarcasm, camp, and smut. Those got me through life, and, deity damn it, They'll get me through death!" Now shut up or I'll stop loving you, and what use will there then have been for your poor, pitiable, pathetic, and apparently prolonged life?. I expected you to write something to make me live in infamy, like Shakespeare promised his poor Elizabethan pushover: "Not marble, nor the gilded monuments of princes, shall outlive this powerful rhyme." Welllllllllll, as it turns out, the gilded monuments of princes are still major tourist attractions, while nobody knows who the hell the sonnets were written for, buuuuuuut—oh, don't cry. I love you. You're brilliant. That was a base canard. You're a wonderful writer. I am less than all that dust upon your laurels. You're probably the greatest living gay playwright. Or with any luck soon *will* be. Look, how's *this* for comfort? We were the last two white people ever to fall in love. That oughta rate some

space in the "Whatever Became Of?" books. And there are no
challengers on the horizon. How can anybody fall in something as
awful as love when they're being careful? Before my condition
started warranting quarantine, I knew two kids: lovers, into safe
sex, monogamous out of terror. One night they were each jerking
themselves off while fucking the other—with vibrators—and one
of them's arms got tired, so he switched hands, and his lover hops
out of bed, screaming, "You switched hands! You might have got
some of your precum on your fingers and it might crawl up the
vibrator into me! Are you trying to kill me?" Naked, except for
rubber gloves and a banana-flavored condom, with an electric dildo
still revolving in his ass. Not quite what one would call "love's
first, fine, careless rapture," now is it? Oh, don't. You're right,
you're always right, yes, yes, of course, love will survive. They
couldn't kill it with those purple hair-do's, they can't kill it with a
plague. Boys will fall in love with each other's earlobes if all else
should fail. Because it was never really about sex, was it? It was
about love? Yes, I know you did. Yes, I know you do. Yes, I do,
too. I'm sorry we broke up, too. I was a fool. No, wait, maybe you
were the fool. How did we break up? You told me we had to cool it
for a week because you caught crabs, and I thought it was a lie
because you didn't love me, and I took up with that jailbait street
meat for revenge, and you went off in a huff to save world drama,
yes, I thought I remembered it being about love. Well, and looky
here now where we are. I love you. You love me. We're having a
deathbed reconciliation fadeout. That oughta satisfy two lifelong
students of montage. Dear Lord, I'm suffering like a living thing.
Sex may be safe, but love never is. *[A church bell rings.]* Ah, saved
from the fate worse than—*[Looks out window.]* Lemme look.
Yeah, there's Mom and Sis, rushing from judgment. *[Bell.]* I can
see the church and the sky And the old International Stud Bar.
[Bell.] No, fool, it's a restaurant now like everything else. How *did*
they clean that back room? *[Bell.]* Probably poured polyurethane
to level the ruts left by my knees. *[Bell.]* No, don't call again. Use
that new phone-sex service. It promises troll-free calls. *[Bell.]* If
you have to do something, write me a funny AIDS play. Sure you
can. *[Bell.]* It's the biggest joke played on us since sex itself—and
with the longest punch line. *[Bell]* I don't want you to call. If God
wanted us to be friends with our old lovers, he wouldn't have made

them such creeps. Goodbye. I love you. Shut up. *[Hangs up.]* Not marble, Bob, not as it turns out. No, not marble at all. *[Feels for the folded paper in his pajama pocket, takes it out, unfolds it, reads it aloud.]* "At least I'll never have to hear the term 'life-style' again." *[He finds scotch tape, tapes the paper to his forehead, hiding his face, and with dignity awaits death.]*

CURTAIN

All performance rights for *Pouf Positive* must be acquired through Samuel French, Inc.

Deborah Ann Percy and Arnold Johnston
Love is Strange

> Love, love is strange.
> Lot of people take it for a game.
> Once you've had it, you never want to quit.
> After you've had it, you're in an awful fix.
> —Mickey & Sylvia, "Love is Strange"

Characters: **MICKEY**, late forties
                   SYLVIA, mid-forties

Setting: A beach at Lake Michigan, mid-afternoon,
                   mid-summer, the present.

*[As the lights rise, we see **MICKEY** and **SYLVIA** sitting
on a sun-bleached log a few feet from the edge of water.
Next to them in the sand is an ornate lavender urn.]*

MICKEY

We watched a lot of television in that waiting room. You know,
there's a shark documentary on television at almost any hour of the
day or night.

SYLVIA

If you're in the ocean, you're a lot closer to a shark than you'd like
to think.

MICKEY

But not in Lake Michigan. No sharks here. We're safe here.

SYLVIA

I'm not afraid of much. You know that. But I can't watch those
shark shows. Crazy divers in metal cages. Some so crazy they're
not even *in* the cages. If I think about it when I'm out there floating
around, I pull my feet up.

MICKEY

In Lake Michigan. You're afraid of sharks in Lake Michigan.

SYLVIA

No. Not really.
        [A beat.]
I imagine one sneaking through the locks. Through the Sault. Living just long enough in the fresh water to find me here. Then, snap!

MICKEY

They've been attacking surfers in California.
        [He gives her a hug.]
In the ocean, of course. From underneath, the surfers on their boards look like sea lions. Big thick bodies. Thin flipper arms.
        [A pause. They look at the lake and lean on each other.]
It was good that I went.
        [A beat.]
Paul was too sick to handle the checkbook. And finances aren't Lane's strong suit. So it was good that I was there.

SYLVIA

I know.

MICKEY

Even though.

SYLVIA

I know. Graduating from high school isn't as big a thing for Rick as it was for us. You'll be there when he graduates from college. He understood. There were the same silly antics as when we were in school. One girl took off her cap and put on one of those arrow-through-the-head deals after she shook the principal's hand.

MICKEY

When Paul graduated, he got his diploma from the principal, then did a cartwheel as he walked across the stage.

SYLVIA

He always did things with flair.

MICKEY

The lavender sheep of the family.

SYLVIA

Rick was talking about what walk he would use. I told him it had better be his normal, regular high-school-graduate walk. He said, "Or what?" I told him it was inappropriate to say "Or what?" to the people paying for your auto insurance.

MICKEY

No dancing? You're one tough mother.

SYLVIA

So he chewed gum.

MICKEY

I should have been there.

SYLVIA

Both you and Paul should have been there.
        [**MICKEY** *rises and goes to squat at the edge of the
        water.* **SYLVIA** *follows and stands behind him.]*

MICKEY

There've been a lot of shark attacks on surfers. There was a famous one—a blonde beach-boy—who was killed right off the public beach in Santa Monica. Big flap about it on TV.

SYLVIA

Rick chewed gum, and when he turned to come back down the stairs after he got his diploma, he flashed that little grin of his.

MICKEY

One surfer said on the news that a lot more surfers are killed by lightning than by sharks.

SYLVIA

Paul's smile. The one he flashed when you introduced me to him. "Mickey and Sylvia," he said. And then he hummed a few bars of "Love is Strange."

MICKEY

[Continuing.]

As if the possibility of getting hit by lightning meant it was foolish to worry about sharks.

> *[He picks something out of the wet sand and hands it up to her.]*

Here. A stone for your collection. A stone with a hole in it.

SYLVIA

> *[Holding it up to the sun to check the hole.]*

I'll take this one out on the boat and give it back to the lake.

> *[She puts it in her pocket.]*

Rick wanted to go with you. Both of us should have gone with you.

MICKEY

For goodness' sake, Sylvia. It was Rick's high school graduation. He shouldn't have gone anywhere. We should all have been *here*.

SYLVIA

Yes. We should all have been here.

> *[She puts a hand on* **MICKEY***'s shoulder. He rises, and they return to the log, where they sit.]*

MICKEY

My *parents* should have been there.

SYLVIA

Your father *was* there.

MICKEY

Eventually.

> *[A beat.]*

Almost too late. After Lane and I had taken care of just about everything Paul wanted taken care of.

SYLVIA

And now that your father's back, he's taken charge of the funeral arrangements.

MICKEY

Now that Paul's safely dead and can't object. Of course, Dad doesn't know about *all* the arrangements.

[He gestures at the urn.]

It never occurred to him we'd slip him a duplicate urn. Paul's last graduation prank.

SYLVIA

[Laughing.]

It seems wrong. This shouldn't be funny.

MICKEY

It's not. Not all of it, anyway.

[A beat.]

Love is strange.

[A beat.]

Paul thought it was funny.

SYLVIA

Lane's really not coming?

MICKEY

Lane's really not invited. That's why Dad had Paul's ashes flown back here. "For Mother's sake," he said.

[A beat.]

Mother, who wouldn't come and be with him when he was dying. We're a family whose checkbooks always balance, though.

SYLVIA

[Quietly.]

I know.

MICKEY

I asked Dad about that. "How could she not come?" I asked him.

[A beat.]

"She wanted to remember him as he was," he said.

[A beat.]

"What?' I said. "Alive?" And he said, "Not—dot-dot-dot—like this."

[A beat.]

"Not gay?" I said. "What? She thinks he wasn't gay all along? Is that what *you* think?" I asked him.

    [A beat.]

He said he'd rather not talk about it.

    [A beat.]

And then this blonde guy on the TV news—the Brian-Wilson-look-alike-only-younger type—said his dumb lightning thing about surfers.

SYLVIA

So you get to be mad at your dad, but Rick can't talk about it with you.

MICKEY

    [Ignoring this.]

There were these televisions in every waiting room, and no one ever has enough initiative to change the channel. No one wants to be rude. So we watched sharks.

SYLVIA

I would have been rude.

    [A beat.]

Once when you were working late—adding up someone else's checkbook for them—I thought I'd be brave and watch *Jaws*. How bad could it be? I thought. I'm a grown-up, and it's only a movie, anyway. I watched the first two minutes, the shark dragging that girl around, and that was it. That was all I could watch.

MICKEY

Lane was like you when it came to balancing their checkbook. There would be Paul's neat, tight hand, all the figures added. And in the middle of a page in the ledger, there would be a check Lane wrote, just like you do, in big sloppy handwriting, just like yours. Or in fat blue felt-tip like you do. And he never did the subtraction. That was always in Paul's hand. It got more and more spidery toward the end.

SYLVIA

I've read reviews of those other *Jaws* movies. I always wondered why the characters in them didn't just stay away from the ocean if they were so worried about sharks.

MICKEY

A lot of the reviewers wondered about that, too.
      [A beat.]
Fate, I guess. The fatal attraction of the ocean.

SYLVIA

Edges. Coasts.

MICKEY

That's what people think, out here in the middle. The heartland.
They think if they stay away from the coasts, they won't be in any
danger, this thing won't get them. It'll only get people like Paul.
And Lane. People like that. That's what my parents think.
      [A beat.]
They need to watch out for land sharks.

SYLVIA

You mean, like Lake Michigan sharks?

MICKEY

Land sharks. Like in that old *Saturday Night Live* sketch? It didn't
matter whether you stayed away from the ocean or not. It would
come to your front door. Disguise its voice. You'd open the door
and, snap!

SYLVIA

Pretend it was someone else. Someone you knew.

MICKEY

Somebody you trusted.

SYLVIA

Someone ordinary.

MICKEY

Somebody normal.
      [Bitterly.]
Normal. Not like Paul. Not like my brother.

SYLVIA

[Quietly.]
Not like their son.
[A beat.]
Not like *our* son.

MICKEY

Don't be silly.

SYLVIA

When we were getting ready to go to graduation, do you know
what he said to me?

MICKEY

[Continuing.]
What a silly thing to say. Why would you say something like that?

SYLVIA

He said he'd heard on TV that a heterosexual male had less chance
of getting AIDS than of getting breast cancer.

MICKEY

That was a dumb thing to say, too. Where did he hear something
like that?

SYLVIA

Some local talk show. That call-in show just before the news.

MICKEY

Did you tell him how dumb it was?

SYLVIA

I told him men *do* get breast cancer. We were on the way out the
door to the graduation ceremony. He had on his cap and gown
with his cap on the back of his head at a goofy angle. We were still
in the middle of our what-kind-of-walk-to-use discussion. That
seemed more immediate.

MICKEY

But you've said something since, haven't you?

SYLVIA

When? When have I had a moment since? You were gone. Your
mother arrived. Then I had to pick up your father at the airport.
Then you. And your father wanted me to help arrange this fake
memorial service for Saturday morning.

MICKEY

It's not a fake service. It's real for them.
     [Gesturing at the urn.]
This one's real for us. For Paul.

SYLVIA

Anyway. I had to work out the food. The phone calls to friends.
While your father arranged having that other urn—the fake one—
buried in the family plot. What? What did you and Paul and Lane
put into it for phony remains?

MICKEY

The day before Dad arrived, Lane and I had Chinese ribs at their
favorite Cuban-Chinese restaurant. We had them box the leftovers.
They still use those goldfish containers, not Styrofoam. The under-
taker cremated them for us. Gave us a deal. Swore us to secrecy.

SYLVIA

Is he gay, too?

MICKEY

I guess. I didn't really think about that.

SYLVIA

So he understood.

MICKEY

I guess.

SYLVIA

     [A beat.]
So your parents are having a memorial service for two Chinese rib
dinners. And burying them in the family plot.

MICKEY

Paul and Lane laughed and laughed about it. Then Paul told me to scatter his ashes on the lake.

[A beat.]

That was Monday. Dad arrived Tuesday. Paul died on Wednesday.

[A beat.]

Mom and Dad are having the service *they* want. Paul's having what *he* wanted.

[A beat.]

And here we are.

SYLVIA

Without Lane.

MICKEY

Lane told me he and Paul had already written their punchlines. He said they trusted me to pull it off.

[A beat.]

So you didn't tell Rick how crazy that stuff was? The talk-show crap?

SYLVIA

When have I had a minute?

[A beat.]

You haven't even told him about his Uncle Paul. All he knows is what your father's told everyone. "Heart failure." Not much better than the blonde surfer and his lightning. Or the radio guy and his breast cancer.

MICKEY

I *will* tell him.

SYLVIA

He deserves to know.

MICKEY

You're right. He does.

[A beat.]

First we have to do this. Then Saturday. Then I'll tell him. *We'll* tell him. About the land sharks.

SYLVIA

We'll tell him.
> *[A beat.]*

How *did* they get rid of it? The one in *Jaws*?

MICKEY

They blew it up.
> *[A beat.]*

They blew it up.
> *[He covers his face with his hands for a few moments, then looks at her.]*

We need to do this. Let's get to the boat and get the sails up.
> *[He rises and picks up the urn.]*

Bring your rock with the hole in it. Come on.
> *[She rises. They stand for a few moments looking out at the water.]*

SYLVIA

Paul knew you would do this for him. And Lane. That you wouldn't let your father have it all his own dumb way.

MICKEY

He was my brother.

SYLVIA

Even though you were afraid of him.

MICKEY

My father?

SYLVIA

Your brother.

MICKEY

> *[Looking at her.]*

Love is strange.
> *[He takes her hand.]*

Come on.
> *[They walk offstage as the lights fade slowly to black.]*

END

Edward Wolf
I Do Not Drive

So the steady stream of things we need:
the cans of soup
ginger ale
rice
bananas
and tapioca
come up the hill
in the black bag slung cross my shoulder.

The walk is good for me.
The air
sun
clouds
trees
faces
headlines
blood pumping
heart
remind.

And when I come in—too quiet—
and do not wake him
his face asleep
mouth open
for a moment my body groans—
I know what it will be like.

I do not drive.
My   hands … grasp
        arms … hold
        legs … carry
our sustenance.
My strong body
sore
says 'I am alive.'

The black bag hangs empty on the hook at night.
I dream of the hill—
We are going down as he clings to my back.

He is lighter than food.

Lesléa Newman

Nutmeg

When you were at work   Guy and I grew
bored   but the only drug in the house
to drop was nutmeg
which we did   dumped the whole container
into a milkshake from McDonalds and drank up
nothing happened   no visions no buzz
a total bust   until we went to pick you up
I noticed it first   waiting
at a stop light   a lady
in fake leopard coat walking her Chihuahua
had your face   a kid
on a Schwinn pumping
up the hill   your face on his face   Guy
noticed it too   turned to tell me
he looked just like you   I twisted
the rear view mirror and stared   you stared back
and winked   At the train station   every passenger
getting off the 6:33   a dead ringer
Will the real Buddy please stand up?
Finally you emerged   somehow we knew
and leapt from the car shrieking   smothering you
with hugs and kisses   bowing down
to the homecoming queen   you were pleased
then embarrassed   then suspicious
"What are you guys on, anyway?"
"Nutmeg!" we roared   giggling like girl scouts
Ten years later I take no drugs   still see your face
everywhere   that kid on a skateboard the boy who pumps
my gas the UPS man with his fancy clipboard
anyone tall dark   and under thirty
Will the real Buddy please stand up?
I'm still waiting for you   to emerge
from anywhere   oh the hugs the kisses
I would give you   your smile making me higher
than the balloons we released

the day you died   standing on the beach
the ocean foamy as a milkshake   Guy's eyes dark wet clouds
the sand under our feet   grainy as nutmeg
Will the real   Buddy please stand up

Aaron Shurin
Some Haunting

> "He is a ghost, a shadow now, the wind by
> Elsinore's rocks or what you will, the sea's
> voice, a voice heard only in the heart of him
> who is the substance of his shadow…"
> —James Joyce, *Ulysses*

If he's sitting there now, it's transparently—*literally* so—and I know he may whiff and re-congeal in another street, another cafe. Most of the time he *(they)* will be seen from the back, or glimpsed, peripherally, in passing; when I come home I'll tell David, "I hallucinated Kenny today," or, "I hallucinated John."

I'm no longer afraid these AIDS apparitions might be real (they've lost the advantage of surprise), but my subsequent clench at the gut or failing of the knees show a terror more truculent than fear of the Impossible. (The Impossible? What, any more, is that?) These particular visitations—these "voices heard in the heart of him"—pursue. They know my name, and my whole shaken body responds to their address.

The ghosts who walk in my city (my ghostly city) are cast as vividly as any childhood stored in a dipped *madeleine*—with that fleeting precision memory affords, and the rubbed-out edges it requires. And they rise just as suddenly. But their appearances are oddly interdependent, communal. They haunt *bodies* rather than places. Born as adults in affectional mutuality—exchanged caresses and comradely struggles—my reappeared friends remain so framed, and show their faces by traversing planes of living faces: faces overlaying faces. Their anxious, drifting outlines cross and merge with passing strangers—strangers filled with similar resonating passions, and hungers large enough to invite in, whole, another's presence. They flash and seize.

During these concentric crossings (I theorize) "Jackson" or "Jose" re-animate toward me, pulse for a passing moment through a flesh they once informed. Alert to the scents of shifting desires that surround them, they tremble, eyes open, through the familiar winds of social heat and social rapport. Shining eyes catch eyes; mine by their corners.

These visions are gone in the next shift of wind, of course—shift of a mouth or shoulder that reroutes the familiar image to the unfamiliar: just somebody else. Too late, for me, who have been stuck by rec-ognition, a *madeleine*-rush of memory that comes, alas, too frequently to be savored, but whose measure is too steady to be ignored.

I am haunted.

§

Like many friends I've lost many friends to AIDS, a range of relations from intimate to "anonymous," but of them all one's inces-sant return puzzles me: why young John? Other friendships were dearer, others longer-lived. Yet in peripheral San Francisco his ap-pearances, quicksilver, are inescapable: on a bicycle there in mud-green knickers, at the cafe with overstuffed art-bag slung, cruising the park with a fresh buzz cut and a goat in his gait. I haven't con-sciously, nostalgically looked for him; didn't *choose* to seek him out above the rest. But—rushed overlays, multiple facets of a shifting center, various frame—I'm surrounded.

It's wise Yolande explains the fact I might have known had my knees held: you *don't* choose. The ghost chooses *you!* My daily wants and needs aren't the occasion of these hauntings. Each ghost has a hunger come to me for his own fulfillment. John hungriest of all, at 28 his torn-out-of-youth death leaving live threads flailing. His compositional eye and draughtsman's hand just begun to merge common power in photography. John, whose innate interrogative restlessness allowed him to distance *and* devour; ravaging and scavenging through artforms, art histories, art communities, affinities, oppositions, to make a map his skillful unlearned feet could walk on...Torqued by the desperate agility of his gymnast's body he dwindled, as he grew, simultaneously, older *and* younger: an apparitional old man in padded baby diapers. John, who documented his bodily demise in a series of dispassionately precise photographs,

[It's hard enough to be shamelessly naked in this body-despising culture, but to be so in a sick body when the same culture paradoxically and faddishly valorizes health takes fearlessness. That the sickness in this case is the dreaded and misunderstood AIDS makes John Davis's straightforward gaze even fiercer. Void of guilt or shame, without seeking pity: these photos do not concede. They insist on being figure studies in which a human body seeks articulation. From a leached 97 pounds to a fluid-swollen 120, John Davis remains a figurative artist, not a disfigured one. The skeleton, the musculature, the skin and eyes: these are the working elements of a photographer/model who catches light and disposes of it formally. The courage to seek such transformations in spite of systemic pain is the heart of Davis's power. The grace of his willfulness matches it pose for pose.

—A.S., for an exhibition, 5/92

John B. Davis leaves us with an outline that is an in-line: the phenomenon of his skeleton's arabesque. This unsentimental view is a gift of mortal presence, one man's self inscription, an alphabet of being. His fearlessness is awakening, and might make us each attend our own hand's particularity. AIDS brought him to this attention, in despite of its ravages. He outlasts it.

—A.S., for an exhibition, 11/93]

and so fused his questions into observations *we* observe, the body's palpable inquiry extended ad infinitum.

Extended beyond those old, fixed borders, to where the gates slide easily, admitting and exiting. If he walks, as ghosts do, if he walks with me now—feeding, searching, feeding: since his very mark was *hunger* he must still be hungry! Caught fleeting and reflected in shards his raw unfinished purpose stalks the crowded streets of my city, "signalling to be opened." Haunting me it seeks completion.

How do I serve this dead young man?

Laurie Novick Sylla
Sideshow

Rack 'em up and break, boys

25 year old with most of his

      brain gone,

           right corner pocket

32 year old losing

      sight from retinitis,

           side left

19 year old junkie

      Banked off the 51 year old

           faggot with Kaposi's

Little black baby

      with PCP

Scratch

Stack those pins,

      set 'em up,

           knock 'em down

Ten off a shared needle
STRIKE

Two longtime lovers

SPLIT

Woman who did not know

                        her lover's other passion

Rolls a gutter ball

Step right this way folks

Three symptoms for a

                        quarter

Get your diarrhea here

It's going fast

Night sweats'll keep 'em

                        hopping

                        every time

Fever, lesions, we can even

Take your breath away

Right this way folks

Right this way

Richard Willett
Boys Will Be Boys

Characters:	**PAUL**, late twenties–early thirties
	SEAN, roughly the same age
	THE HANDSOME MAN, sexy
	NANCY, Sean's older sister, thirties
Scene:	An apartment building in New York City
Time:	Now

Scene 1

> *[The lights come up on the first-floor hallway of an apartment building in New York City. Two apartment doors face each other.* **SEAN** *is sprawled in front of* **PAUL***'s door. He has been beaten about the face.* **PAUL** *opens his door and is shocked to find* **SEAN** *there.* **SEAN** *gets up and limps across the hall, deliberately keeping his face turned away from* **PAUL***.]*

SEAN
[immediately; as he walks away]
C-c-could you call the super, please?

PAUL
Huh?

SEAN
[referring to the door across the hall]
I lost my keys.

PAUL
Oh...Sure. *[***SEAN*** sinks down to sit on the floor opposite.]* Are you OK?

SEAN

Yeah. I'm fine.

PAUL

Did you...fall or something?

SEAN

Y-y-yeah. I fell.

PAUL

Do you want to come in and sit down?

SEAN
[showing more anger than he wants to]
I'm fine. Could you please just call the super?

PAUL

Sure. No problem. *[He exits back into his apartment.]* I'm just going to close this so the cat won't get out, OK?

*[**SEAN** doesn't respond.]*

[Blackout.]

Scene 2

[A week later.

Lights up on the other side of **PAUL***'s door, where he sits in a chair, addressing* **THE HANDSOME MAN***, who is at a slight remove, listening a little but saying nothing, continually trying to seduce* **PAUL** *by striking flirtatious, even pornographic, poses. It's a struggle, but until the end of his speech,* **PAUL** *resists* **THE HANDSOME MAN***'s suggestions. They never touch.]*

PAUL

I assume he's gay. I mean, he goes to the beach so often. And when he goes, he's always so colorfully dressed. Plus I've heard him...

you know ... bringing men home. I'm up writing at four in the morning and I hear him come in with somebody. It's a different voice every time. They talk for a while on the other side of his door, and then they stop talking. *[Pause.]* What gets me is how long he's probably lived here without me even knowing it. It's very hard for me to talk to other people in the building. I believe they think I'm strange. They walk by and hear me either typing or talking to ... myself. *[Pause.]* Funny to just open my door and find him lying there, like an offering for the gods. *[Pause.]* That's the other reason I know he's gay. I mean, why else would someone be attacked in Greenwich Village? *[Pause.]* He's cute. I think. But naturally I can't get it together to really approach him. And I don't think he likes me either or something. I mean, the only reason I found out he was attacked was that I overheard him saying it to a friend outside my door. Why didn't he tell me what had happened? Does he think I'm straight? *[Pause.]* So much work. *[Pause. To* **THE HANDSOME MAN**.*]* You're a lot simpler. *[Not especially seductive.]* Take your clothes off. *[***THE HANDSOME MAN*** takes off his shirt as* **PAUL** *watches.]*

[Blackout.]

Scene 3

[Two months later. The middle of the night.

In the darkness, a door buzzer sounds repeatedly. Lights up dimly on **PAUL**, *obviously just awakened, opening his door and seeing* **SEAN**, *dressed for bed, at the end of the hallway between the doors (on the other side of the outside door to the building). The door to* **SEAN**'s *apartment is ajar.* **PAUL** *buzzes him in.]*

SEAN
[a little disoriented]
Sorry. Did I wake you? I got locked out.

PAUL

[groggily]
That's OK.

SEAN

There was an accident. I heard the sirens, didn't you?

PAUL

No. Not really.

SEAN

[entering his apartment quickly]
Thanks.

[He exits behind his door. Pause.]

[Blackout.]

Scene 4

[The next day.

Lights up on **PAUL** *and* **THE HANDSOME MAN**.*]*

PAUL

He looked so sweet in his little pajamas. He looked so thin. It's the oddest thing—his appearance seems to change or something every time I see him. Plus it was cold last night. I just wanted to put my arms around him and hold him till morning. *[To* **THE HAND-SOME MAN**. *Almost nasty.]* Which I never want to do with you.

[Blackout.]

Scene 5

[Two weeks later. The middle of the night.

Lights up on **PAUL** *and* **THE HANDSOME MAN**. *We hear the sound of* **PAUL**'*s answering machine, which he is monitoring as it records the message of someone saying softly, maybe a little drunkenly,* "*Paul...Paul...Paul... Paul...Paul. Pick up, Paul. Come on, pick up, pick up. I know you're there.*"]

PAUL

The machine has been taking this call off and on all night. I don't know who it is. *[He moves to stand just inside his door.]* A friend of mine was once on an airplane, sitting next to a man he didn't know, when one of the two women behind them said to the other, "Those two men up front are gay." When her friend asked her how she knew, the woman said, "They're not making conversation. Gay men are always shy with each other." *[Pause. The following is said to* **THE HANDSOME MAN** *as a kind of escape.]* Take your clothes off. *[Again,* **THE HANDSOME MAN** *obliges.]*

[Blackout.]

Scene 6

[A few days later.

Lights up as **SEAN** *waits nervously on the other side of his door. When* **PAUL** *opens his door,* **SEAN** *opens his at the same time.]*

PAUL and SEAN

Oh...hi.

*[***PAUL***, who is on his way to get his mail, stands awk- wardly, not knowing what to do.* **SEAN** *is on his way out of the building and locking the door after himself.]*

SEAN

A-a-actually...I'd l-l-like to give you a set of keys to my apartment.

PAUL

You would?

SEAN

Yeah...S-s-so that if I get locked out again, I know you have a set.

PAUL

Oh...OK.

[SEAN hands keys to PAUL.]

SEAN

I don't know, I seem to be p-p-pretty forgetful recently.

PAUL

I know the feeling.

SEAN

You don't mind, do you?

PAUL

No, I'd be—That's fine. Thanks. I mean—Yeah. Sure.

[They stand for a moment in awkward silence.]

SEAN
[leaving the building]
I'll see you around then.

PAUL

Okey-dokey. *[Then, after SEAN has gone; disgusted with himself.]* Okey-dokey?!

[Blackout.]

Scene 7

[Two weeks later.

Lights up on **NANCY** *standing outside* **SEAN***'s door with a suitcase. She fiddles with keys, trying to get the door open.* **PAUL** *listens on the other side of his door.* **NANCY** *finally gets the door open and takes her suitcase in.* **PAUL** *frantically tries to think of an excuse to enter the hallway. He grabs a bag of garbage and heads out.]*

PAUL

Hi.

NANCY

Hi.

PAUL

Are you a friend of Sean's?

NANCY

I'm his sister.

PAUL

Oh.

NANCY

I just got here from Wisconsin.

PAUL

Oh. Did Sean go away on a trip or something? I haven't seen him around.

NANCY

No... he's in the hospital.

PAUL

Oh. *[For lack of anything better to say.]* Which one?

NANCY

Cabrini?

PAUL

Oh. Is this... a long stay, do you think?

NANCY

They say maybe he can come home Saturday.

PAUL

Good. *[Moving out.]* Um...Tell him I said hi, OK?

NANCY

I will. What's your name?

PAUL

Oh...sorry. Paul. My name's Paul.

NANCY

I'm Nancy.

PAUL

[as if to explain why he isn't shaking hands]
Garbage.

NANCY

I understand.

[Blackout.]

Scene 8

[That night.

Lights up on **PAUL** *lifting a dumbbell and talking to* **THE HANDSOME MAN.***]*

PAUL

Of course. I feel like the idiot of all time. His appearance doesn't change every time I see him—he's losing weight. Jesus, you can be around it for years and not even know when it's staring you in the face. *[Pause. He stops exercising and drops the dumbbell, exhausted. He looks at* **THE HANDSOME MAN**. *With a sigh.]* Take your clothes off. *[***THE HANDSOME MAN*** obliges.]*

[Blackout.]

Scene 9

[A few days later.

Lights up as **SEAN***, quite a bit weaker now, exits his apartment.* **PAUL** *hears him, throws on a coat, and exits his.]*

PAUL

Hi.

SEAN

Oh...hi.

PAUL

You're back.

SEAN

Yeah.

PAUL

Are you feeling better?

SEAN
[too enthusiastic]
Yeah, I am. I think that's it. I think it's over now.

PAUL
[as they walk toward the front door]
Oh...great. I... um...A play of mine is being produced. I was wondering if you'd like to come see it.

SEAN
[excited]
Sure. That would be great.

PAUL

[handing him one]
Here's a flyer.

SEAN

Thanks. *[Pause. As they start out the front door.]* You don't have shoes on.

*[**PAUL** looks down, startled.]*

[Blackout.]

Scene 10

[A week later.

*Lights up on **PAUL** and **THE HANDSOME MAN**.]*

PAUL

It's hard to know what to do for him. I mean, he's never even said he has AIDS. He told me he was having a reaction to a flu shot. He doesn't seem to want any help. It's like that first day, when he was beaten up. He doesn't want to be thought of as helpless. *[To* **THE HANDSOME MAN***; fed up.]* What do you know about it? *[On the other side of the stage, **SEAN** quietly leaves his apartment carrying a note. **PAUL** continues to speak to **THE HANDSOME MAN**.]* What do you know about…compassion? *[**SEAN** slips the note under **PAUL***'s door and returns to his apartment. **PAUL** sees the note and goes and picks it up. Reading.]* "See you tonight at the play. Good luck. Sean." *[He turns and **THE HANDSOME MAN** is being especially seductive.]* No!

[Blackout.]

Scene 11

[A month later.

In the darkness we hear the sound of a wracking cough as heard from the apartment across the hall all night. Lights up on **PAUL** *and* **SEAN** *in the hallway.* **SEAN** *continues to cough and must continually lean against the wall.* **PAUL** *is fiddling with keys at his door.]*

PAUL

It was nice of you to volunteer to take care of her while I'm gone. *[He looks hesitantly at* **SEAN**, *who is collapsed against the wall coughing.]* Um…I guess it won't be too much trouble. *[***SEAN*** *continues to cough.]* Hmn? *[Turning back to the door.]* Anyway, I'll just— *[He gets an idea. Pretending.]* Damn! This one doesn't fit either. I'm having the hardest time getting a copy made of this key. I think I gave the original to another friend the last time I was away. And you can't make a copy of a copy. *[He takes a smaller key off his ring.]* I tell you what. If you could just take in the mail for me a couple times, that would be great. And I'll get my friend with the key to look in on the cat, OK?

SEAN

[very weary; taking the key]

OK.

[Blackout.]

Scene 12

[Two weeks later. Morning.

In the darkness, we hear the sound of another voice and someone knocking on **SEAN**'*s door.]*

VOICE

Hey, Sean! Open up! It's Ray and Fred from GMHC, Sean. *[Sound of* **SEAN**'*s door opening. Pause.]* Oh, come on, Sean, what's going on in here? You're just giving up, that's all. You should be thinking about what a great summer you're going to have, not moping around like this.

[*Lights up on* **PAUL** *and* **THE HANDSOME MAN**. *It is later that day.*]

PAUL

It was loud enough to wake me up. Don't they realize he doesn't want everybody to know? [*Pause.*] Maybe in their position you get so you just automatically break down barriers. [*He moves to stand just inside his door.*] I think growing up gay, you get to be too good at loving people from a distance.

[*Slow fade.*]

Scene 13

[*A week later.*

Lights up on **PAUL** *at his door and* **SEAN** *and* **NANCY** *at* **SEAN***'s with suitcases.*]

NANCY

So I'm taking Sean back to Wisconsin with me for a bit.

[*She bends down to tie* **SEAN***'s shoe. He is leaned against the doorjamb.*]

SEAN
[*embarrassed that she is doing this*]
Do you have a key to my mailbox?

NANCY

Yeah. We gave him that, remember?

SEAN

We did?

NANCY
[*getting up*]
Yeah. That's all set.

SEAN
[looking back into the apartment]
Do we have everything?

NANCY
Yeah. I think we're all set, Sean.

> *[She sees that* **SEAN** *wants a moment alone with* **PAUL**. *Somewhat reluctantly she hefts the suitcases out the front door.]*

SEAN
[to **PAUL***; quite boisterous, given his obvious debility]*
All right then. I'll see you in a couple of weeks. *[He offers his hand and* **PAUL** *shakes it.]*
> *[Pause.]*

PAUL
OK. See you.

SEAN
> *[exiting]*
Okey-dokey.
> *[Slow fade.]*

Scene 14

> *[Three months later.*
>
> *Lights up on* **NANCY** *handing* **PAUL** *a box through* **SEAN**'s *doorway.* **PAUL**'s *door is open.]*

NANCY
I'd rather you have this stuff than give it to some stranger. I appreciate all your help.

PAUL
But I haven't done anything. I never felt I could do anything for him. He always seemed to want to do things on his own.

NANCY

I know. *[Pause. Looking back into the apartment.]* How about a barbell set?

PAUL

Oh... I have one, thanks.

NANCY

You know, Sean always talked about how glad he was that he got to see that play of yours.

PAUL

You're kidding.

NANCY

No. He said he thought that's what living in New York was all about. He was doing some writing himself, you know.

PAUL

Really?

NANCY

Yeah. *[She is leaving and locking up.]* It's too bad you two didn't get to know each other better, actually. I think you had quite a bit in common. *[She heads out.]* I'll be back with the movers.

PAUL

OK.

> *[*NANCY *exits.* PAUL *stands a moment in the hall, hesitating, then, looking around a little guiltily, he withdraws* SEAN*'s keys from his pocket and enters* SEAN*'s apartment. He looks around a bit, then crouches near a box. He peeks in and pulls out some of* SEAN*'s writing. He looks at this with interest. But his eye is caught by something else in the box. He digs and pulls out some pornographic magazines. He flips through one and lies on the floor, leaving* SEAN*'s writing for now, completely absorbed by the*

photographs. In **PAUL***'s apartment,* **THE HANDSOME MAN** *rises, strips off his shirt, and poses provocatively, a triumphant look on his face as the lights go down.]*

END OF PLAY

Ezekiel Weaver
The Tattoo

[A living room in Philadelphia. Late evening, late spring. A sofa. **NIKOS** *sits on one end.* **BUZZ** *sits on the other. Awkward silence.* **BUZZ** *moves towards* **NIKOS**. **NIKOS** *moves away. A beat.* **BUZZ** *moves towards* **NIKOS** *again.* **NIKOS** *moves away again.* **BUZZ** *moves towards* **NIKOS** *again, this time more aggressively.* **NIKOS** *evades him again.]*

BUZZ
I don't want you to think I'm insensitive...

NIKOS
I don't think that.

BUZZ
Good. Because I've had twenty-three years of therapy.

NIKOS
You told me.

BUZZ
[A beat]
Nikos, I think we need to clarify...you know, where things are.

NIKOS
You're disappointed. I'm sorry.

BUZZ
I'm not disappointed. I'm just confused. Not that I'm trying to pressure you. If you'd rather leave...

NIKOS
I don't want to leave. I like you.

BUZZ

I like you too. But the question is, in what way do you like me?

NIKOS

I want you.

BUZZ

You want me?

NIKOS

Of course I do.

BUZZ

Great. Great.
[*A beat.* **BUZZ** *kisses* **NIKOS**. *A beat.* **NIKOS** *responds.*
BUZZ, *encouraged, continues. He starts to undo* **NIKOS**'
belt. **NIKOS** *pulls away.]*
What's wrong?

NIKOS

Nothing's wrong.

BUZZ

Tell me. If you're positive, I can handle it.

NIKOS

I'm negative. But I can't take my clothes off.

BUZZ

Arthritis?

NIKOS

That's not what I meant.

BUZZ

Oh. No rush. We'll just cuddle.

NIKOS

I can't. I'm sorry. I have a tattoo. On my ass.

BUZZ

A tattoo?

NIKOS

Yes.

BUZZ

That's what you're afraid of? That I'll see your tattoo?

NIKOS

Yes. No.

BUZZ

Nikos, I don't care what you've got as long as most of you works.

NIKOS

You don't understand.
        [A beat]
It keeps changing.

BUZZ

Changing?

NIKOS

I'm not making this up.

BUZZ

What do you mean it keeps changing?

NIKOS

It's a heart. And it changes. Not the heart, the name.

BUZZ

What name?

NIKOS

There's a little area in the middle where you put someone's name.

BUZZ

And the name changes?

NIKOS

Yes. Every time I go out with a new guy.

BUZZ

You mean, you have it changed?

NIKOS

No, I mean it changes all by itself.

BUZZ

Oh, come on.

NIKOS

It does. And then horrible things happen.

BUZZ

[*Skeptical*]
Like what?

NIKOS

Loss.

BUZZ

Loss?

NIKOS

It's not the normal thing, is it? The normal thing is accumulation:
more money, more things. If you have any brains, more knowledge. If you have any luck, more love.

BUZZ

How could a tattoo...?

NIKOS

I'm not making this up. I swear to you. It starts with small disap-
pearances. Forgetting things. Losing the car keys.

BUZZ

That's ridiculous.

NIKOS

But then the car disappears. Then the table the keys were on. Then the whole apartment. Then friends. Memories. Consciousness. Finally, the body. Entire lives wiped out physically, metaphysically. I guess I should have said something.

BUZZ

I don't understand.

NIKOS

Of course you don't understand. I don't understand. But that's the way it is.

BUZZ

But it doesn't make sense.

NIKOS

What makes sense? Nothing makes sense.

BUZZ

Some things make sense.

NIKOS

Name one?

BUZZ

I don't know. There are some.

NIKOS

It doesn't matter. It's not the point.

BUZZ

What is the point?

NIKOS

The point is we can't do this. I'm sorry.

BUZZ

Then why did you go out with me?

NIKOS

I don't know. Habit.

BUZZ

Habit?

NIKOS

I liked you. I still like you. I really should go.

BUZZ

No. Don't go.
        [A beat. He grabs **NIKOS** *and kisses him.]*
I don't care.

NIKOS

But…

BUZZ

I don't care about loss. Whatever there is disappears. Absence is all there is.
        [He kisses **NIKOS.***]*

NIKOS

But I think…

BUZZ

Quiet.

        [Kissing **NIKOS**, **BUZZ** *undresses him. Ultimately, he is naked. The tattoo on* **NIKOS**'*ass is visible.* **BUZZ** *looks at it and sees his name.* **BUZZ** *kisses the tattoo. A beat. Realizing he's misplaced something, he searches around the room.]*

NIKOS

What are you looking for?

BUZZ

I can't find the…uh…
        [He can't remember.]

NIKOS

The rubbers?

BUZZ

Right. Well, it doesn't matter. I'll run out and buy some.
        [Looks around]
Where are the car keys?

*[**BLACKOUT***]*

Perry Brass
Phoebus Apollo Anoints

"Marc'Antonio Pasqualini Crowned by Apollo"

The Metropolitan Museum:
A Painting by Andrea Sacchi,
"Marc'Antonio Pasqualini Crowned by Apollo"
(Who is portrayed here completely, gorgeously, nude,
in comparison to Marc'Antonio, primly dressed in his
choir boy outfit.)

Sucking Apollo's dick, who would
deny it? Dangling and uncut
right there, in *plein air,* tempting
man beyond music, and the honey
and cream of the god's skin, all golden,
kissed by every favor of Heaven and Earth,

must speak to Ages of men in
an ancient language best blotted
out by Church and profitable corporation.

"So, Apollo now will crown me,
while shadows run across my face,
and I have thoughts grave
and counterpointal in order
to save myself the ruddy grape
of blushing cheeks that say:

'Apollo, bend yr silken face and let
me stretch my mouth unto yr handsome neck:
Crown me with thy Leaves as yr favorite:

I will think of Thee different tonight!'"

May, 1986
The Metropolitan Museum, New York

1996–2000

1996 *Newsweek* rather optimistically runs a cover story that—due to HAART therapy—AIDS will soon be over. • *Rent* opens on Broadway, and *ER* features the first major recurring character with HIV on television. Poet Essex Hemphill dies. • Sapphire publishes *Push* (later made into the hit movie, *Precious*). • Dr. David Ho, pioneer researcher of protease inhibitors, is hailed a hero by *Time* and other magazines. • The FDA approves several new AIDS drugs. • Triple combination therapy becomes the standard. • HIV-positive skater Rudy Galindo wins the U.S. national title and the bronze at Worlds.

1997 Nigerian Afrobeat superstar Fela dies from AIDS-related complications. • Tony and Emmy-winner Michael Jeter discloses his positive serostatus. • Pearl Cleage publishes *What Looks Like Crazy on an Ordinary Day*. • Edmund White publishes *Farewell Symphony*. • Brazil is the first developing country to provide free combination therapy to its citizens.

1998 The FDA approves the first human trial of an AIDS vaccine. • The Alliance for Microbicide Development is formed. • BET and the Kaiser Family Foundation partner to form the Rap-It-Up Campaign. • Zackie Achmat cofounds Treatment Action Campaign in South Africa. • The Ricky Ray Hemophilia Relief Fund Act of 1998 is authorized.

1999 AIDS is declared the fifth-leading cause of death for persons aged 25–44. • Origin of HIV-1 discovered. • AIDS activist Reggie Williams dies. • The Black AIDS Institute launches.

2000 February 7 is named the first National Black HIV/AIDS Awareness Day. • President Thabo Mbeki of South Africa breaks ranks with other world leaders and announces his support for AIDS dissidents. • *Queer As Folk* debuts on American television, featuring a major character who is HIV-positive. • Singer Ofra Haza dies.

Randi Triant
The Pecking Order

I used to have coffee with my friend James every day at three o'clock at the same café in Provincetown. We'd call it coffee, but I mostly drank hot chocolate and James only ordered herbal tea.

I liked meeting James for coffee. Our talk would drift between dish and literature. Sometimes the two would meld when James relayed some racy tidbit about this or that author who had had a wild weekend stay in town.

The café sits across the street from a hot-bed of lascivious looks and full-force cruising: the Post Office. One day James eyed a group of men on the P.O.'s steps so conspicuously it was embarrassing. Cruising was okay—but only as long as it was within reason. James, though, wasn't keeping his staring to a subtle gaze and it made me so uncomfortable I knocked my cup, spilling the hot chocolate all over our wrought iron table.

"The goddamn pecking order," James muttered, handing me his napkin, his eyes never leaving the men.

"What?" I asked. I blotted at the dark creamy mess with the clump of wet paper napkins.

James raised his rail thin brown hand and slowly pointed towards a group of heart-stopping attractive men sitting on the P.O.'s steps. They looked like different versions of Ken dolls, blond and brunette, all with the same chiseled faces, broad shoulders, thin waists, tight butts, and lean thighs. They wore shorts—khakis or jean cut-offs—that caught their groins and showed off their oiled and tanned legs. T-shirts pulled across their chests or lay wrapped around their necks like yokes.

"The goddamn pecking order," James said again. "Six months ago I would've been sitting there with them."

I glanced at his sunken eyes. "So why aren't you sitting there today," I asked, balling up my mess into a small pile.

"Shut up," he said.

I played with the dry end of one of the napkins that stuck out. He fiddled with his box of Dunhill Blue cigarettes and then twirled it around as if he was playing spin the bottle.

"Sorry. I didn't mean that. I'm not sitting there because my looks just don't pass the test anymore, girlfriend."

"That's disgusting," I said.

"Like you wouldn't jump at the chance to belong to the best looking group this side of the Atlantic. Come on."

"Oh please. You know I don't give a shit about that."

"Yeah right. You girls are too P.C. for all this, right?" He squinted one of his murky eyes at me. "Bullshit. Everyone wants to belong," he whispered as if he was letting me in on a big secret.

I swallowed the teaspoonful of hot chocolate that was left in the cup. He tapped the end of a cigarette against the box, his tapered fingers curled around the smoothly rolled paper like they held a pen.

"The pecking order dictates everything. Where you sit. Who is approached first. Who decides what club or party you will all go to." He lit up his cigarette and dragged long and deep, his hollow cheeks filling out. What did it matter at this point anyway?

"The healthiest, most beautiful one is smack dab in the fucking middle," James went on. "The ones next to him are our up and coming stars of tomorrow. Beautiful boys with T-cell counts to die for."

"James, for Christ's sakes."

"You *asked*," he said. He waved his cigarette dismissively at me. "The ones on the outside of the circle are the foot soldiers. Poor dears, their looks just aren't what they were last season, are they? I give them two more seasons at best." He dragged on his cigarette as if it were a joint. "Last year I was next to Guy Chalmers. He's the one in the middle. Six months ago I was on the outside ring. Today, I'm *here*, sitting with the only person who'll sit with me in this damn town."

"Stop it. Self pity doesn't become you."

He smiled. His gums were splotchy and swollen. "It used to, remember?"

I did remember, all too clearly. I remembered seeing him for years at the Boatslip at T-Dance every afternoon, fresh from the beach, all muscles, lean and tall and godawful, gut-wrenching beautiful. His mouth set in a perpetual come hither pout, his cheekbones were high and wide, his eyes huge, a piercing green. His chest was broad enough to sit comfortably on. I did that one late afternoon on the beach, kidding around, when he and I could still kid around and I could still sit on him without any thought of crushing his body.

"So what would happen exactly if you picked yourself up and sat down with them?" I asked defiantly.

He laughed loudly. "It's just not done, m'dear." He waved his cigarette like a bad Bette Davis impersonator. "Besides, I prefer your company over theirs any day."

I heard him say these words even as I saw him look longingly back towards the men. They were too busy eyeing a rollerblading man in a thong bathing suit to notice James or me.

"So, have you read anything good lately?" I asked.

"Nice try," James said, his dark eyebrows becoming pointed over the bridge of his nose, his face a scowl of reproof. He opened his mouth to say something more, but then his eyes moved over my right shoulder.

"Hey, James," a man's voice said behind me. I turned and recognized one of the group from across the street, one of the ones on the outside ring.

"Hi, Thomas," James answered back.

"Feel like coming back to my apartment? A few of us are going back to smoke a little." Thomas glanced around the other tables nervously.

"Um, well," James hesitated and shot me a look.

"Go on," I said.

"Great, well, I'll call you later," he said in a self-assured voice, though he stood up from the table a little too quickly, a little too eagerly.

Thomas suddenly backed away from the table. "Um, we'll meet you there, okay James?" Without waiting for an answer, he took off down the street. Two of the other foot soldiers bounded down the Post Office steps after him. The three of them turned quickly down an alley as if they were trying to lose someone tailing them.

I looked at James and didn't say a word.

"Oh, they're probably just picking up some beer or something," he offered and smiled painfully.

"Or a porno movie," I suggested.

He breathed a sigh of relief. "Yeah, right. A porno movie," he murmured and looked away. He stared over at Guy Chalmers and the rest of them on the steps. Guy said something and they all laughed.

"You could come home with me. I'll make you lasagna," I said.

"What?" James turned back to me. "Oh, no, no, that's all right. I think I'll just go for a little while, you know. Say hello. I mean he did come over and invite me. It would be rude if I didn't go." His voice sounded sharp, strained.

He lit another cigarette, even though his other one was still burning in the gold foil ashtray. He ran his hand over his stubbly head. His brown thick hair had withered just like his body until he had finally shaved it all off.

"He used to worship me, you know." James looked forlornly back to the turn-off for the alley. "Thomas, I mean. He was relentless in his pursuit. Finally, one night, we were all doing Ecstasy and I let him come home with me. Now the bastard doesn't even want to walk down Commercial Street with me."

James dropped his cigarette and crushed it with his beat-up army boot. He snorted loudly and turned his cavernous eyes on me. "So, I'm off."

"James, wait."

He shook his head. "You're not gonna get serious on me now, are you?"

"James."

He held up his hand. It was trembling slightly. "I have to do this."

"Don't forget to call me," I shot at him as he walked away. His back to me, he held up his gossamer hand and turned it slightly like a

Queen Elizabeth wave. I watched him until I lost him in the crowd. I wondered if that was what it was like when you finally crossed over into heaven. A slight wave of the hand and a resigned walk through crowds of people until you disappeared from sight.

It was the last time that I had coffee with him.

§

At his memorial I turned around in my front pew seat and scanned the thick crowd sticking together in their slickers and damp wool suits and leather jackets. Thomas stood in a corner in the back, alone even while surrounded by others. No one else from the pecking order had come. He looked drug addict haggard, thinner than I had remembered him from the summer before. Across the church, he recognized me and shyly lifted his hand up. I turned my back on him.

§

This summer I saw Guy Chalmers and the rest of his groupies once more commandeering Commercial Street, the small battalion in lock step on their confident way to conquer all in their path. Thomas was not with them.

I saw a lot of another group too—a clique of young girls. I had heard about this group. They were called "the pretty ones." Depending on whom you asked they were also known as the fems, the lipstick lesbians, or sometimes, inaccurately, the Montreal girls, for none of them were actually from Canada. They just looked like they couldn't possibly be from nearby.

Every day at four, on their way to T-Dance, they walked the length of Commercial Street as if it were their own personal fashion runway. The ruler of the group was a twenty-five year old woman from New York City—Justine Winters. She was a petite powerhouse who ruled over her girls like a goose with her goslings, giving them a sharp peck if they got out of line. She walked slightly ahead of them in expectation that they would always follow. Her hair was black, cut straight across at the shoulders, her face small with hard, blue eyes that were set a little too widely apart. Every day she wore a different brightly colored box hat as a crown. It was rumored that she lived off a trust fund left by a great grandfather who had invent-ed a machine that could cut industrial size wall-to-wall carpeting. She certainly acted as if she always knew what was under her feet; she had a surefooted model's glide.

The rest of the group were five long-haired blonds—Sharon Stone types who made Justine's dark appearance even more strik-ing. They all looked alike in their tight little boy's white T-shirts and their modestly ripped jeans. They strode along to the sides and in back of Justine—bouncy, full of life, glib. They beamed mouthfuls of teeth a la Claudia Schiffer at no one in particular. As we watched them glide by, it seemed as though they took away our thoughts and our breaths for the few moments that they passed in front of us.

One day I watched the pretty ones parade by again, only this time I stood up from the Post Office steps and followed them. They turned left into the Boatslip where T-Dance was already in full groove. Justine led the other five out to the crush of sweating bodies on the dance floor. I watched from behind a bar railing. Miraculous-ly, the writhing, surging, dancing bodies in the middle of the floor seemed to ebb back to leave a free area for Justine and her minions. They quickly formed themselves into a daisy chain, each holding on to another from behind as they began to grind themselves into each other, one long caterpillar. I stared openly at them in their sensual dance. At Justine particularly, who was in the middle, one blond girl grinding into her from the front, another holding onto her from behind, as Prince filled the room.

Justine's head was thrown slightly back so it rested on the shoulder of the girl behind her. Her eyes were closed, her lips barely apart. I stared until those blue eyes opened. She saw that I was watching. She smiled, still grinding into the girl behind her, still moving so smoothly to the music. Then she took her hand away from the other girl's hip and she crooked her finger at me in a come here motion.

I slid through the crowd and Justine pulled me in between her and the girl that had been in front of her. She surrounded my waist with her thin forearm and hand and guided me into hips, which were moving moving moving. I closed my eyes and felt the music, felt Justine, felt the girl in front of me who hadn't paused the whole time. That girl leaned her head on my shoulder and her blond hair intermingled with mine by my neck.

I wanted to think of nothing then, just feel the heavy bass beat and Justine's swaying body, her hands pulling me further and further into her. Prince's song fed into the next, the continuous beat drew us on, tighter and tighter, one body, one being. I opened my eyes as if I were drugged. A man in the cheering crowd was staring at us, smiling. Without warning, my hips shifted slightly.

"You're losing it, girlfriend," Justine hissed into my ear. I shook my head and pushed away from her abruptly, making the chain lose its rhythm, its force, its bearing. I blindly shoved my way through the crowd and then I was outside in the cool, cool sea breeze on Commercial Street. I sat down on a curb and, hugging my knees to my chest, I began to rock gently back and forth, my heart pounding along with the deep bass still audible from the dance floor within.

Tom O'Leary
Memorial

Characters: **STEPHEN SMITH:** 38, acidic in his humor
and outlook on life.
BILLY HODGE: 35, innocent until provoked.
MARTIN STUART: 42

1996. Late Afternoon.

*[Lights come up on The Common Room of St. Stephen's
Episcopal Church. Rear of stage is a long banquet table
littered with food.* **BILLY HODGE** *stands alone, staring
off.* **STEPHEN SMITH** *enters.]*

STEPHEN

William.

BILLY

Stephen.

STEPHEN

Delish food.

BILLY

I haven't eaten.

STEPHEN

Try the wine. It's frisky as a puppy.

BILLY

I keep meaning to eat. Something. Small.

STEPHEN

One never knows if it's bad form. Chowing down. There's so much
food.

BILLY

It's a waste.

STEPHEN

Tragic.

BILLY

I'm sure they'll donate it. To something.

STEPHEN

Everything gets donated to something these days.
    [Pause.]
The music was just…

BILLY

Brahms.

STEPHEN

…perfection.

BILLY

Cello Sonatas.

STEPHEN

Perfect.

BILLY

Really.

STEPHEN

Exquisite.

BILLY

Brahms.

STEPHEN

I often think memorials are the only proof we have of civilization,
now.
    [Nearly uncomfortable pause.]

His mother looks nothing like him.

BILLY

No.

STEPHEN

She's big. Her head.

BILLY

His father's head is small.

STEPHEN

Very.

BILLY

Small.

STEPHEN

Glass of wine?

BILLY

I keep looking at the food.

STEPHEN

Come to think of it, he never listened to Brahms.

BILLY

All this food, just begging for attention.

STEPHEN

So that's what I have in common with food.

BILLY

His musical taste...to be honest...

STEPHEN

Was abysmal.

BILLY

He liked that woman with the season for a last name.

STEPHEN

Yes. That woman.

BILLY

[touching his head]
The plethora of food is giving me a headache.

STEPHEN

She was always sharp on the phone. She didn't believe in small talk. "Joseph, it's your mother. Call."

BILLY

Even when I close my eyes I can still see the food.
[Pause.]

STEPHEN

So, how's the TV business? Billy?

BILLY

What?

STEPHEN

How is the wide world of television?

BILLY

Oh. Fine.

STEPHEN

I see your Ms. Walters is combing down and over. Perfect choice.

BILLY

Thanks.

STEPHEN

No "Hi, Stephen, how's the hair business?" No "Hi, Billy, how's the television business? Your Ms. Walters is combing her hair down and over. Very becoming." Nothing idle from that one. That little one with the big head. Wine, Billy? Dry as dessert wine?

BILLY

Coffee.

STEPHEN

Ixnay. Lactose intolerant. Can't stand it black. Had you met her?

BILLY

His parents didn't come east during our...

STEPHEN

Moment of bliss?

BILLY

I don't...

STEPHEN

Bumping of uglies?

BILLY

...think...

STEPHEN

Roll in the hay?

BILLY

No, they didn't visit.

STEPHEN

Yes, Tucson as center of civilization. Oh, Binky is here.

BILLY

He's gained weight. How lovely.

STEPHEN

Please, God, don't let him come over. One former lover's former lover at a time.

BILLY

Are we all here?

STEPHEN

I haven't seen Charles yet.

BILLY

Charles is in L.A. He has a great position with ICM.

STEPHEN

The food here is rather blinding, now that you mention it.

BILLY

Had you met her?

STEPHEN

No. They were in the city for one day. On their way to County Cork. I made an excuse. Joey seemed relieved.

BILLY

He hated confrontation.

STEPHEN

Didn't he just.

BILLY

She seems harmless now. His mother.

STEPHEN

Except for the large head. Glass of wine?

BILLY

Sober. Two years. Three months. I thought everyone knew.

STEPHEN

Dear. One of the sober ones.

BILLY

It must be hell for his parents.

STEPHEN

I wouldn't think your sobriety would affect them one way or the other.

BILLY

His passing.

STEPHEN

Oh. Yes. That.

BILLY

Michael is here.

STEPHEN

Yes. I see. If he's expecting that hair color will bring back his long lost youth he's mistaken.

BILLY

How many former boyfriends do you suppose there are?

STEPHEN

Oh, not many. Just enough to fill Noah's Ark.

BILLY

Joe was popular.

STEPHEN

Yes.

BILLY

You heard his Elton John story.

STEPHEN

Not from him. He hid all of that from me. He thought I was this mature, settled figure. Thought I wouldn't approve of his youthful indiscretions. I did hear the story eventually. One always hears those stories eventually.

BILLY

I hated that she never bothered to learn my name. Granted, our shelf life was just two years. Joe had a two year limit. As you know.

STEPHEN

Oh, look, Martin is still alive.
  [*They smile at an unseen* **MARTIN.**]

BILLY

Joe would have been...

STEPHEN

Thirty-four. Just.

BILLY

Thirty-four. Yes. When I first laid eyes on him I actually said out loud, That is the best looking boy I've ever seen. He sparkled.

STEPHEN

One needed sunglasses.
  [*Pause.*]
When you say two years, are you saying twenty-four full months on the dot?

BILLY

Perhaps a sandwich. They look so inconsequential.

STEPHEN

Wouldn't it be nice to clear the air? Everyone else seemed to know at the time. Everyone but us.

BILLY

It was a dozen years ago.

STEPHEN

Call me Cathy Curious.

BILLY

Martin is on a new regimen. Louis was telling me. He's doing that tea thing everyone is doing. They look like pods. You boil them. Or something. I'd be afraid the pods would come and crawl on your face in the dead of night. You'd wake looking like Cathy Lee Rigby. Very Rod Serling. What was your question again?

STEPHEN

All of '84 and the winter, spring and the beginning of the summer of '85 he was with me. You came along, as the world knows. You. Bathsheba. Came along. But you didn't arrive until after the summer began. You couldn't have.

BILLY

Professionally speaking, what would you do with Frank's hair?

STEPHEN

Set it on fire.

BILLY

How do you define the beginning of summer?

STEPHEN

Joey and I were with Rick and Jason on the Island the weekend of the Fourth.

BILLY

Seriously? July 4th? Where was I?

STEPHEN

I can't possibly know. I'm not sure I know where you are now.

BILLY

To be perfectly honest, since you insist, I met Joe the day before Mother's Day.

STEPHEN

[shocked]

You can't have. You must be thinking the Fourth. After the Fourth.

BILLY

They're wrapping things. I should grab something.

STEPHEN

Let me!
    *[**STEPHEN** goes off. He returns with a tray of pastries.]*

BILLY

Stephen, really! You've returned with a plate of sin. I couldn't.

STEPHEN

Don't be precious. You, Jerry Hall, you.

BILLY

They're watery.

STEPHEN

They're sweating. Pastries sweat. It's how they mourn.

BILLY

Just one tiny one.
    *[**BILLY** eats a pastry.]*

STEPHEN

He spent Labor Day with me.

BILLY

That's a lie! We were on the Grove with Sally and Cherise. I was reading *A Tale of Two Cities*. These sweaty pastries are beyond delicious. Just one more.

STEPHEN

Explain Mother's Day.

BILLY

Explain Labor Day.

STEPHEN

I asked first.

BILLY

I could eat a hundred of these.

STEPHEN

If you do not explain Mother's Day, I will rip the perfect eyes out of your perfect head.

BILLY

Wait. Last one. If I reach for another cut my hand off.

STEPHEN

Oh, why stop at the hand?

BILLY

Wait. Where is your glass of white wine?

STEPHEN

[smile]
Darling, I finished that ages ago.

BILLY

Stephen, you had a full glass when you went for the pastries.

STEPHEN

Really, Billy. It doesn't take an Academy Award winning performance to finish a glass of wine.
[Pause. **BILLY**'s face turns white.]

BILLY

WHORE!
[**BILLY** rushes off. **MARTIN STUART** enters.]

MARTIN

Did someone call me?

STEPHEN

Hello, Martin. How are you?

MARTIN

Alive, Stephen. How are you?

STEPHEN

Oh, I'm presently going through a Bette Davis phase. Mischief. Mischief. Mischief.

MARTIN

How does one manage to be mischievous these days?

STEPHEN

It takes great thought and planning.
> *[**BILLY** returns, out of breath and red in the face.]*

BILLY

COW! BENEATH PEASANTRY!

MARTIN

William, really. All of the other boyfriends are looking.

BILLY

YOU KNEW I WAS SOBER!

STEPHEN

I had heard tell.
> *[**BILLY** lunges at **STEPHEN**.]*

BILLY

I'll rip every processed hair out of your skull!

STEPHEN

Get off me, animal!

MARTIN

Darlings, what the hell are you thinking? Everyone is watching! Stop it! Now! You heard me!
> *[**BILLY** and **STEPHEN** pull apart.]*
> *[**BILLY** takes **MARTIN**'s glass.]*

BILLY

What is this?

MARTIN

Water.
>   [**BILLY** *drinks, gargles, spits behind him.*]
>   [*They stare at him as if he were from another planet.*]

Have you lost your slender mind?

BILLY

No.
>   [*to* **STEPHEN**]

I slept with him the day before Mother's Day. So there.

STEPHEN

I slept with him Labor Day weekend. So there.

MARTIN

Girls, girls. We are not in a Bavarian Beer Hall.

STEPHEN

You were nowhere near him on Mother's Day.

BILLY

No, but I was on top of him the day before.

STEPHEN

Slattern!

BILLY

Mendicant!

STEPHEN

Slavophile!

BILLY

We met at the skinny card shop at Eighteenth and Seventh. He was
late with his Mother's Day card. He cruised me like a sailor who's
been at sea for decades.

STEPHEN

I don't believe it. Not a word. Your brain has obviously been dam-
aged thanks to the decades you've been pickling it.

MARTIN

Oh, no.

STEPHEN & BILLY

What?

MARTIN

She's crying.

STEPHEN & BILLY

Who?

MARTIN

The mother.

STEPHEN

Oh, God, no.

BILLY

I hate that.

MARTIN

The father is going to say a few words.

STEPHEN

I really hate that.
　　　[Pause.]

MARTIN

Very few words.

BILLY

They're both crying now.

STEPHEN
Not fair.

MARTIN
The entire room is crying.

STEPHEN
I hate it when they thank us for being family too.

MARTIN
That always kills me.

BILLY
Stephen, your mascara is running.

MARTIN
My God, it is.

STEPHEN
That's impossible. This is tear-proof.

MARTIN
You, butch-fem, you.
> *[Pause.]*

BILLY
Heard you were doing the tea thing, Martin.

MARTIN
Yes. It's fabulous.

STEPHEN
Your color is thrilling.

MARTIN
Thank heaven; it's been a grand month. Excepting Joseph.

BILLY
Yes.

STEPHEN

Excepting.

BILLY

Joe.
  [Pause.]

MARTIN

Did he tell you his Elton John story?

STEPHEN

No.

BILLY

Yes.

STEPHEN

I heard it.

MARTIN

Yes. One does.
  [Pause.]

STEPHEN

Anyone going uptown?

MARTIN & BILLY

No.

STEPHEN

Well. Then.

MARTIN

How about a movie? An old movie. One of the bad Julie Andrews musicals. Something overblown and witless.

STEPHEN

Like us.
  [They stare off.]
One often feels like a dinosaur.

MARTIN
Surviving the crunch.

BILLY
Leave it to Sondheim to have the last word.

STEPHEN
Let's not do this again soon.

MARTIN & BILLY
Agreed.

> *[Pause. They stare off.]*

CURTAIN

Tobias Maxwell
The Mary Play

The Characters: **MARY**, a man
ZACK, a medical intern
DR. FELD, a voice over the phone

Scene: The set consists of two playing areas. Stage left is
an interview room with a small rectangular table
with two chairs. There is a therapy poster on the
upstage wall. It is a grid made up of cartoon faces
depicting different human feelings in each of the
square boxes. Stage right is an office with a desk,
two chairs, one behind and one in front of the desk,
and an analyst's couch along the upstage wall.
There is a picture of Freud above the couch.

[*At rise: The lights come up on as* **MARY** *enters.* **MARY**
*is a man in his 30s. He has a goatee and mustache, and
wears a long, red-haired, curly wig styled with a modest
bouffant shape on top of it. He is dressed in a light-
colored, sixties "mod" dress with white sheer stockings,
two-inch heels, and a long shoulder evening bag. The
effect should be neither "drag" nor "crazy street person".*
MARY *should have a very real and matter-of-fact quality
about his being a man who happens to have dressed up in
this particular outfit that day.* **MARY** *enters from stage
left and pauses for a second. He looks around and glances
back offstage as if he were being followed. He breathes a
sigh of relief and does a quick sign of the cross with his
right hand, immediately followed by both hands doing a
movement best described as a "limp wristed, girl-have-
I-got-some-dish-for-you" gesture. The movement should
flow as one—sign of the cross/bend of the wrists.*

MARY *walks over to the poster and admires all the
different faces on it. He begins to mime faces.*]

MARY

Happy. *[Mimes it]* Angry. *[Mimes it]*

> *[As **MARY** is doing his repertoire, **ZACK** enters. **ZACK** is a young-looking* MD *intern, who has just recently begun his psychiatry rotation. **ZACK** is not prepared for **MARY** and stands there, observing him.]*

MARY

Depressed. *[Mimes it]* Anxious. *[Mimes it]* *[**ZACK** clears his throat and **MARY** jumps.]*

MARY

You startled me. *[Laughs]*

ZACH

I'm…sorry…I…uh…was enjoying your…uh…

> *[**MARY** looks at him suspiciously, and goes and sits down at the interview table. **ZACK** walks to the table, picks up a clipboard and pencil and sits opposite **MARY**.]*

ZACH

So…umm…is this your first time at St. Mike's?

> *[**MARY** gives him a deadpan stare.]*

ZACH

Is there something wrong? *[Straightens his tie]*

MARY

No…no. Nothing's wrong. What's the middle initial stand for?

ZACH

Middle initial?

MARY

Yeah. Your tag says "Z.J. Nader." What's the middle initial stand for?

ZACH

My middle name. Is that...important?

MARY

For who?

ZACH

For you?

MARY

I don't know. Maybe. For you, maybe?

ZACH

Well then, shall we begin? *[***MARY*** nods once]* Okay. Uh, name?

MARY

Mary.

ZACH

[Tries to be casual] Mary? Ummm. *[Starts to write it down, stops, erases it with small chuckle to himself.]*

MARY

[Looking over onto his clipboard] Anything wrong?

ZACH

Well no...nothing wrong. But...I'm going to need uh...you know, your full name. First and last. *[Beat]* Middle. Uh, legal name. You know.

MARY

Oh it's just Mary. That's all.

ZACH

That's all. Just...Mary. Mary?

*[***MARY*** nods and smiles innocently.]*

ZACH

Has it always been...Mary?

MARY

Oh no.

ZACH

Oh...good. Good. Uh, why don't you give me your old name? You know—the one you got at birth? Just for the record.

MARY

Well...I'm not sure I should.

ZACH

Why not? Are you afraid? Is it...something...with the law?

MARY

Well...no. Not man's laws. No.

ZACH

Man's laws? Uh...*[Chuckles]* Anybody else's laws we should know about?

> [**MARY** *smiles and looks upward towards the ceiling.*
> **ZACK** *looks at* **MARY** *for a second and hesitantly glances upward and quickly looks down at his questionnaire.]*

ZACH

Listen, uh...

MARY

Please, call me Mary.

ZACH

I can call you Mary, it's just that—

MARY

Good.

[**ZACK** *feels stuck with this Mental Status Examination.
He tries another tactic. He writes down* **MARY** *on the
form with quotes.* **MARY** *looks over and sees this.* **MARY**
looks at **ZACK** *with a sad, questioning look.*]

ZACH

Yes?

[**MARY** *continues to stare at him.*]

ZACH

What?

[**MARY** *mimes "quotes" with his fingers.* **ZACK** *exhales,
takes his pencil and erases the quotes.*]

ZACH

There. No quotes. Are you satisfied? [**MARY** *smiles happily.*] So,
tell me, Mary—what might happen if you told me your full name?

MARY

[*Conspiratorially*] You really want to know?

ZACH

Uh, yes. Sure. Why not? Try me.

MARY

I don't know, really. All of this has been pretty confusing to me so
far.

ZACH

Confusing? So far? Can you elaborate?

[**MARY** *suddenly rises.* **ZACK** *jumps up, thinking*
MARY *is making a run for it.*]

MARY

[*Looks at* **ZACK**, *surprised.*] I'm just getting up to stretch. What
did you think?
[**ZACK** *feels foolish as he sits back down.*]

MARY

It's so uncomfortable sitting down lately.

ZACH

Oh, of course. No, please. Be my guest.

> [**MARY** *stretches a bit, takes some deep breaths, and pats his stomach a few times.*]

ZACH

So...you were saying, about...confusion?

> [**MARY** *walks to the poster and searches the faces intently.*]

MARY

There's no face there for me.

ZACH

No face? What do you mean?

MARY

I'm not there. There's no face for what I'm feeling.

ZACH

Which is...?

MARY

[Philosophically] Oh...fucked?!

ZACH

Really? Are you sure?

> [**MARY** *looks at the poster again, then realizes* **ZACK** *is pulling his leg.*]

MARY

You had me there. For a second. Fucked! *[Laughs]* No, I don't think they'd put up a face like that. They'd have to put *my* face up there for that one.

*[**MARY** does a profile pose, lifting up some of his wig ringlets for effect. **ZACK** laughs.]*

MARY

*[Stares at **ZACK**]* Glad you can laugh. It's not you that's fucked!

ZACH

[Regaining his neutral, professional demeanor] I, uh...wasn't laughing at you. Honestly...I'm sorry. I was being inappropriate there. I...I...

MARY

Gotcha! *[Laughs]*

ZACH

[Laughs warily] So...we're not going to get a full name, then?

MARY

It doesn't really matter. I'm Mary now. That's all that counts.

ZACH

That's why you're uh...screwed?

MARY

*[Looks at **ZACK**, breathless. He is suddenly in awe of **ZACK**'s astuteness.]* How did you know?

ZACH

[Puzzled] A lucky guess?

MARY

You know then?

ZACH

Uh...know...what?

MARY

About my getting fucked...well, not exactly *[Whispers]* fucked, fucked. *[Regular tone]* Obviously. Otherwise I wouldn't be so fucked. I mean, well, you know. *[Laughs uproariously]*

ZACH

[*Pause*] Mary, are you sure you wouldn't want to share with me your full name? Do you know what day it is?

MARY

I know this is my ... [*Pauses and counts on his fingers*] Fourth month.

ZACH

[*Very lost*] Fourth month ... for what?

MARY

Since ... you know.

> [**MARY** *does a head gesture as if something was next to them.* **ZACK** *does a quick take to the side and looks back at* **MARY**.]

ZACH

Know ... what?! Mary, you're going to have to spell it out for me. Are you seeing things? Do you hear any voices talking to you now? I mean do you see anyone else here?

> [**MARY** *glances around very quickly and does the sign of the cross/bend at the wrists gesture. He gets up and looks into his shoulder bag.*]

MARY

I can smoke in here, right?

ZACH

No, no. I'm sorry. No smoking allowed.

MARY

Oh what am I saying? I promised Gabriel anyway. And you know he hears everything!

ZACH

Gabriel? He's your ... "friend."

MARY

[Laughs] I never thought of him like that. *[Pause]* Yeah, why not? It's not like we're not involved here, right?

ZACH

So…Mary. Won't you sit down? You seem pretty on edge to me.

MARY

[Points to a face on the poster and mimics a frenzied look] Damn it. You'd be too. In my state! I'm gonna need all the help I can get.

ZACH

We're here for you, Mary. Come on. Sit down.

MARY

[Sits] You got kids?

ZACH

Is that important for you? *[**MARY** nods quickly]* Now, let's stay focused on you.

MARY

[Nods disappointingly] If you do, you had them out of wedlock. *[Points to his left hand ring finger]* No ring, Doctor. Shame on you.

ZACH

*[Getting frustrated, looks at **MARY** for a second, trying to figure out a new approach]* So, Mary. Can you tell me why they brought you in?

MARY

Goddamn priests! Between you and me? They need to get laid. They get ugly—fast!!

ZACH

Yes, well…how does a priest have anything to do with your being here? Do you remember?

MARY

Of course I remember. I went to mass this morning—

ZACH

Dressed...like that?

MARY

[Looks at his shoes] It's the shoes, right? They don't match? It's
not easy, you know. These last few months, I've had to get a whole
new wardrobe, if you know what I mean.

ZACH

I don't know what you mean. Mary, I'm going to ask you to stay
focused here. Or we'll be here all night.

MARY

You gotta hot date waiting out there? What about those poor kids.
Oh, the sins of the father—

ZACH

Mary, stay focused. What about the priest?

MARY

I went to confession. Before mass. It's Holy Week, for Christ's
sake! *[Suddenly stops, looks upwards, clutches at stomach]* Oops.
Sorry about that. Bad habit. Well, anyway. I'm confessing my
sins—next thing you know, I've got this old geezer practically
yelling at me through the slot in the confessional. He's telling me
I'm gonna burn in hell. That I'm the filthiest whore—

ZACH

Why was the priest saying those things to you? Did you say
something? Do something...provoking?

MARY

I was just trying to get some guidance on my personal problem. I
figured—a priest could help, right? But no!! This old buzzard starts
to pry about my sex life! Like he hasn't got one—so he's gotta get
it secondhand! *[Pause. Straight-faced]* I mean, God doesn't mind
me having sex with guys. I just never thought he'd want me to get
pregnant!

ZACH

Pregnant?!

MARY

Yeah. You act surprised. I thought you knew.

ZACH

Knew? What? How?

MARY

Well...guessed it then. I thought, you know, you guessed it somehow. You know, a minute ago?

ZACH

Uh...sorry, Mary. No.

MARY

Oh, well. Whatever. Listen, is this going to take long? I'm very tired. In my condition.

ZACH

No...not too much longer. We just have to get a few more answers. So...Mary...you think you're pregnant?

MARY

Think!? Oh, get real. This is no psychosis. In my wildest dreams! The closest maternal instinct I ever had was with my sister's Barbie doll. And that ended quick enough when I found her Ken doll, let me tell ya.

ZACH

When did you start...becoming...pregnant?

MARY

I told you. I'm in my fourth month.

ZACH

Oh, that's what that was all about. *[Pause]* So, Gabriel's the father?

MARY

[Gasps audibly and does the sign of the cross/bending of the wrists gesture.] Bite your tongue. You're going to get us into trouble here.

ZACH

No one's here. It's just you and me, Mary. You're safe.

MARY

Boy, you don't get it, do you?

ZACH

Mary, you seem a bit...paranoid.

MARY

Paranoid? Bullshit! You go through what I've gone through. Then you talk to me about paranoia! Jesus Chr...*[Looks upwards]* Oops. Sorry.

ZACH

You keep looking up. Do you see anything up there?

MARY

It's out of habit. Gabriel tends to come in from an upward angle. You know...the wings? *[Does a fluffy gesture with his hands.]*

ZACH

Uh...the wings?

MARY

Yeah. Gabriel's wings. He's an angel, right? He's got wings. Big ones! Let me tell ya.

ZACH

Oh...of course. *That* Gabriel.

MARY

You don't know your Bible, do you?

ZACH

I know it. Some.

MARY

New Testament?

ZACH

Okay. So you got me there. *[Looks at* **MARY***, waiting for some kind of information.]* Anything I should know?

MARY

[Quotes] "The Angel Gabriel was sent by God to a town in Galilee called Nazareth, to a virgin betrothed to a man named Joseph, of the house of David; and the virgin's name was Mary." *[He extends his palm out to* **ZACK***, waiting for him to shake it]* Go ahead. Make my day.

*[***ZACK*** hesitates, then limply shakes* **MARY***'s hand.]*

MARY

Pleased to make your acquaintance.

[Blackout. Next day. Lights come up on stage right. **ZACK** *is at his desk, flipping through a chart, looking puzzled, anxious and confused.* **ZACK** *closes the chart and reaches for a large Jerusalem Bible and opens it where he has placed a bookmark.* **ZACK** *reads it silently as the phone RINGS. He presses the speaker button.]*

ZACH

Dr. Nader.

DR. FELD

Zack, what's this on...this Mary guy?

ZACK

Uh, Dr. Feld, yes. Uh, what about Mary?

DR. FELD

No other name?

ZACK

No. Just Mary, for now.

DR. FELD

Christ! These loonies. Is he a screamer?

ZACK

He's actually very...mild-mannered, rather nice.

DR. FELD

You ruled out paranoid schiz, but you want to extend his hold? What's going on?

ZACK

Dr. Feld, Mary is a very interesting case—

DR. FELD

Zack, this isn't your specialty. You're going into pediatrics, right?

ZACK

Obstetrics. But there's something unique about this...case. It's just a hunch, but—

DR. FELD

Listen, Dr. Nader. By the end of your rotation you'll be thinking to yourself, "Same ole, same ole", trust me. The psychoses, the delusions, the paranoia. It will all blend into one giant ball of *mishegoss*. You'll see. This Mary guy—he's no danger to self or others?

ZACK

He attacked a priest.

DR. FELD

Doesn't sound too crazy to me.

ZACK

Dr. Feld, his psychosis is pretty—

DR. FELD

Listen Zack, he's the fourth Virgin Mary I've had this year. Trust me. I'll take Mary over a Hitler any day. We need the bed space.

[DR. FELD hangs up. ZACK hangs up and opens the Bible again, reading aloud.]

ZACK

"Gabriel went in and said to her, 'Rejoice, so highly favored! The Lord is with you.' She was deeply disturbed by these words and asked herself what this greeting could mean but the angel said to her, 'Mary do not be afraid; you have won God's favor. Listen! You are to conceive and bear a son, and you must name him Jesus. He will be great and will be called Son of the Most High. The Lord God will give him the throne of his ancestor David; he will rule over the House of Jacob forever and his reign will have no end.' Mary said to the angel, 'But how can this come about, since I am a virgin?' 'The Holy Spirit will come upon you,' the angel answered, 'and the power of the Most High will cover you with its shadow, and so the child will be holy and will be called Son of God.'"

[ZACK shuts the Bible, goes back to the chart on his desk, opens it, picks up the phone and dials an extension.]

ZACK

Hi, this is Dr. Nader. Has the male patient, Mary, been released yet? *[Pause]* Great. Listen. Bring him down to my office. I want to see him before he leaves. *[Listens]* Yeah, right away is fine. Thanks.

[ZACK hangs up, looks at the file once more and shuts it quickly. He paces around the office and suddenly realizes how manic he is. He lies down on the analyst's couch in a fetal position and takes a few deep breaths before facing away from the door. MARY enters. MARY is dressed the same as before, but he has no makeup on today; the look is softer.]

MARY

Shouldn't I be the one lying down?

ZACH

[Jumps up, startled] Mary, I didn't hear you come in.

MARY

I must be getting the hang of these heels. Finally!

ZACH

Please, sit down.

> [**ZACK** *points to the chair in front of the desk.* **MARY** *hesitates, then sits as* **ZACK** *returns to the chair behind the desk.*]

ZACH

You look different today, somehow.

MARY

I do? Uh…oh, my makeup. Someone here stole my makeup.

ZACH

Really? Who?

MARY

[Does a take] Little Moe, if you ask me!

ZACH

We have someone on the staff here called Little Moe?

MARY

This is "The Snake Pit," right?

> [**ZACK** *gives* **MARY** *a look.*]

MARY

It might as well be, the way they lock you up at night.

ZACH

That's what this is—a locked facility. It's kind of understood? You come in; we lock you up.

MARY

And shoot you up!

ZACH

[*Beat*] Sometimes.

MARY

They wanted to medicate me last night. Me! In my condition.

ZACH

How are you feeling today?

MARY

I'm getting out of here, thank God. [*Realizes what he's said and laughs*] Thanks, God.

ZACH

But you're feeling okay?

MARY

Why are you so concerned all of a sudden?

ZACH

[*Lying*] I've always been concerned.

MARY

No, you haven't. And yes, I am feeling fine. No thanks to your medications.

ZACH

It's just standard procedure here, I'm afraid.

MARY

Standard?! What would I do if I gave birth...premature? Or worse...

ZACH

Gabriel would...help you...right?

> [**MARY** *stares at* **ZACK** *with gaping mouth, and slowly looks all around the room. Glances up quickly at ceiling before looking back at* **ZACK.***]*

MARY

You too?

ZACH

Me too, what? *[Quickly]* Oh...no. No!

MARY

Phew, I was getting worried there for a second. I mean, how many Mary's can there be, right? Unless we've got one sick angel making the rounds. *[Thinks about this]* I never thought of that one...

> **[ZACK** *reaches for the Bible and opens it to Luke 1:28, reading aloud.]*

ZACH

"Rejoice oh highly favored! The Lord is with you."

MARY

[Gets up and starts to pace] Please, do I have to go through that again?! The Holy Spirit already came on me once. Trust me. That was enough. Why are you doing this? Is this how you get your kicks? *[Quickly]* Don't answer!

ZACH

Mary, please. Don't get yourself all worked up again. Why don't you lie down?

> **[ZACK** *gets up, and starts towards* **MARY** *with Bible in hand.]*

MARY

Oh, you are sick! *[Tries to cover his ears.]*

ZACH

[Reading from the Bible again] "Know this too; your kinswoman Elizabeth has, in her old age, herself conceived a son, and she whom people called barren is now in her sixth month, for nothing is impossible to God."

[**MARY** *goes towards the door, when* **ZACK** *notices a big, red spot in the seat of* **MARY***'s dress.*]

ZACH

Mary, hold on. You're ... bleeding.

[**MARY** *backs away from* **ZACK** *towards the couch, stands there with a dumbfounded look and plunks down onto the couch, staring out blankly into space.*]

MARY

What are you saying?

ZACH

You're bleeding. Rectally ... I think ... I guess. I really don't know. It's on your—

MARY

No, no, not that. I'm just spotting. No, the other stuff. The Bible quotes. What are you getting at? What are you trying to say here?

ZACH

I don't know, Mary. I'm confused. *[Beat]* What do you mean, spotting?

MARY

Spotting. Ever since, you know ... that night ... with the Holy Spirit? I've been spotting, on and off.

ZACH

This looks a lot worse than just spotting to me.

MARY

It's probably those fucking meds from last night.

ZACH

Well, let me look. I'll just check ...

[**ZACK** *tries to approach* **MARY**. **MARY** *jumps up from him.*]

MARY

No! Don't touch me.

ZACH

I'm a doctor. I'm in obstetrics. This is my specialty, well sort of, will be...

[**ZACH** *gets up and goes towards* **MARY**.*]*

MARY

[Runs behind the desk] You can't touch me like that. I don't want you to touch—

ZACH

Mary, you're overreacting. This is...unique, I'll grant you that much. I did a workup on your blood. According to that, you're pregnant all right. *[Pause]* Makes no sense, but I'm worried about your health. *[He moves a few steps closer.]*

MARY

It's not what you think. It's not safe.

ZACH

Safe? I'll be gentle. Trust me.

MARY

Not safe like that. It's not safe...to touch my...blood...

ZACH

[Pauses as the information sinks in.] Ohh...

[**ZACH** *stands there as* **MARY** *comes around the desk and begins walking towards the door.]*

ZACH

Where are you going? *[Goes in front of* **MARY** *and stops him.]* I can help you. Somehow. *[Pause]* Sit down. You should be lying down. Your feet should be up. *[Slowly leads* **MARY** *to the couch and sits him down.]* I don't understand any of this. It doesn't make any sense.

MARY

You're telling me!? Four months ago, I'd never have been caught dead in heels.

ZACH

Really? I thought...

MARY

What? That this is me? Oh, hello?! Pilot to tower...come in...come in.

ZACH

I just thought...I don't know.

MARY

Come on, say it. You think I don't know? You thought, "Gay...Fag...Queen". Right?

ZACH

No, no. I didn't think...
          [**MARY** *clears his throat.*]

ZACH

Well...you have to admit, your get-up is a bit—

MARY

[Defensive] What?!

ZACH

Well, you're not exactly dressed as a nun.

MARY

Under the circumstances? I don't think so.

ZACH

What I meant was...you look like an outrageous, flamboyant—

MARY

All right, all right. I get the picture. So, I have poor taste. I thought I'd go with this Sixties retro thing. I didn't think I'd stand out as much.

[ZACK looks at MARY with an incredulous stare.]

MARY

All right, so I have a soft spot for Fellini. Jesus could do worse for a mother. Anyway, I'm due in October. Jesus is going to be a Libra this time. He'll love all of this!

[They both pause, assessing each other.]

ZACH

So why didn't God choose a drag queen? It would have been easier it seems.

MARY

And lose her figure? Not the queens I know! *[Laughs, then does a small movement indicating some activity in his stomach.]*

ZACH

You okay?

MARY

Yeah, yeah. I'm getting used to this. Really. *[ZACK tries to touch MARY.]* I don't want you to get infected.

ZACH

I can't see God choosing an HIV positive man for this ordeal, so that he would somehow put others at risk along the way. I won't get infected.

MARY

Where do you think I got the HIV from?

ZACH

[Incredulous] What?! What are you saying? Oh, you've been listening to one too many televangelists!

MARY

The baby's infected with the virus, that's the whole plan. That's why this one's going down like it is.

ZACH

Now I'm really confused.

MARY

Well, get in line!

ZACH

You got infected with the HIV virus through the Holy Spirit?

MARY

Indirectly. Yeah. And I don't really know if I'm HIV positive yet. I just assume I am. In utero. Reverse-like, you know?

ZACH

You don't know? You didn't ask Gabriel?

MARY

I'm in bed. A large fucking angel with very large, ff... *[Looks upwards]* fluffy wings shows up in my bedroom. Tells me I've been chosen to bear baby Jesus. And the baby's going to be HIV positive! You don't ask questions. You just stay in a big state of "awe-ness", you know, like after a very bad perm.

ZACH

Maybe this is a Jewish thing. But I would.

MARY

[Sheepishly] If you want to know the truth. I'd smoked some reefer that night. *[Defensively]* I never, ever anymore. It was just... one of those things. How do you think I felt?! Talk about timing. *[Pause]* You know, I kept thinking—Gabriel must know that I'm wasted here. It was like being a teenager and living at home all over again. It was awkward, trust me.

ZACH

I'll buy that. *[Silence]* So, let me get this right. God went to a gay male, but who's not a queen, who occasionally smokes dope, and who was HIV negative, to be the mother—

MARY

Bearer. I'm the...bearer.

ZACH

Okay. No, I'm okay with that. *[Pause]* I hate to ask this one. Really. Really. I hate to ask...but...

MARY

Go ahead.

ZACH

You're...a...virgin?

MARY

Uh...*[Looks at **ZACK** funnily]* Technically.

ZACH

Oh, you're going to have to help me with that one too.

MARY

Well, I've never been...penetrated...anally?

ZACH

Yes?

MARY

[Quickly] But I've gone down and jacked off a hell of a lot of guys.

ZACH

Oh, kind of like a 1950s definition of a virgin.

MARY

Yeah, I like that.

ZACH

[Confused] I guess. I mean, if God's okay with it—

MARY

Hey, it's not like the Holy Spirit is some horndog, you know? Working on his own, making the rounds. There is some kind of choosing going on here. I do believe God has a plan. Difficult as that may seem now.

> *[Silence. **ZACK** and **MARY** look at each other as if for the first time.]*

MARY

You don't have any kids?

> *[**ZACK** shakes his head.]*

MARY

I can leave today? Now?

> *[**ZACK** nods his head. **MARY** slowly rises from the couch and begins to work towards the door.]*

ZACH

Am I supposed to be like John the Baptist?

MARY

Ask Gabriel. I can't tell you that.

ZACH

[Gets up and stands in front of the desk] Why is this happening?

MARY

Gabriel said it needed to happen again. Everyone's forgotten the original message. It's going to be . . . very interesting.

ZACH

The baby, you don't know how long it will live?

MARY

That isn't for us to question.

ZACH

[*Pause*] How are you going to endure all of this?

MARY

I'm gay, Zack. This is nothing! Try being a gay, Baptist teenager in the South. [*At the door*] It's all part of the plan. The new Redemption, with a new cross to bear.

ZACH

Wait . . . I want to help.

[**MARY** *stops and looks at* **ZACK** *very seriously.*]

ZACH

What can I do?

MARY

Know any good inns? [*Pause*] Joseph.

[**ZACK** *does a slow take to* **MARY**.]

CURTAIN

Mark Bibbins
Ghosts

I forgot to tell you,
you talk in your sleep,
translations
from the milky language
of the dead
curdled on your pillow.
When there is nothing
else of you here, I wash
the sheets, hang them
on the line. They ripple
in August light
like ghosts undone.

Jerry Rosco
The White Dog
for Jack

Finally, the things that once kept them from being closer no longer mattered. What remained was simply their souls stripped bare, and that their love, despite everything, was true.

Will looked out the bay window behind him and watched all the activity around the bird feeder twenty yards away. As usual, three squirrels were there. Every day one would jump onto the plastic hood of the large oval feeder, shaking black seeds to the ground. Then all three would feed alongside the undaunted birds. The usual pair of large, light-brown mourning doves was there, and three red-winged black birds. A familiar pair of bright yellow finches moved back and forth from tree branches to the base of the feeder. Other times there were large bluebirds, and even a magnificent crimson-colored cardinal.

Will had been watching the woods and fields behind his lover John's family home for months, from mid-winter through most of the spring. Now he looked away from it, back to the silent living room. He was sitting at the end of the long sofa, and beside him his young lover was stretched out asleep under a red plaid blanket. Will looked at John's handsome face. He needed a shave and his dark curly hair was flattened against the pillow, but his face was as boyish as it had been when they first met seven years ago. His small hands were clasped together in sleep, resting on his chest above the blanket.

Spring. Late spring. It wasn't supposed to be like this. In early

December John had decided to leave their city home and stay at his parent's house in the country for two or three months. Will could only agree. John's illness was no longer manageable, his weight loss was serious, and his city doctor seemed indifferent. But he'd met his parents' doctor in the country and the young physician was aggressive, and optimistic. He wanted John to stay at his parents' house, to get at least a few months of TPN weight-gaining treatment. Then he could return to the city, or at least alternate back and forth. But it hadn't worked out that way.

A large wall clock chimed in the adjoining parlor. John stirred but fell back to sleep. His parents were off to an early dinner with relatives. Will felt useful, giving John's youngish parents a break, a night out. That was better than feeling like a constant intruder in their home, like the long-haired, 40-year-old, somber, brainy, city person he was. Or like the looming presence he no doubt seemed . . . a vigilant big dog sitting forever by their son's side.

Still, they had all gotten along somehow. For over five months Will had been here more than he'd been at his city apartment a hundred miles away. He'd given up most of his work and income. Friends had taken care of their apartment, their mail, cats, and the white doves John had brought home last summer as a surprise. There'd been endless bus trips back and forth, some welcome visits from their young friends, and many nights in the sleeping bag on the floor beside John's bed.

All that seemed like a lot, but it was nothing. After the bad news that struck them halfway through this stay in the country, all that mattered now was being together. Will remembered that's how it had been seven years earlier, when their first months together were such a simple joy. He realized that they'd come full circle, back to the pure understanding of the night they'd met.

John, ten years younger, had made the first brave move. Small, with dark eyes and hair and a pretty face, he'd stood by himself in the dim-lit balcony of an old rock club. It was a weekly rock music night, and on the main floor below were hundreds of dancers and strobe-lit go-go boys.

Will noticed John, standing about 30 feet away in the smoke and shadows, and imagined the young man's first impression: that Will was bigger, dark with long hair, older, maybe too serious looking, but attractive, sexy. And Will saw a cute kid who cautiously moved a little closer, then suddenly walked directly over and looked into his eyes as he said hello.

Right away the differences between them didn't matter because Will saw that John was sweet, honest and attractive, and John could see that Will was the masculine but gentle type he liked. That night they were both there truly looking for love, and they found each other.

There were the early good times meeting each other's friends, learning about each other's world, taking short trips together. One day John left a hand-painted card on Will's table. On the back he'd written, "I think I'm in heaven."

It was months before the honeymoon ended. Then the relationship began, with all the usual fights and compromises, and then some. There were times it seemed as if it were over. But it was never over. Years passed in a quiet sort of happiness. Will saw that now. And later, when the bad news shrouded their lives, a deeper kind of love moved in.

First there'd been a year of fighting the illness while trying to hold onto their daily routines. By instinct they both knew that's what mattered most. Then, after a few months at his parents' home, John actually put it in words. "It isn't the big things I miss," he'd said months earlier. "Not California or Key West or Cherry Grove. Or going to concerts or plays. It's the little things. Like when you'd go rent a video and I'd get ice cream to surprise you. And the cats. I miss them."

"We'll have all that again," Will had said. At the time it seemed true. But then...John's eyesight...and soon after that, the worst news.

Then Will learned good things he had rather never come to—because the only way there was through months of the worst pain and most tears he'd ever know. But he got there—and learned that only those who have been through such grief know about the humbling beauty at the heart of it. When fear, terror, pain and loss have done their worst, and love and dignity are still there, then, he discovered, you can only feel awe. Whatever it is that is greater than our small lives, is there in that pure instinct to make love sacred and to give reverence to life.

§

A few months earlier, on a bright white February morning, the surrounding yards and fields white with snow, the sky clear and brilliant, they had decided to take a walk. This was in the brief period of time halfway between hope and the end of it. Weeks earlier, the sudden, merciless loss of his vision in the days between Christmas and New Years seemed to end the recovery plan and any expectations. Then, ten days later, some shadowy patterns of sight began to return, sometimes flickering to a black and white clarity for just a second. Will sat right beside the doctor when he said this was a miraculous event, and that John's vision would return over a period of months. "You'll be driving a car again," the young doctor said with real joy. But Will, believing it, noticed that John's expression did not change; it was too much, too much to accept or hope for all at once, after all he'd been through. And after all the medical mistakes and misstatements.

But still, there they were, in that brief moment of time, when John was feeling stronger, when cloudy silhouettes and fields of gray gave some hope that his vision was indeed coming back. Will understood why John didn't want to talk about things…too much was at stake to allow the jinx of loose talk. Everything hung in the balance. But Will allowed himself to think of it, of months ahead when they might be back in their city home, when John would be ill but better, his sight limited but improving by degrees. Visits from and to friends. Some sacred, miraculous recapturing of a bit of their normal life together.

And so, on a February morning when everything was beautiful and silent after a snowfall, they decided to go outdoors. Will and John put on their coats and boots in a sort of ritual of hope and optimism, which was not lost on the parents. John was feeling a little stronger, the walk would do him good. And after the terrible recent weeks of bad news and dependence, it was good to have a little time together at last.

They stepped out the front door to the sound of snow under their feet and fresh cold air. "I can see the walkway," John said, one arm locked in Will's arm. There was just enough snow to cover everything in all directions. The sunlight hit the cement walk that stretched in front of them leading to the driveway, making a flat white plane against the rolling white shape of lawn and low shrubs.

"It's pretty," Will said, "a real winter's day, everything's really white, not the way it is in the city."

"I know," John said, glad to share the moment, acknowledging the verbal gesture by city boy Will toward the country.

Little understatements always went far with them. But the big questions were always difficult. Both could talk just at the edges of something sensitive, and let the other either infer an answer or ignore it. Will had sensed only the smallest bit of cautious optimism from John on his chance for returning vision, but that was something. And Will delicately expressed back that he shared John's mixed feelings of anger, loss of all trust in doctors, fear, and courage. In the past, in happier times, Will always had a knack for carefully picking the right words with John who, younger and less confident, had a hair-trigger temper. Now, with all that had happened, they'd both become expert at handling each other with the most lovingly delicate choices of words.

And the really big questions were just not touched in words. John's strength and courage were amazing, it turned out, but neither of them could bear to hurt the other with any direct talk of possible finality. And they never did. Everyone and every couple is different, but between them their care and reticence with words, and their silences, were the greatest expression of their love.

It had been that way for nearly two years, to a fault. And now all the chips were pushed to the center of the table and here they were, in silence, side by side on this snowy path.

They stepped from the driveway onto the country road, which had little traffic in the winter months. "We'll walk to the end of the road and back," Will said, looking ahead at the hundred yards between them and the turnoff for the busier street that led to the highway.

Snow crunched under their boots as they walked in the center of the road. Wind brushed through the treetops, and tall old trees sounded the hard creak of wood you hear only in the stillness of the country in winter.

John's step was slow but steady, Will noticed. The weeks of TPN and his mother's cooking had helped a little. There was that whisper of hope again, like the soft wind in the high barren treetops.

But should they have a serious talk, Will wondered. He understood they'd always spared each other's feelings through the ordeal. But he knew John had spoken more frankly with a few friends. Between them, what they'd done instead was focus on each crisis, each savage assault on John's slight young body. Crypto. Fevers. Gallbladder. Shingles. Weight loss. Eyesight. Staggered, they struggled through each episode as if that were the whole problem.

Will asked himself, where is the wisdom in silence now? He thought of the expression he'd heard at a caregivers' meeting in the city: "Start the conversation." The conversation didn't have to be about "when," it could be about "what if."

He glanced at the handsome young face of his lover and his heart sank. This is my baby, he thought—he knew John liked to hear that endearing name out loud. For himself, he realized, the whisper of hope was better than words about the unimaginable, the unendurable.

But what about John? Did he need to talk about it, about what was very possible, even probable? Here was their chance. The vast white stillness around them seemed to portend something, something beyond their weighty homebound routine and tedious doctor visits.

John, maybe sensing Will's thoughts, kept silent for another moment. Then, still looking ahead, he said, "See that house on your left, the one that's way off the road, next to a small barn?" And he told Will about his neighbors, whose family this old road was named for.

And so it was, just that clearly, that no big important words would be spoken now. They came to the end of the road—the sound of a car on the highway could be heard—and John held onto his lover's arm as they slowly turned.

Just then, Will stopped, surprised by the large stocky white dog that stood before them. For a stunned second he thought it was a wolf. It seemed to come from nowhere, pure white as the snow all around them, and it waited, its pale blue eyes looking directly at him.

"There's a big dog here, a white dog," he said.

"That's just old Madison," John said, taking the first step toward home, "he lives at the corner house. He just likes to walk around the neighborhood."

As they walked, the white dog fell in right beside Will. It hobbled on its right front paw in the few inches of snow but stayed just ahead, as if leading them. This seemed strange or silly to Will, or make-believe, like following a dog in a fable. It had a sweet gentle expression, but was methodical, not playful, as if they'd done this before. It put its head down and pushed forward, old and arthritic in the snow as it barely stayed ahead of their slow pace.

The dreamlike stillness of the cold morning seemed even stranger now. Something clutched at Will. He didn't know why. He wanted to stop and grab John in his arms and hold onto him. But he knew it was the wrong time. Anything he did like that now would upset him. Instead he made sure to stay in step, to keep their arms linked, to hide his emotion. Everything blurred in front of him, but he didn't think his lover could see him rub his free hand against his eyes. The old white dog looked up again with that friendly grin and calm, gentle expression.

Up ahead, Will could see John's father get in his car and back down the driveway. The dog stayed beside them as they moved to the side of the road. "That's your father," Will said, "wave as he drives by." And John brought up his arm at just the right moment.

When they got to the house, Will stroked the dog's thick, coarse white fur. It watched them as they went inside, then hobbled off across the lawn.

§

After the final bad news there was just the waiting, which they didn't speak of, some emotional visits from friends and family, and finally their precious quiet days and nights together.

It was spring, then late spring. John's waking hours gave way more and more to the sleep of time-released morphine. Finally the bed was moved downstairs to the parlor, the chimes of the big clock were stilled. That night they hugged arm in arm, Will saying words of love, John nodding.

On the last day, Will said into John's ear, "We'll always stay together. You're staying with me and I'm staying with you. That's the way it's going to be." John heard the words.

Will sat on the room's little sofa and wept. The good local priest sat beside him. Outside the window, the white dog moved with a limp across the green lawn.

Lisa Freedman

Last Night on Earth No. 56

Why bother with lipstick?
> Why adjust the lights
> when the words these lips
> hafta utter
> blind like a flashbulb
> and snap that border love shares with death?

> "I am living with HIV"
> glares like a July noon sun.
> We're not here forever
> and there's only so much space
> between our first breath and our last.

> So, I unwind my lipstick
>> and dim down the lights.

Arlene McKanic
Getting On With It

Albert Hyttenberg lay prostrate on the livingroom floor of the townhouse he'd just sold. The room was empty and silent. Squares of sunlight fell on the parquet and climbed the soft, peach-colored walls. He'd lived here for years with Michael and then with their son Augustine. Now Michael was dead and Albert could no longer bear to stay.

He sat up after a few minutes, rubbed his face, squinted against a beam of sunlight. He drew his knees to his chest and listened to the stillness that pressed against his ears like pillows. He'd sold the townhouse to his nephew and his wife and didn't know whether selling to a relative had been wise. He'd have to come back. He'd have to endure another family's celebrations and even tragedies in a place where he'd lived through his own. He'd be tasked by the sight of another family taking possession of rooms that had once been his and Michael's and Auggie's. The walls would absorb the sounds of another family's life: laughter, whispers, screams, quiet talk about nothing, the sizzle of something frying on the cooking island, the tumult of two other little boys. Soon, Albert thought this townhouse would forget him. He wouldn't be allowed to forget it.

He heard the front door being unlocked, distantly, and he got to his feet. He waited till his nephew appeared at the room's entrance.

They greeted each other quietly; David's hand lingered a while on Albert's back in a gesture of consolation and support. They left the townhouse and drove to Albert's parents' summer home in Long Island. Auggie had been farmed out to them during the move to enjoy their affection, their big house, their pool, their dogs, and the noisy comings and goings of the extended family. They had dinner then, Albert, Auggie and David drove back to Manhattan. Albert dropped David off at the apartment building he was soon to vacate then continued on to the building he and Auggie had moved into, a high-rise in the upper West Village with a nice view of both the Twin Towers and the Empire State Building. After Albert parked in the underground garage he and Auggie rode the elevator to the top floor and entered the apartment in nearly reverential silence. Auggie went straight to his new bedroom. He'd been worried that his things would be misplaced during the move, but his old bed was there, as were his toys. His Power Rangers posters were on the walls, his clothes were in the closets and in the chest of drawers, his bicycle stood by the window in the sunset light. His books were on their shelves and his desk with his computer and gooseneck lamp waited, dustless, against a wall.

He dropped his knapsack on the floor and plumped down on the bed.

"Like it?" Albert asked.

Auggie nodded. He looked up at Albert. "Are we gonna stay here?"

"Of course we are," his father said. "What kinda question is that?" But he asked it gently. He'd always treated Auggie with gentleness. Now, in these weeks after Michael's death, he was conscious of it, careful of it. Tenderness was all.

Auggie shrugged. Albert watched him. He was only seven and looked small and lost, sitting there. The room was bigger than the one he'd had at the townhouse and its newness made it vaguely unfriendly. Albert sat next to Auggie on the bed and put an arm around him as if to protect him from it.

"Let's check this place out," Albert suggested. "Okay?"

"Yeah," Auggie nodded.

They investigated like good spelunkers. They inspected the bedrooms, the living room, the salon and reception room, the kitchen, the dining room and library, the pantry, the private hallway that led to the two servants' bedrooms. The rooms felt enormous to Albert and also unwelcoming; somehow the townhouse had been cozier.

'That's because three people had lived there,' he thought, and was struck by a grief so terrible that he had to lean against the door-jamb of the *au pair*'s room to bear it. Albert had learned that grief, after its initial bulldozing and grinding down of one, became like a flare star, with periods of simmering unease interrupted by spikes of pure agony. Grief didn't feel like fear at all, he'd learned. Fear felt like grief—fear was, in fact, the anticipation of grief. Grief felt like nothing but itself. 'Oh my God,' he thought. 'I can't believe this. I just can't believe this.'

He pulled himself together before Auggie noticed. They resumed the tour of their home. Auggie unlocked the terrace door but it wouldn't open, and after some exertion Albert managed to unstick it. They stepped out and stood looking at the buildings around them, at windows and roofs and roof gardens. They watched the traffic crawl up 6th Avenue and flocks of pigeons swoop down to rooftop dovecotes. They saw a corner of their building's playground.

They returned to the living room and watched TV for a while. Albert sat on the sofa and Auggie lay with his head in his lap. By the time the Saturday night movie was over he was asleep. Albert carried him to his room, laid him on the bed, and gently woke him. He could have changed Auggie into his pajamas, but Auggie was too dignified for that sort of thing now.

"Time to get ready for bed," Albert whispered as his son's eyes fluttered open.

Auggie took his bath and brushed his teeth and changed into his pajamas while Albert waited in the bedroom; he missed bathing Auggie. He felt a need to do so now, to relive that intensity of care and tenderness, but he couldn't. Auggie was a big boy. When he came back to his room Abert only helped him get under the covers.

"It feels weird," Auggie said.

"What? The bed? But this is the bed you had before."

"Yeah, but... it still does," Auggie said.

"Yeah, I know," Albert said, stroking his hair. "I know."

He went to bed reluctantly. When Michael died he'd immediately sold their old bed for a new, smaller one, and it still felt alien after a month of use. It was just a strange bed in a strange room. Albert felt he was in a place less hospitable than a roadside motel. He couldn't sleep well. When he did sleep grief wrung his dreams.

He woke early and fixed his and Auggie's breakfast. At around eleven they left the building and walked three blocks to Auggie's new school. The building was officially closed, but after some wheedling Albert had a security guard show them around the big sunny classrooms with desks for no more than twenty children, the gym, the cafeteria, the computer and science labs, the auditorium, the art studio, the rooftop atrium and the small playground.

'This is what we're supposed to be doing,' Albert told himself. 'Getting on with it.'

"What'd you think?" he asked Auggie as they walked back home.

"It's okay," the boy shrugged, but his eyes were on the little stores they passed: the Chinese takeout place, the stationer's, the dry cleaner's, the shoe store, the women's and children's boutiques, the patisserie, the flower shop with its explosions of blooms in the windows, the antique store. Albert was grateful for them all. He'd moved into a real neighborhood.

They didn't go upstairs right away but visited the playground. Auggie approached a trio of boys his age who were clambering over one of the jungle gyms. Albert sat on a bench beneath a plane tree and watched him. He found something unbelievably poignant about the back of his head and the softness of his shoulders as he approached the other boys; he seemed like a wary fawn. But soon Auggie was climbing with them. He made friends easily. Albert knew of only one parent who'd forbade his child to play with Auggie because of his living situation. That had been back in Gramercy Park.

Albert let Auggie play for about half an hour before he caught his eye and gestured to him. The bells of the neighborhood church were tolling by then.

When Auggie came over Albert reminded him it was time for lunch. Auggie didn't want to leave. Albert saw this, too, as a good sign.

"Tell them you'll be back down. They're probably going in for lunch too in a few minutes," Albert whispered to him. Auggie nodded, mollified, and ran back to his new friends.

Albert got an idea as he fixed Auggie's sandwich at the kitchen's work island after they'd come upstairs. He said nothing to Auggie about it as they ate; he forgot what they did talk about, except that it was all comforting father-son banalities. After lunch Auggie rushed back downstairs to find his new friends. Albert felt the children would be well supervised by the security guard, so he stayed upstairs and let his plan take delicious form in his head; the pleasure of it felt like a piece of pottery that was both beautiful and useful taking shape between his hands.

§

Auggie started school the next day. On Tuesday, Albert took the afternoon off from his job at his father's downtown law firm, drove to an AKA certified kennel in Larchmont and bought a samoyed puppy. Albert had always wanted a samoyed because they were fluffy and smiled up at you adoringly and of all the dogs he'd owned he'd never had one. Auggie loved dogs and liked fluffy things—he'd never admit this, but Albert knew—so Albert picked the healthiest looking of the balls of thistledown that leapt at him ecstatically from behind the wires of their cages. When the salesman took the puppy out Albert saw that his dark little eyes were brilliant and his tongue was pink and his nose and behind were dry, and bought him.

He got home before Auggie and let the puppy out of his box—he shot like a comet into the apartment's cavernousness. Albert didn't run after him but he and one of the building's maintenance men set up his little wicker bed with is tartan cushions and blanket in a sunny corner of the kitchen and arranged his toys—a ball, a rawhide bone—around it. He put his food and water bowls in another corner of the kitchen near the fridge, and filled them. Albert was elated; infact, he was smug. He was going to spring an absolutely wonderful surprise on his son!

When the maintenance man left, Albert wandered around the apartment, whistling and singing out, "Here boy! Here boy!" He finally found the puppy in the largest bathroom. He'd yanked down one of the towels from the rack and was dragging it about the floor, growling. "No no no," Albert said. "Come on." He took one end of the towel and tugged gently—of course the puppy tugged back, thrilled at the new game. Albert kept this up for some moments before he let go. When he did, the puppy let go too, and Albert scooped him up. He wriggled in Albert's arms so much that he let him down before he dropped him. The puppy took the opportunity to go tearing off again.

"Oh geez," Albert muttered, and went after him

The puppy found his food bowl and had stopped momentarily to refuel. Albert noticed he'd left a puddle on the tiled kitchen floor. "Damn," he said.

He'd just finished mopping up the mess when he heard the key in the door. Improbably, the puppy got to the entry hall first, yapping.

"Oh wow!" Auggie screamed. "Oh Dad, is he ours!?"

"He's yours," Albert said. "Take your stuff off first—how'd he get out here that fast?"

Auggie tore off his jacket and knapsack, then got down on the floor with the dog. Hammily, he threw himself in Auggie's arms and licked his face as if he were along lost relative. Just looking at him made Albert tired. But Auggie's giggles caused him another, sweeter pain. He hadn't heard his son giggle so joyfully in a long time (Albert reminded himself that this was exactly what he'd meant to happen). The puppy squirmed out of Auggie's arms and took off again and Auggie, laughing, took off after him.

Albert picked up his son's jacket and knapsack from the floor. He hung the jacket in the foyer closet and carried the knapsack to Auggie's room and tossed it wearily to the bed. Then he went to look for his son and his dog.

They were in the living room. Albert could see that something was wrong immediately.

"Auggie?" he demanded.

Auggie sat on the rug and the puppy was snuggling in his lap. He raised his head and looked at his father. His features were pinched, and he was wheezing.

"Oh Christ!" Albert hurried to him. He was appalled; he hadn't been gone for five minutes. He pushed the puppy out of the way, or tried to—the sammy bounced right back to them. "Auggie, are you okay? Oh God." He cupped the little boy's face in his hands. "You can't breathe? Should I call Dr. Wasser?"

Auggie's eyes widened with anxiety and Albert knew the little boy was more afraid of the dog having to go than not being able to breathe. "N-no!" he gasped.

"You can't breathe, honey," Albert said, more brusquely than he meant to. He got up and carried Auggie to the nearest bathroom. The puppy followed and Albert had to stop himself from kicking him in fury; he did manage to lock him out of the room. He sat Auggie on the bench and turned on the hot water shower. He heard Auggie gasp over the roar of the water. His small chest was spasming.

"Take it easy, okay?" Albert said.

Auggie nodded. The room began to fill up with steam.

Albert ran to the telephone in the master bedroom and called Auggie's pediatrician. Dr. Wasser agreed to send an ambulance.

He intercepted the puppy in the hallway on his way back to the bathroom. He snatched him up, carried him back to his bedroom, tossed him to the floor as gently as his anger would allow, then shut the door on him before he could dash out. He hurried back to Auggie. The billowy wall of steam smelled of metal. Albert sat down next to Auggie and pulled him into his lap.

"It's all right," Albert said. The boy's body trembled as he fought to breathe. "The ambulance is coming. You comfortable?" Auggie nodded. "You can breathe like this?" Auggie nodded again. Albert remembered. He'd never been allergic to animals before. "Daddy's here, honey," he said. He rocked Auggie in his arms. "He's here."

He was allowed to ride in the back of the ambulance. One of the EMS workers had fitted Auggie with a nasal cannula. In the hard ambulance light Albert could see Auggie's lips and the wings of his nose had turned blue, as if he'd been swimming for a long time in cold water. As humidified oxygen was poured into him, the blue disappeared and his eyes shut in nearly drugged relief. Albert couldn't believe he was in the back of an ambulance again, this soon. 'No,' he thought. His heart hurt like a running gear with sharp edges. 'Christ!' He reached out; his son's hand disappeared into his.

When they arrived at the hospital Dr. Wasser gave Auggie a shot of cortisone in the emergency room. Albert called his parents. When he heard his father's voice over the phone he broke down. The phone was on a wall near the elevator bank and everyone who passed saw Albert's tears. He couldn't care; grief had affected his dignity. Even before Michael's death, Albert had suspected this was another thing grief did—he'd been to his share of funerals—but he was unprepared for how debased grief left you. A howling dog was less shameful than a human being overwhelmed by his own sorrow. Albert was forty-three years old and he blubbered to his father like a child.

"Oh hell, Albert, he'll get over an asthma attack," Jordan said.

"Oh my God, Papa," he wept. "He couldn't breathe! He couldn't freakin' breathe! It was like…"

At the end, Michael couldn't breathe either. A colony of proto-zoa had clogged and scarred his lungs.

"He can breathe now," Jordan said, cutting him off. "Look, you want me to come down? I'll at least pick up the mutt. You shouldn't have a dog in your apartment anyway."

"But he's never… Auggie's been around dogs. He's around your dogs all the time," Albert said. "I don't know why now."

"Maybe it's the stress of moving and starting school and all that and the dog just overloaded everything," Jordan said reasonably.

Albert wiped his eyes with the back of his hand, again, like a child. He saw an orderly wheel a gurney past him and and steer it through the swinging doors of a room across the hall. The figure beneath the white sheets was child-sized. "I… I think he's back."

"Okay. Go see him. I'll be there."

Albert didn't know if he was allowed to enter the room, but he pushed through the doors anyway. His son had been put in a bed. He was asleep and his breathing was even and deep. Albert rolled up a chair and sat next to him, watched him. God, the universe, some-thing ws toying with both of them. Albert was beginning to believe that the lower you sank the harder the universe kicked you. And why? Didn't God have anything better to do?

'I can't stand this. When the fuck is this gonna end?' he thought.

Dr. Wasser came in a few minutes later. He woke Auggie gently and checked him. He told him and Albert that he saw no reason why Auggie couldn't go home that night. The episode seemed to be isolated.

"I guess I can't keep the dog," Auggie whispered.

"'Fraid not," Albert said. He'd regained enough self-restraint to make Auggie think he was in control. "Grandpa'll take it. It's better for a dog to be out in the country anyway."

Albert's parents arrived later that evening. Jordan was calm as usual, but Googie's face was ashen when she saw her grandson in that hospital bed. Michael's death had been hard on her.

Albert gave Jordan his set of keys to the apartment so his parents could get the dog—he didn't want him to be there when Auggie returned.

"How are you going to get back in?" Googie asked just before she and her husband left.

"Leave the keys with the doorman," Albert told her, calmly.

Googie nodded uncertainly; Jordan's nod was firm. He bent down and kissed Auggie's hair, and to Albert's surprise, walked around the bed and bent down to kiss Albert's as well. His hand lingered a moment on his son's cheek and Albert had to fight not to weep again.

"See you later," Jordan said

"Thanks for everything," Albert murmured. His voice was raspy. He cleared his throat. His mother was so undone that she forgot to kiss anyone.

Auggie was discharged later that night. When they got home Albert put him to bed. For the first time in a while he asked Albert to tell him a story, then to wait at the bedside while he silently said his prayers. Albert was surprised; prayers hadn't been one of the usual bedtime rituals. Then he realized, 'It's because...'

He couldn't finish the thought.

Later, Albert washed the dishes and damp-mopped the kitchen floor, especially the places where the dog's bowls and bed had been. He was grateful for how fast he was forgetting him. He took a shower, brushed his teeth, then crawled into that strange bed. He was numb. He was like a lab animal so tormented by its handlers that it won't leave its cage even after the door has been opened. Later, Albert would describe himself as punch drunk. Maybe this was a mercy. Maybe it was better to be anesthetized than in such chaotic anguish that you couldn't function. Albert had a young child; he had to function. He was grateful also for even the drudgery needed to keep a young child properly cared for. He realized he'd have to get out of bed the next morning. He'd check on Auggie to see if he was well enough to go to school, and if he wasn't Albert would have to take off from work, for the *au pair* wasn't due till Friday. He'd fix the meals, he'd clean a little. Perhaps he and Auggie would watch cable or play video games, or perhaps they'd lie together on his bed and talk about nothing, and Albert would at last feel the fabric of their life being stitched back together, quietly.

Robert Vazquez-Pacheco
Juan Diego

I spend my time scratching spontaneous rashes
that appear like miraculous sightings of the Virgin,
apparitions that blossom like Juan Diego's roses,
and then disappear leaving their images on my skin
and the scent of hydrocortisone in the air.

My skin is now covered with these discolorations
dark spots where rashes appeared then vanished,
marking the miraculous moment of discomfort forever,
these marks could form some intricate pattern
from head to toe, which my fingers follow
like a blind man seeking meaning through touch.

If each strain were to be connected
a variation of a game I played in school
what message, written on my skin in lines of fire,
will this viral messenger disclose to me
words that I try to wipe from my skin,
like reading Braille written in sand,
while seeking the momentary grace of scratching.

I wonder if my skin were to be flayed
and my hide dried out and stretched,
perhaps volumes of text would be revealed
on the pink underside of my brown skin,
pulsing nerve endings now fashioned into
an elegant viral script, like Arabic
or Sanskrit, telling us about the cure
or the reason why this happens.

Or perhaps showing us a picture,
the image of another Black Mother or
an Aztec goddess, wine-dark as lesions,
Our Lady of the Plague, to whom we pray

to for protection from the evils of breathlessness,
diarrhea and dementia, in hopes of salvation
or perhaps just the simple end of pain.

Gary R. McClain
Key West in the Last Days

Saturday morning slips in through the narrow slats of the mini-blinds. I wake up to find myself curled up on the edge of the bed and when I look over my shoulder I see that Alby is facing away from me. He's way at the other side, so far away his head almost hangs over the mattress and bumps against the wall. There's room for two more people in the middle, maybe the two people we used to be, the two who a long time ago used to wake up curled together, arms and legs entwined, or if not, soon found their way to each other.

I turn over to watch him, rest my head on my elbow. He's pulled the covers up around his throat, the little wisps of hair are matted to one side, he must have done some tossing and turning. A few wisps are left on the pillow; I try to brush them off before he notices, just in case he cares anymore.

I want to reach over and put my hand on his shoulder but I'll wait a moment or two. It's not time yet. Something inside me is telling me to savor this moment, store this image in my mind: Alby sleeping so peacefully, the covers rising up and down to rhythm of his breathing. He's congested, almost wheezy, and he swallows occasionally, sniffles, before the rhythm returns. It's one of those moments, I know it is now, that I want to freeze in time, one of those moments that will quickly slip away, maybe to sneak back and torture me sometime later. He's so calm, my handsome man sleeping through the morning. As good as it gets, the voice reminds me.

I look up at our clock radio and see that it's almost 10 a.m. I figure eleven hours ought to hold him, at least until lunch, so I lean in closer, curling my body into the same shape as his, moving just within a few inches of him. I breathe with him, steal his rhythm, then softly, barely, touch his neck with my lips. I leave them there, feel his pulse as it beats against my mouth, then press in harder. He pushes himself toward me, and I fold my arms around him, wrap my leg over his.

"How do you feel, buddy?" I ask. "Did you sleep okay?"

"Yeah," he answers.

"Are you hungry?"

"Not yet."

He reaches up and takes one of my hands, moves his butt against me. "You feel good," he says.

"So do you. You always feel good."

I crane my neck around to try and figure out what the weather is. A few clouds maybe and, yes, even some snow flakes. The windows are filthy, I don't have time to worry about them anymore, and a few flakes have stuck to the dirt. They remain in place only for a few seconds, then start to melt, leaving tiny streaks as they ease their way downward.

I snuggle closer into him. Did it snow like this last winter? I don't remember. I was too near-sighted to notice, hiding behind my rose-colored glasses, trying to pretend that reality was a temporary bad dream. A bad dream that we tried to escape, for a few days, through our annual Key West trip. A few days, that's all I wanted, after all, there would be more. I told myself.

At breakfast, Alby sits next to me, in his usual chair. He picks at the scrambled eggs covered with melted cheddar cheese, ignores the bagel and fruit. I try to hold my tongue to keep from nagging at him. We have a whole day ahead of us, no reason to get him irritated this early on.

The phone rings. His sister Marla, calling to check up on us.

"How's that brother of mine doing?" she asks. There's a forced cheerfulness to her voice, but I think she's just hiding her worry.

"He's fantastic."

Alby sits straight up, one leg crossed over the other, drinking his coffee. Jaunty. A cocky bastard, even. For a few seconds, it's like any other Saturday morning. I could almost pretend...but not quite.

"That's good," she says.

"Who is it?" he asks me. I mouth her name to him, and he smiles and winks, then lifts the newspaper up in front of his face.

"Do you want to speak with him?"

"In a second," Marla answers. "First I want to tell you to have a good week with my brother. Keep spoiling the hell out of him if that's possible."

I laugh. Too loud. It crosses my mind how much a laugh and a sob are alike, and how easily mine could turn. I look over at Alby. He's unfolded the paper, and is looking through it. I wonder if he can see well enough to read.

"I don't think I should go too easy on him."

"What are you two conspiring about?" he asks through the newspaper.

"And my brother is going to be with us for a long time, isn't he?" she asks.

"Yes he is," I answer. "He sure the hell is."

"He may want to stay longer than a week," Marla says.

"He knows he's welcome."

Alby lowers the newspaper. With mock impatience, he says, "May I please speak with my own damn sister?"

This is the middle of winter, February. And when I compare how he is now to how he was on our last Key West trip, a year ago, I know that he really has changed. He can't get up and walk across the room without help anymore. Me, or somebody, has to stand next to him, gently touch an arm, and be ready to grab when he gets off balance. When did this start? I can't remember. I was measuring time in milestones for awhile: first symptom, more symptoms, first AZT, first hospitalization, chemotherapy, second hospitalization. Good days, bad days, self-delusion days, all part of the routine of his life, and mine.

Life is starting to seem like a gentle, maybe not so gentle, down-ward spiral.

Each step has propelled me forward in the knowledge that this is for real. It's happening. I think about the people around us and how I've been closer to Alby than anybody else, the first person he told, the one who has walked with him every step of this mess. His friends Ken and Darren were among the last to know, and they knew as soon as they saw him on that trip to Key West, of course they did. For me, his illness remains a bunch of facts that stay in my head but that I struggle to keep from sinking down into my gut and becoming real.

And then I wonder if I'm still not the last to know.

It was a four-day weekend, President's Day. I was well into

the spring semester and needing a break from students and dreary weather, Alby was already on disability. We had gone to Key West with Ken and Darren the two previous years, and he wanted to do it again. I didn't want to go, I wanted the time alone with Alby, and looking back, I also wanted to hide him away from the rest of the world, avoid the stares and whispers, yes, hide away with him, as if his illness were our private matter. (And maybe, if we didn't go public with it, it might just slink away on its own.) But they were two of his best friends. Alby wanted to see them again, maybe for the last time. And I guess he wanted them to know.

I had hoped he might tell them ahead of time. 'I don't want you to be shocked old chaps but I'm not in the best of shape, you'll see.' Get the Big Revelation out of the way before we got there. But that was Alby's choice to make, he had at least that much control over his life.

By then, Alby and I had developed a routine around his condition. We knew what we could talk about and how to step around the difficult stuff. I could ask him how he felt, and when he said "okay today," I knew he was gonna have enough energy to make it through until his afternoon nap. I knew how to look for any changes in his appearance without staring him down.

Two other people could interfere with that routine, through sideways glances that lingered too long, and knowing uncomfortable looks at each other, tip-toe questions. Would that be better than saying the words out loud and admitting that the man was sick? Maybe we could somehow leave them with doubts, words left unsaid. That might be better, I thought, than acknowledging the truth. Leave us all self-deluded but hopeful.

Alby and I flew in with the masses on a Friday night. Since school had started a couple of days before that, I couldn't leave any earlier. Ken and Darren had arrived the day before, and Ken was going to meet us at the airport.

As we walked off the plane, we scanned the crowd for signs of him.

I felt myself becoming anxious. Crowded places, with staring eyes and disapproving glances, felt threatening to me by then. "They may be running late. They should be here."

"Patience, my son," Alby said.

We pushed through the hugging children and grandparents and followed the rest of the crowd toward the baggage claim. In the distance, I saw Ken running toward us. He had had a chance to hit the sun. As he got closer, I could see that his scalp was red under the thinning reddish spiky-cut hair, and his nose and cheekbones, and his arms, were equally bright red. It was a farmer's burn. He must have had a tee shirt on through most of it; the burn line was apparent at the edge of his open-necked sport shirt.

Ken waved, lifting his arm straight up in the air. "Hey," he yelled.

"Hey," I yelled back, lifting up my hand high and waving it back and forth back and forth like a drowning victim going down for the third time. And while I did this, I had the urge to wave it in the other direction, to wave him away. You're not ready for this. His big innocent smile confirmed to me that Alby hadn't told him yet.

Ken looked away from me to find Alby, who was a few steps behind me, carrying the smaller duffel bag in one hand, and my briefcase in the other. I watched Ken's face as he got closer to Alby.

The wide smile held, at first. Ken has a way of smiling so hard his eyes almost close shut, and a mouth full of too many teeth, all a bit yellowed from his chain-smoking.

When he was within a few yards of Alby, Ken opened his eyes wider, as if trying to focus. The smile disappeared, and he frowned. His hand dropped to his side.

He looked back at me, rushed toward me and hugged me, after first grabbing the biggest bag from my hand and setting it down to hold me in both arms. He kissed me on the cheek, and then squeezed me hard again.

"Glad to see you," I said, the pressure of his squeeze making me catch my breath. Hope you're still glad.

Alby was watching us, smiling, oblivious of the looks of the crowd as they pushed their way around us. My hands went up to Ken's shoulders and I gently pushed him away. Then I reached over and took Alby's arm and brought him closer.

Ken tried to smile again but he couldn't pull it off. Instead, he had a look, slightly frowning, disappointed, that said: not you too. Or maybe: don't do this to us.

Alby moved toward him and they embraced. Ken reached up and put his hand on Alby's cheek, then pressed Alby's face against his own. He stood back, his hands on Alby's shoulders.

"Sorry about all of this," Alby said.

"Don't apologize," Ken answered. "It's okay, Alby."

Ken reached down and picked up the bag he had taken from me, and then offered to take the duffel bag from Alby.

"I can handle this," Alby said.

"Okay, my friend."

We started to make our way through the crowd, Ken walking first, Alby in the middle, with me taking up the rear. Ken kept looking over his shoulder and smiling to make sure we were following close. Face after face, in the oncoming crowds, frowned, or stared curiously, as they caught a glimpse of Alby. Even in this land of leather-skinned natives, his face was a little too thin, the lines too deep, the eyes slightly too big. They knew something was wrong. Most of the faces then registered guilt as I gave them an evil glare that let them know they were caught in the act. As if I haven't done my share of staring at somebody else's misfortune. But back off, this time it's mine.

As we got closer to the exit doors, a voice on the loudspeaker broke into the noise of the crowd. A voice reminded us—first in English and then in Spanish—that we were all responsible for our own baggage.

It's Tuesday. Alby slept through the morning. His lunch seems to have perked him up.

"Can you give me my bath now?" he asks me.

"Yeah, baby."

I get the water temperature just the way he likes it, then help him step into the tub. Alby leans all the way back, letting the water level come to just below his chin. I reach underneath his head and let it rest on my hand.

"Is my head too heavy for you?" he asks me.

"Never."

"You won't let me drown, will you?" He smiles contentedly as he relaxes his weight all the way into my hand.

"Nope."

"Good. It's a shitty way to go."

"You're telling me. I'm the one who's hydrophobic, remember?"

With my other hand, I take the soap and gently scrub him down, then lightly splash water to rinse away the lather. Alby sniffs some of the soap bubbles that have crept up into his nose.

"Would you rather sit here and soak and listen to the radio?" I ask him.

"No. I want you with me. Maybe you can wash my hair. Do you mind?"

"I'd love to."

I dip the washcloth into the warm water and gently tip his head back while I squeeze it out onto his wispy hair. He closes his eyes while the water runs over his face. Then I place one hand on the back of his neck while I work a few drops of shampoo into his head. I gently work in the shampoo, massaging his scalp back and forth with my fingertips.

"That's good," Alby says. "Did you see that Spike Lee movie where he says getting your hair plaited is better than sex?"

"I do remember that. Is it true?"

"I think it might be. Laying in this warm water, having you hold me and rub my head. I don't think life gets any better."

I hold the washcloth over his eyes while I rinse the shampoo out.

"I'm glad you're happy."

"I love being in water. I always have." He reaches up and brings my hand to his mouth and kisses it. "Not like you, right?"

"You got that right. I'll stick with showers so I can jump out if the water gets above my ankles."

He leans back and closes his eyes. "I've been thinking about our last trip to Key West. It was great, wasn't it?"

On that Key West weekend, Darren saw Alby's condition clearer than anybody. He's a social worker in some kind of drug treatment program. While in the past I'd always found his empathy to be pushing the envelope rapidly in the direction of nausea, it was welcome this time.

He was at the hotel waiting for us. We walked in and he took one look at Alby and said: "You've got HIV."

"That's a real ice breaker," I said, relieved that we weren't going to be dancing around the obvious.

"Yeah," Alby answered. "I do."

"This isn't a bad time to have it." Darren's voice dripped with an optimism only a member of the compassion crowd can muster. "Great treatments." Darren is a couple of inches shorter than Alby. After a summer of sunbathing, his skin was darkly tanned, contrasting nicely with his light blue shirt, and his blond hair was bleached almost white. He leaned in close to give Alby's face a clinical once-over, his eyes obviously lingering over swollen lymph nodes in Alby's neck. "You can beat this bullshit."

"I'm trying."

"Good. Attitude is important."

"He's really doing fantastic," I added. "He's got a lot of energy."

Alby gave me a little cuff on one arm just as Darren was reaching up to cuff the other. They both gave me a half smile that almost seemed patronizing.

"Mr. Optimistic," Alby said.

Ken continued to look shell-shocked, reeling under the shadow of death. He was usually the optimistic one, full of jokes. He sat on the edge of the bed and watched us with a sullen expression, crossing his arms as if holding himself and rocking back and forth. Darren looked over at him and raised his eyebrows like he expected him to make a move.

"How about a beer?" Ken asked, then, after looking at Alby, he added, "or a Coke."

"I'll have a beer," Alby answered, with some defiance in his voice. "Not a damn Coke. And then we're heading for the Keys."

Late one night, after Ken and Darren had gone to bed, Alby asked me if I wanted to go for a walk. He had taken a nap while the rest of us watched TV, and his energy was back. We both threw on Polo shirts, his light green and mine pink. Alby wanted to take advantage of the cover of darkness to avoid the long sleeved KS-covering shirts for a while.

Duval Street was quiet that late in the evening. The families were safely tucked away in their motel rooms, most of the nightlife crowd was milling around on the way to the next scene, the couples were looking for a nightcap, and those who were still unaccompanied were looking for another chance at a conquest.

The gay boys owned the streets again.

A drag queen saw Alby and hollered, "Hey, tall, dark and handsome." She had a tight fitting chartreuse minidress on, and make-up to look like Betty Davis. I put my arm around him possessively and we both laughed.

"You'd like to think you can hang onto that man," the drag queen warned, shaking her finger at me as she passed.

I walked slowly so that Alby could keep up with me, and we didn't talk much. We passed the closed up tee-shirt shops and frozen yogurt shops, the so-called galleries stocked with shopping mall poster store art. Every time we hit a dark area, or slipped down a side street, I would hold his hand, even for a few seconds, sneak a quick kiss, and then let go of it when we were under the streetlights again.

I had unconsciously started walking faster again, and Alby reached over and touched my arm. "You have to slow down for me, my friend. Remember?"

I was caught off guard by a memory that popped into my mind about how I used to have to speed to keep up with him, how we used to leave everybody else behind in our dust. I stopped in the middle of my next step, and then brought my foot down in an exaggerated way, as if caught in slow motion. I knew right away it was a cheap shot.

"I'm sorry," I said. "I don't mind slowing down."

We came to the end of Duval Street, turned around, and started back on the other side of the street. We had survived one promenade; the return trip would be easier. I paced myself with his rhythm. We didn't talk; there wasn't much to say. It seemed more important to reach over and touch hands and to feel each other's presence.

On the way back through the Keys we stopped at one of those gator farm tourist traps. Alby dragged us to a cage with a cobra in it. He stood in front of the cage and tapped on the glass to get its

attention. Then he weaved back and forth, slowly, until the cobra focused its eyes on him. Gradually, the cobra began to coil and, finally,
opened its hood. When the owners weren't looking, Alby slapped
his hand up against the glass. The cobra struck at him. Alby held up
his hand and we high-fived each other, while the venom dribbled
down the glass like cum.

"I am invincible," he said to us.

"Yes you are, baby," I answered. I looked over at Ken and Darren, who were watching me. They smiled, sadly and indulgently,
like they had something on me. "Yes you are, Alby," I said to them.

He's lying in our bed, on his side now, facing toward the wall.
I sit at the edge of the bed, and watch him for a few minutes. I get
in and wrap myself around him, push my face up against the back
of his neck. He reaches around and touches my face. His hands are
cold, not overheated like the rest of him, and the coolness feels good
on my skin. I move my lips around to kiss his fingers.

"Mike?"

"I'm here, Alby."

"I was thinking about Key West again. How much fun we had.
I was thinking about how we all went into the water, even you. The
guy who hates water. Do you remember that?"

"I remember, Alby. I sure do."

"And I was thinking how you should keep remembering that
day and not stand on the shore while everybody else is splashing
around."

I pull him into me close and kiss his hand again.

"I'll go swimming with you, Alby, if you want. We'll take lessons, right?"

"You know that's not what I mean, Mike," he says gently. "I won't be there with you, buddy. You can't save me." He finds my hand and squeezes it. "But you have to dive in and get wet again. You know. With life. You promise?"

"Alby, I don't want to—"

"Dive in, Mikie. You're not gonna drown."

I press my face, hard, into the back of his tee shirt. The emotion flows out of me in sobs, sobs that rack my whole body, and shoot out in tears. I can hear myself, moaning and choking and convulsing like a kid after a good beating.

"It's okay, Mikie," he whispers. "It's okay."

We hit the beach, somewhere along the Keys where we'd stopped to take an afternoon break on the long drive back to Miami.

The four of us were in a fairly deserted area, past the families and tourists, even beyond a section the gays had staked out as their very own. Darren brought along a cooler filled with all the food we haven't yet gotten around to eating that weekend; it took the combined muscle power of both of us to lug it that far, with Alby and Ken following along behind us with beach bags. We stretched out on a couple of old sheets.

Alby jumped up and threw his shirt off.

"What are you doing?" I asked.

He stood in front of me, legs slightly apart, and swung the shirt around and around over his head, then held it in front of himself like a bullfighter.

"It's a beach," he said. "Life's a bitch. I'm going swimming."

Ken and Darren glanced up at Alby, then over at me. It was the first time he had taken his shirt off in front of them, the first time they'd seen the splotches of KS on his chest. When he turned around, his back looked like the abstract art of a slasher, big, bold, angry splotches in red—the newer ones, and dark purple—the older ones. They stood out against his brown skin; the sunlight over the last few days had sneaked through his white cotton shirts to give it a darker, coppery tone. It was out in the open now, so to speak. They could see how far the KS had progressed, no secrets. Darren looked away, pretending not to notice. Ken kept watching.

"I don't know about the water temperature. Isn't it too cold?" I asked Alby.

"You think too much. Stop worrying about me."

Alby tossed his shirt at me and half walked, half ran, down toward the beach. I hadn't looked at him from a distance before. His red boxers hung loosely around his hops. He was becoming more skeletal—there was no other word for it. His legs looked more spindly than I remembered, his rib cage protruded out over a gap where his flat stomach used to be. His head was starting to look too big for the rest of his body.

"Alby always liked the water," Ken said, "even in high school. We used to go down to Dewey Beach when it started to get warm." I heard his voice catch.

When I looked over at him, he was still staring at Alby. I imagined what he must be thinking, something like what was going through my own mind, how time passes and we are too fucking stupid to know when life is good, too caught up with ourselves, and what we think we need and don't have, to appreciate it. Until something walks in and changes it all.

Ken must have been remembering times in high school, things that Alby had already told me about, smoking in the boy's room, sneaking out during the day to go to a movie. Typical high school stuff. He must have been remembering all of that, hoping like me that someday the memories would give him something besides pain. Good luck with that one.

I looked in the same direction as Ken. Alby had waded out to his knees, angrily kicking the waves out of his way as he moved forward. When the water reached to just below his waist, he bent down and began splashing.

It was late afternoon, the sun was starting to drop from the sky and spiral into the ocean, casting a glare out over the water. From where I was sitting it was almost even with my eyes, making me squint. On the horizon I watched as Alby scooped up the water with his hands, poured it out over his head, over his shoulders, down his back. He was illuminated with an aura of yellow and turquoise that hid the lesions, and, for a moment or two, I let myself pretend that the KS had disappeared, that his body was perfectly sculptured again, that the sun and the ocean had taken pity on him and decided he'd suffered enough.

But then two joggers went by, two men in spandex. As they passed, one of them nudged the other and pointed toward Alby. Ken also saw them and his protective instinct kicked in before mine did.

"I'm gonna go play with Alby," he said.

He ran toward the beach, throwing off his shirt and leaving it on the sand as he approached the water. This would be Ken's time with Alby.

Darren offered me a beer and I sucked it back, swallowing it in deep chugs that I knew with this sun would give me a nauseous head-ache, without taking my eyes off Alby and Ken. I thought about a time months and years ago, when Alby first told me about the HIV. I was sitting alone in my office, staring at the print of a sailboat out on the open seas. I remembered imagining him out in that sailboat with no oars, venturing further into the sea, where the waves would sweep him away to wherever he was supposed to go. Maybe he was testing the waters, feeling what it was like as the water pulled him down, closed in on him, lulled him into letting go.

I felt a flash of panic, as if this was really going to happen, as if he'd been planning this all along and had chosen this day for an exit. And the panic sped up my heart and made me look out across the beach to find him. I was prepared to run, throw myself into the water and dive until I found him.

"Not today, Alby," I'd scream. "Today is not the day for the sea."

The glare was directly in my eyes and I had to use my hand to shield my vision. And when I did, I saw the figures of Ken and Alby. They were standing in water up to their knees and, as each wave came toward them, they stood up against it as if trying to meet it head on and push it back out into the ocean. They splashed each other and laughed loudly, they were talking but I couldn't hear what they were saying over the crashing of the waves. I watched Alby duck under water, then resurface again a few feet from Ken, who reached out and put his arms around him.

Alby waved at me. "Come on in," he yelled.

Darren watched them. We looked at each other and he asked, "Why should those two have all the fun?"

I stood up and crossed my arms over my chest.

Darren screwed his beer can into the sand to keep it from tipping over, pulled on his baseball cap and asked, "Afraid you'll melt?"

I kicked off my flip-flops and Darren and I raced each other across the sand and out into the water. Ken and Alby stood side by side; Ken had a hand on his shoulder. They had just been soaked by a wave, which was now in retreat. Alby had water running off his face; his trunks clung to his bony hips. He grinned at me, and I gave him a quick hug and grabbed his hand.

"Look Kenny," Alby said. "Mike is getting wet."

"I'll alert the media," Ken said as another wave came crashing toward us.

The four of us stood together, giggling like little boys, as the foamy water rose above our waists, then higher, almost to our necks. I stood firm against the force of the wave and the coldness of the water, the roar drowning out our laughter and our voices. The water rose higher and higher as it crashed into us, high enough to splash foam into my face. I tasted the saltiness and howled. I looked over at Alby and he was watching me.

"See?" Alby said. "It's only water. Once you take the plunge it's not so bad."

"You're right, Alby. It's not so bad."

He pulled me against him and we held each other. When the wave subsided, Ken, Darren and I made a circle around Alby as if he were the birthday boy. We danced around and around, laughing and splashing him, and splashing each other. "Alby. Alby. Alby," we chanted in unison. Alby turned with our circle, his eyes looking into mine, his lips puckered into that half kiss that said: we're a team.

"I love you," he said.

"Me too."

Then I squeezed his hand hard and we braced ourselves against the next wave.

George Koschel
The Test

The dinner party was wonderful. Our friends had left, and my lover, Josh, and I sat on the sofa. His arm around me, I leaned into him.

"Tonight was perfect," I said.

"There's only one way to cap it off," Josh said, as he placed his lips on my neck and playfully tried to give me a hickey.

I felt a sudden rush of passion. "Let's just not forget to play it safe." The safe sex line was meant to be funny, implying that we had both had a lot of wine to drink, but Josh misunderstood.

"Goddamn, Glenn, never mind. I don't want to infect you." He got up suddenly, and had to stop myself from falling over on my side.

"I wasn't serious. I only said it as a joke."

"Sure." He stormed out of the living room, slamming the door, then into the bedroom slamming that door. The evening ended with each of us huddled in opposite corners of the bed.

I had met Josh jogging in the park one Sunday morning. We had both finished running, but from opposite directions. We both wore yin and yang tee shirts. I also wore a lambda earring.

"Love your earring too," he said, "lifting my ear lobe with his index finger.

We talked and decided to have breakfast together. We drove our cars to a small restaurant where a lot of gay people had breakfast on Sunday mornings.

Over scrambled eggs, we made a date to run together the next Sunday. It became a regular part of my weekly schedule. After we ran, we went out to breakfast. Usually we ordered bacon, eggs, and grits—the only variation was how we ordered our eggs. It was our little joke with the waiter.

Besides running, Josh and I also enjoyed the movies, everything from old Republic Serials that could be purchased on videotape to the contemporary.

Although I found Josh attractive, I feared that if I had sex with him, it would ruin our friendship. Anyway I didn't think I wanted a lover.

One day at breakfast, Josh was praising some old Victor Mature biblical epic. "It was crap," I said teasing.

As we left the restaurant, he walked a few feet ahead of me. There was no one outside, but I could still hear the polite chatter emanating from inside.

"This is what I think of your criticism," he said. He quickly dropped his running shorts and mooned me. It was over in a second.

I think I actually swooned. He turned around smiling, but stopped. My face must have told him something.

"Didn't mean to embarrass you."

"You didn't. I think I briefly entered Henry James territory."

"What?"

"Nothing. Forget it," I said, sticking my tongue out at him.

Later, I was surprised I missed Josh as much as I did when he was gone for a month visiting his parents.

"I have to go home this week. My father is having cancer surgery," he had told me as we started running one day before he left.

I stopped. "I'm sorry. You know they have all sorts of treatments these days. It's not an automatic death sentence. God, I sound like one of those awful cheery types I can't stand."

"You mean well," he said smiling faintly. "Come on. Let's run."

"One thing I do know is that I have an uncle who is dying from lung cancer, and my aunt has been taking care of him. According to my mother, my aunt and mother are sisters, this disease has brought my aunt and uncle closer together."

"Right." That's all Josh said. We ran the rest of the way in silence. When we finished Josh said, "I'm glad you're my friend, Glenn."

After Josh returned, he was quiet, almost to the point of being withdrawn.

"Do you want to talk?" I asked as we finished one mile.

"No, let's just run."

He put in an extra kick into it, and I had to struggle to keep up for the next two miles.

"That felt good," he said, toweling the sweat off his face when we finished. "Let's eat."

At the restaurant, the waiter gave each of us a cup of coffee and two menus. As always, he stood next to the table, pen in hand.

"Give me a few minutes. I want to order something different," Josh said.

"Uh-oh, the world is coming to an end," the waiter said. "Call me when you're ready."

"There's something I need to tell you," Josh said.

"Your father, right?"

"Glenn, I'm HIV positive," Josh said.

I was quiet for a very long time, looking at this man who in the past few months had become such an important part of my life. I said, "It doesn't matter to me because I'm in love with you." The words, *because I'm in love with you*, came out automatically. It wasn't that they weren't true; it's just the way they came out. I don't know who was more surprised, Josh or me.

I reached across the table and touched his hand.

"Are you infected?" he asked.

"No," I said. "I was such a hypochondriac I used to get tested every three months. Every cough or sneeze gave me an anxiety attack. Then I realized I wasn't doing anything to endanger myself and thought how stupid I was."

We downed our coffee, left an outrageously big tip, hurried to Josh's house and made love. The next day on my movie calendar, which hung on the wall next to my bed, I wrote Josh's name. Behind it I put an exclamation point. The scene that month was from *Casablanca*.

I was grateful to God, fate, or whatever for letting me have Josh. We were both in our forties and I felt nothing could happen to him as long as we had each other.

In the wee hours of the morning we lay in bed with my arms around his shoulders. A dog barked at a siren in the distance. I was on the verge of sleep. I felt content.

"I'm afraid," Josh whispered.

"Of what?" I asked, suddenly pulled away from slumber. I could feel his body tense as he backed in closer to me.

"Afraid of dying alone."

"Do you think I'd let that happen to you? Do you think I'd leave?"

"My ex, Ted, told me that he wouldn't leave me when I told him I was going to be tested, but when I told him I was positive, he walked out the door."

"I'm not Ted. I'm with you in sickness and in health."

"Glenn, are you asking me to marry you?" he asked, smiling as he turned around to face me.

"If I asked you to marry me, would you?"

"In a minute," Josh said.

"Then, will you marry me?"

"Of course."

Perhaps I would have waited longer to move in with Josh, but I saw time slipping away, like a string being pulled through my hand by a powerful airborne kite. I was ready to make the leap and did.

In the weeks after we had the argument over my crack about safe sex, Josh would warm up a little, I would be happy, but he would withdraw. No matter how happy he seemed to get, he always withdrew. He reminded me of a little puppy I got off the streets when I was a kid. He'd play a little, but always remained cautious until he finally realized he could trust me.

I grew impatient. I came home one afternoon, threw down a bunch of rubbers that were sealed in golden disks, making them look like cheap doubloons, and said, "I want you to fuck me."

"What?"

"You heard me. I want you to fuck me and I want it now." I grabbed his hand and started to pull him into the bedroom. He resisted a little. "If you don't want to do it in the bedroom we can do it right here on the living room floor."

"No," he said, laughing a little, "the bedroom is fine."

We entered the bedroom; he sat on the bed, and started to remove his shirt.

"Let me do that," I said.

For the next few minutes, between long wet kisses, I slowly undressed him. For the past few months, since Josh and I had been together, the more I got to know him and the little rituals we all do to get through life, the more I grew to love him. Friends had told me that for romance to last, there has to be some mystery, but for me, the turn-on was getting to know Josh better. It was as though I were reading a long novel page by page.

After we were undressed, I broke open one of the gold doubloons to remove the condom. There was enough pre-cum on his dick so I didn't need to use any lubricant to get it on him. Slowly I worked it down his shaft. After the condom was on, my mouth went up and down on his latex-enclosed dick to lubricate it. His dick glistened from the moisture from my mouth.

I rolled onto my back and pulled my legs back over my head. Slowly he worked his way into me. We found our rhythm, and I felt as though I were riding the waves in some vast ocean.

Josh panted, "I'm coming."

He came and a few seconds later I did too. The afternoon sun splayed across the bed through the double windows seeming to celebrate the world of erotic love.

"Have to get up," Josh said, "need to go to the bathroom. Stay there, don't move."

I lay in the bed, spent, yet happy, contemplating another round with Josh. "Taking a long time in there," I yelled. "You drown?"

I was all smiles when Josh came out of the bathroom ashen-faced.

"What's wrong?"

"Glenn, the rubber broke." He sat on the side of the bed and began to cry. I sat on the bed next to him, and put my arm around him. But I felt this coldness at the back of my neck that worked its way down me. My hand trembled on his shoulder.

"Maybe you should try to clean yourself out," Josh said.

Knees wobbly, I stood up, walked to the bathroom, and closed the door. I stared at the john, white and antiseptic. In one convulsive move, I dropped to my knees, and threw up. Tears rolled off my face into the john with the remains of my lunch. I tried to muffle my crying.

"Come out of there, Glenn. We have to talk," Josh said on the other side of the door.

I came out to the bathroom and sat on the edge of the bed. "At least we didn't forget to use the rubber," I said.

"Yeah, right." Josh got up, got dressed, and stormed out of the house.

I lay there on the bed, my knees brought up to my chin, thinking another lame joke gone flat. I thought of the joke because to think of anything else at that point would have terrified me.

For the next few days we cautiously moved around one another. My fear was that I would see Josh die which would mirror the type of death I would have to face.

As a teenager, after I realized I was gay, I remember the litany of shame that ran through my head: you're a homosexual, you're a homosexual, you're a homosexual. Over and over I heard that cry. Now the litany changed to: you're going to die, you're going to die. I didn't know whether this one had to do with shame or with bottom-of-the-gut, primal fear. But like the earlier one, it was ever present.

Josh tried to break the ice when he brought home a video tape of *Dark Victory*.

"You can't be the only one around here with a twisted sense of humor," he said.

We snuggled on the sofa looking at the movie. It brought out my worst anxieties.

"I'll pop some popcorn," I said.

Josh took the remote to stop the tape.

"Let it play. I'll only be a minute," I said.

I went into the kitchen, and put the popcorn in the microwave. The bag came to life as the kernels began to pop. As I watched the bag enlarge my anxiety level began to increase. I had palpitations, and my hands became clammy. There was a pain in my chest.

"Josh, I'm having a heart attack," I screamed.

A few hours later we returned from the emergency room with my prescription for Xanax.

"Heart attack," Josh said jokingly. "Do you want to finish seeing the movie?"

"I'm going to bed," I said wanly. I curled up on my side. All night long I heard the litany over and over: you're going to die, you're going to die, you're going to die.

The week after my supposed heart attack, if Josh touched me, I didn't respond, or worse, I pulled away. In bed, if he fondled me, I remained flaccid. I was frightened now more then ever. I wanted to be out and away from Josh. But how could I tell him in such a way that wouldn't hurt him?

As we finished washing and drying the dinner dishes one night, I said, "Josh, I have to move away. It's not forever, just for the time being to get my bearings. I want to come back," I lied.

He dropped the plate he was about to give me to dry back into the soapy water. "What!"

So much for my attempt not to hurt him, I thought. "I'm not good for you right now. I'm unhappy and I'm making you miserable. Now rinse off the plate and give it to me to dry."

The flat of his hand hit the counter causing suds to shoot out over the kitchen. "Don't you understand? I love you. I know you're overwhelmed but don't leave. I'll give you room," he said, his voice suddenly softening.

"I've already put a deposit on an apartment."

"Oh, I see." He was quiet for a moment. "Well, here it is: if you leave, don't come back. You won't be welcome."

"That's your decision," I said, walking out of the kitchen.

He picked up the plate out of the water and held it in both hands as though he were trying to see his reflection. "Please, just go."

Watching him broke my heart, but I left.

I was relieved to be away, and I did it in such a way, that it was Josh's decision, not mine. I should have been ashamed but wasn't. My only concern was to live.

Like practically every gay man on the planet, I knew there would have to be a waiting period before I got tested. I called the AIDS hotline and an infectious disease doctor to make sure. I would get tested in three months and then again in another three—to be safe.

I started to read everything I could about the virus. I wanted answers in black and white, but all I seemed to get were answers colored in various shades of gray. I didn't sleep well. When I did, I dreamed about Josh who was smiling. But was it a smile of pity or contempt?

Suddenly death assaulted me on another front. For years now I had girded myself against the sorrow of seeing gay friends and acquaintances dying of AIDS. My aunt, about whom I had told Josh, had a massive stroke. For a week she lay in the intensive care unit of the hospital while her husband, on another floor, breathed oxygen out of a tank. Our family, my mother and father among them, camped out at the hospital. The family alternated between floors as both husband and wife lay dying, their flesh mortified in a vain attempt to keep them alive. A few weeks after my aunt died, my uncle passed away.

At her father's funeral, my cousin, who was too exhausted for tears, told me, "This really brings it home. You realize that after your mother and father die, you're next."

After the funeral, alone in my apartment, I cried so much I didn't think I would stop. The day after, a phlebotomist drew my blood to see if I was infected.

Before my blood draw, the volunteer counselor told me, "You want to be very cautious about telling anyone you've been tested. However, if there is someone you trust, I mean really trust, you may want to bring him or her here with you when you get your results in a week."

In bed with my fingers clasped behind my head, unable to sleep, I was mesmerized by the ceiling fan's circulation. I thought about what the counselor told me. Who could I trust? Three months ago the answer would have been simple. Now I was confused.

Images of my aunt and uncle also ran through my head. They were paragons of middle class American virtue, but that didn't prevent them from suffering long, drawn out deaths. Yet they had each other.

I thought about other deaths I had known about in my middle aged life, not deaths related to AIDS, but mainly deaths of older relatives and parents of friends. Very few people, I realized, had pleasant deaths. They all involved suffering, but usually family and friends came together, unified, perhaps briefly, by their pain. Unfortunately, that wasn't always the case with AIDS-related deaths.

I wasn't confused; I knew what I had to do.

Early the next morning, on a bright beautiful day, I knocked at Josh's door. I was impatient. Then I rang on the doorbell, pressing on it longer than I should.

From behind the door I heard Josh. "I'm coming. Hold on will you?"

I heard the sound of the men's voices and the trucks as they picked up the morning garbage. The door opened; my stomach knotted. Before I could say anything, Josh asked coldly, "What do you want?" His hair was askew and he wore an old Mickey Mouse tee shirt he used for sleeping.

"At least you didn't slam the door in my face," I said.

"I have more class than that."

"That you do. May I come in? I need to talk."

I sat on the sofa, the same sofa I sat on when I made the safe sex remark that started everything in my life moving downhill. It seemed like a lifetime.

Josh sat opposite me. I clasped my hands and put them between my knees. I looked at Josh, feeling small and insignificant.

"Here goes nothing," I said. Josh's face remained impassive. I looked into his eyes. "Walking out on you was the biggest mistake of my life." He had been sitting back in his chair, one leg casually draped over the other, but suddenly he sat upright.

"Just walk back in, and pretend nothing ever happened. 'Sorry Josh, but everything's okay. I'm back.' Thanks but no thanks," Josh said.

"We could try dating again, a Sunday morning run in the park," I said lamely.

"Let me guess: you got your test results, and they were negative. And everything will be fine until another rubber breaks, or you get the flu. And you'll be thinking, the son of a bitch is killing me."

"If I say, 'you have every right to be mad,' it will only make you angrier."

"Nail on the head, Glenn."

"My aunt loved my uncle very much, and caring for him killed her. She actually died before he did."

"What in the hell are you talking about?"

"I've done a lot of thinking. My aunt and uncle—I told you about them a while ago—both died. She ran herself ragged at the hospital caring for him, and stroked out. I'd like to think she wouldn't have had it any other way, but I don't know. What I do know is that most of us don't have nice clean deaths. Most of them are long, drawn out, painful affairs.

"If you're trying to cheer me up, it's not working," Josh said.

"And no, I don't know my test results in response to what you said a few minutes ago. When they drew my blood, the counselor told me I should be careful about telling anyone I was tested. But if there was someone I could really trust, bring that person with me to get my results." Josh was about to speak. "Let me finish. That person is you. You are one of the few people I know who knows what I'm going through."

"Nice speech, Glenn, but I feel I need someone I can trust too. Someone who will be with me in sickness and in health. Remember?"

"I deserve that, but please let me try to explain." I knotted my fists so Josh wouldn't see my hands shaking. "This isn't easy. It was more than the fear that I might be infected that made me leave. Or run. I thought I'd see my death in yours." Shame made me look away.

"Can you deal with this?" He lifted his shirt. A half dozen or so lesions—some as big as quarters, others a bit smaller or larger—dotted his chest. They looked like drying scabs or blood blisters.

I fell to my knees, and buried my face into the pale hair covering his stomach. "I love you."

"Don't do this." He tried to push me away.

"I'm afraid, scared to death, but I won't leave you if you'll have me." I kissed his stomach, and I reached up to touch his chest, my fingers splayed over a few of the lesions. I felt his tee shirt slide down his body onto the nape of my neck as I pressed my face more gently into his stomach.

Samuel R. Friedman

AIDS Researchers

On alternate Mondays, scattershot Tuesdays,
and three times a year on days that are primes,
numberless friends whisper in our ears
that our work matters, that lives
balance in our hanging eyelids and twitching
jaws,
reminding us of scenes from ancient Rome,
of triumphs where they whispered "You are not
a god"
to those who butchered lives,
of crucifixions where lugging your lumber
was a prelude to others' hammers,
of ruins more beautiful than retroviruses,
of epidemics lost
in the runes of time.

Migdalia Cruz
So...

A commission by Sean San Jose Blackman for the Names Project, an AIDS benefit, sponsored by Bay Package Productions and the Magic Theatre, San Francisco.

Cast of Characters: **A WOMAN**—30s, beautiful in a robust way, a hopeless romantic
A MAN—30s, beautiful in a sculpted way, a tender fatalist
ANOTHER WOMAN—20s, Latina, wasted looking though once beautiful, a grounded realist
ANOTHER MAN—20s, Latino, beautiful in a brutal way, a scared pragmatist

Time: The Present
Place: In a place of worship where one kneels before one's God. Each character speaks to God in his or her own way. God is a shaft of light that slowly fades.

In a place of worship, four people are caught in separate shafts of light. The light comes on as each one begins to speak, then stays on as the others speak. Each one speaks to the light as if it were God.

A WOMAN
So...finally...I'm in love.

A MAN
So...I'll always love him.

ANOTHER WOMAN
So? I'm still in love with the son-of-a-bitch.

ANOTHER MAN
So, of course I still love him.

A WOMAN

He has blondish hair—what's left of it. And a bald spot suitable for kissing.

A MAN

He has brownish hair—what's left of it. And a bald spot suitable for licking.

ANOTHER WOMAN

He has black hair and a hardass heart let me tell you

ANOTHER MAN

He has my same mouth and nose and looks just like me when he smiles.

[As **A WOMAN** *continues, the others are lost in thought and prayer.*]

A WOMAN

There's too much hair on his back and shoulders—but that's part of his charm. Too much and too little of something or other. His eyes are blue—not scary shark blue, but azure like the sky—like the sky on a good day. His fingers are long and good for giving people the finger—not that he does—he wouldn't, I mean, not so they could see him do it anyway. He's what we used to call a pushover—now we'd say a wuss or a pussy. And what's that about?! Pussies are good things—as far as I'm concerned anyway. I know I like and admire my own. But it's no good without the proper stroking. The cajoling of my inner thighs is simple for the loved one to master. The object of my desire has a really goofy laugh. I think it must be genetic. A midwestern "I find really stupid things funny" kind of laugh. A laugh that's not afraid to be laughed at. A laugh that registers on the Richter scale a full 4.0 kind of laugh. We have walked through cemeteries together, admiring the flowers which grow wild over the most forgotten graves. I will write him a beautiful eulogy—because girls always live longer than boys. So I'm told.

A MAN

He has so much hair on his legs and inner thighs. I have a made a porridge of his fluids on that nest of his hair. And boy do I have

a thirst for his breakfast cereal. It is composed of tears and pain.
But I'm strong for him. He knows this so he tortures me. He sends
me away from him when he needs me the most. "Get used it", he
whispers. "Get used to life without me." But I don't want to. I still
smell him on me wherever I go. I haven't washed my pillowcases
in six months because he lingers there like a new scent by Nina
Ricci—too many flowers and not enough herbs. In its faintness,
it grows sweeter and easier to remember. In its faintness, I am
reminded of how soon he will leave me. I ask for just one thing.
He wants to leave me his collection of North African pop on vinyl.
He thinks I crave the exotic. I just crave him. A hand in mine, a
head on my shoulder, a walk to the toilet in the middle of the night
because he can't hold it in anymore. "You don't have to hold it in
around me, baby. I love every bit of you." This he will not believe.
He is embarrassed by his own weakness as I could never be. This
he cannot believe. So he sends me away.

ANOTHER WOMAN

He's killed eighteen people. He said he kilt them because they
were white and whites don't have no feelings—not like the rest
of us. I think he had to kill the thing he most wanned to be. And
anyway, he was killing himself the whole time same as them. I
don't shoot up anymore. Without him it's not the same. I did it for
him and with him. And now he's alone in there. I know he's dying
in prison because I'm dying out here and that's how it works. I
tried to see him, got as far as the bus. Turned around. I'm too ugly
anymore for anybody to love me. My daughter, Lizzie, says I got
number eleven legs because they so skinny, like sticks. I used to be
fine. We loved to go out dancing—all dressed and looking sharp.
But then the killing started and I couldn't go there with him. I had
Lizzie to keep those bad things out of my mind. I could still see the
good in people with Lizzie to show me how. He never liked her—
from the day she was born all he wanted was for her to be quiet. I
think it's because she reminded him of good things too. Things he
thought he didn't deserve to feel. That's what I think. I think the
State will kill him before it does. I hope I don't go before him. I
don't got nobody to care for Lizzie. But I'm looking. So maybe I'll
find somebody soon.

ANOTHER MAN

What's that stupid social worker think? That a man don't love his brother just because he's dying. I can't help it that I can't see him. I don't want to remember a crazy faggot in a bed hooked up to a machine. Don't get me wrong—I mean he's not a real faggot, that's just a figure of speech. Sure he used drugs, but that's all. He got hooked in the army when he was in Germany. They give you drugs to stay in the army. That's what he told me anyway. People assume you're a faggot because you got it but that's not the truth—not in this case. I just wanted to be clear on that with you. Anyway, I want to remember the guy I went out and picked up girls with. The guy I took trick or treating. He always wanted to be a ghost. I made him all his costumes. One Halloween we got a real good one when our sister Wandi got her period and we used her sheet—boy, we grossed a lot of people out that year. It was a good year. And I hate to say it but I guess he got his wish now, huh? That's like a joke but it's not a joke because I bet he looks dead already—and why would I need to see that? I know he doesn't want me to see him like that. She said he's been asking for me, but I say she's lying. How can somebody who's already dead ask for anything? She just thinks a family member or some shit needs to be there to see him die. I don't gotta see that because I see it already in my head. So what would you do?

A WOMAN

I know what I'm going to do. I'm going to declare myself to him. He's stopped drinking so I know he can hear me now. I heard him all those times he declared himself to me in his drunkeness. He'd grab for a body part and say he could hold me so good like nobody else ever could. But I didn't believe it coming out of those vodka scented lips that have kissed more mouths than I could count— more moustaches too. That's the sad part.

ANOTHER WOMAN

I'm gonna go see him next week. It's my birthday present to myself. Might be a good time—might be the only time. But I don'know, he's jus'gonna look at me and scream. I've never looked so bad that a little make-up didn't help. But make-up just ain't working no more. I keep smearing my lipstick when I cough and then I look like a clown. Lizzie tells me that too. "Ma, you're looking like Bozo today," she says. I wish I looked as good as Bozo these days...

A MAN

I'm going to go and buy myself some new pillowcases. The ones with his smell on them, I'll sew them up at the end like a secret and put them inside my new cases and I'll sleep there on them and only I will know what's on the inside.

ANOTHER MAN

I'm just not going to go. That's why I came here. I wanned to explain myself to someone who'd listen.

[The lights begin to fade slowly.]

ALL FOUR

Hey, don't go.

[The lights stay on at their lower level.]

ANOTHER MAN

Are you mad at me now? I'm just being honest. Men shouldn't see other men looking weak. Brings the strong ones down. Let the girls go see that—they like to cry. I got no use for that. He'd feel the same about me. I wouldn't want him anywhere near me.

A MAN

I tried real hard the last time I saw him—I tried to give him a kiss but he turned away from me and started coughing. I think it was on purpose. He thought I'd get all grossed out by his mucus and blood, but I just wished I could suck it all out of him and make him better. I would do anything to kiss him. I kept trying but he kept coughing and motioned me out the door. I rested my lips on the other side of that door and left a kiss for him anyway. In my head I see him kissing me back.

ANOTHER WOMAN

You think they let people on death row get kissed by other people? I'd have to kiss him if I got in to see him but I bet I'd have to kiss him through plastic or somefin. Oh, it's okay to kiss. My doctor tole me it's okay with Lizzie and everyfin. I would die if I couldn't kiss her. Right now, right here, I would jus'die.

A WOMAN

I wish for a sweet four minute long open-mouthed kiss. That's all. Then I could die happy. I know it's four minutes because I practiced with his picture and that's how long I could keep his face in my head without opening my eyes. Four minutes in heaven. The only thing is he won't let me kiss him, because he thinks he's diseased—but that's not how you get it, right? By kissing? I know you don't get it like that. But still he won't let me.

ANOTHER MAN

I think about his hands sometimes. They were so delicate. I would tease him about those hands all the time. Sweet, faggoty hands. And then I'd chase him and kiss those hands if I caught him. I'd kiss them now if I could. He knows I would if I could. But I can't...

ALL FOUR

So...what's a kiss?

[The lights fade slowly out.]

ALL FOUR

Don't go.

End of Play for now...

Dean Kostos
Hiding in Intervals

I fled your room each time I cried,
though of course, you couldn't hear me.
(With the door closed, I cracked inside.)

I tried to compose myself, tied
up like rubber-banded daisies—cheery.
I cheerily fled your room each time I cried.

This architecture of going to hide
in intervals provided walls of safety—feeble theory!
The hospice door closed; I crumbled outside.

Five days I sat in vigil, tugged by the tides:
need-fear, need-fear, need you near me.
As in a ritual, I solemnly rose to cry,

knowing it made no sense to—your sense had died.
As if disembodied, I watched my own motions, teary-
eyed, as I closed the door and collapsed inside.

The day of morphine, you metamorphosed beside
me into an infant. Could I have cradled you more dearly?
Quitting the room *and* my face that lied,
I was the door and the man it kept outside.

A One-Act Play by Craig Lucas
with Music & Lyrics by Patrick Barnes
The Boom Box

Characters:	**RICK**, a ghost
	JAY, a ghost

Time & Place: The play takes place on the spirit level. The ghosts
are the only things visible to the audience; they
stand upon nothing and float against nothing
in a soundless universe save for their own ghost
voices. They are capable of perceiving the earthly
plane which will remain invisible to us throughout:
it consists of an open field covered with thousands
of quilt panels and the thousands of people who
come to see them. The sounds the crowd makes,
the music they play, their individual movements,
are entirely unseen and unheard. We may only
glean what is out there by what the ghosts do and
say in response.

[**JAY** and **RICK**, side by side.]

JAY

Hey.
    [Short pause.]
New here?
    [A little nod.]
A little overwhelming, huh?
    [Another nod.]
I'm Jay.

RICK

Rick.

JAY

Nice to meet you, Rick.
    [**RICK** *looks down at the ground before him, behind him.*]

RICK

Wow.

JAY

Oh, you haven't seen it.

RICK

No.

JAY

It's beautiful.

RICK

God.

JAY

Astonishing, isn't it? What they can do?

RICK

Oh my God.

JAY

All the detail....

RICK

It's actually...incredibly beautiful.
> [**RICK** *looks further, at the ground beneath* **JAY**, *then all around.*]

JAY

All the effort. Well, I mean, take a stroll around the whole place. You won't believe it...before it gets more crowded.
> [*Short pause.*]
You didn't see them working on it at all?
> [*A little headshake from* **JAY**.]
Wanted to be surprised?
> [*Short pause.*]
What were you...I mean...where were you when they were working on it?
> [*Pause.*]

RICK

Oh, I was...I was taking the Grand Tour.

JAY

Of?

RICK

All the places I'd traveled with my boyfriend....Um, some in Italy, some in, oh, you know, all kinds of places...gardens...San Francisco....

JAY

How long has it been?

RICK

About uh...about....

JAY

I know, time...really—

RICK

I can't get a hold of it.

JAY

Me either.

     [Silence. **JAY** *indicates the ground under* **RICK**.*]*
Are you happy with it?

RICK

That...I mean, the whole idea of being satisfied has, it's all changed for me.

JAY

Uh-huh.

RICK

It isn't, what is sort of....

JAY

Is.

RICK

So, yes, I am. Because it's what it is.
[Pause.]

JAY

But not because it's what you would have wanted.

RICK

What...I would have wanted has become....It's not even as solid
as smoke. I can see it in my memory, but it has no substance,
anymore than I can touch you or feel this...fabric.

JAY

It goes on for miles, literally, square miles now.
[Pause.]

RICK

Let it cover the planet.

JAY

Oh, don't say that.

RICK

Why? We're all coming here anyway.

JAY

Were you surprised?

RICK

What?

JAY

That there was anything. After.
[Pause.]

RICK

Surprised, see, that's it. I can remember my wondering, my
doubts, and...but now...it's all...it's a movie. Their lives, their
movements, suffering, cracked ribs, wars, chapped lips, everything
they go through, their orgasms...it's a movie. A really long,

really complicated, insufferable foreign film. A million times more complicated than one of those Russian epics based on a nineteenth-century novel where everybody has a diminutive and patronymic....

 [**JAY** *looks at him quizzically.*]

Oh, you know, those names like Maria Marinovich, little Maria, what the nurse calls her, her contemptuous sisters....

JAY

What kind of work do you do?

RICK

Well, I haven't resumed. I haven't quite gotten the knack of what it is, I mean, why it is we do it here. You see the doctors running around pretending they're taking care of the little tiny dead babies and the teachers teaching the dead babies once they've been pretend-reborn and pretended to grow....

JAY

It's just practice.

RICK

It's no more sensible or clear or—I feel less enlightened than I did when I was living.

JAY

This is living.

RICK

Okay.

JAY

This is just...another—

RICK

[*Same time.*] A different plane.

JAY

Level. Yeah.

 [*Pause.*]

RICK

I miss fucking.

JAY

Oh, here they come.
> *[They look off into the distance.]*

RICK

I don't look, I never look.

JAY

At the ... ?

RICK

People.
> *[Pause.]*

JAY

Really?

RICK

Never. I look at buildings. The only living things I can stand are trees.

JAY

Why?

RICK

They live longer. They don't scream when they're dying.
> *[Pause.]*

JAY

You won't be reborn with that attitude.
> *[Pause.]*
Is that your strategy?
> *[Pause.]*
You're making it harder on yourself hanging around here at your panel if you don't want to see your loved ones.

RICK

I'm testing myself. Building my resolve. If I can stand here and see past them, then I can withstand anything.

JAY

But...I mean, there's gotta be something better than this...limbo here; don't you want to be a saint or break the cycle of rebirth forever?

    [Pause.]

RICK

I want the living to come screaming after me and put me back in my life which I loved more than anything anyone has ever loved...I want my eyes and my gift for languages and my dick...I don't want to see what happens in a hundred years because I know what it is already, it's horrible suffering, I want Rick. I want me. I want exactly what I had.

JAY

Well, here...I mean, isn't that what they're bringing, don't you want to look—

RICK

At what there is of everything I had except me in the middle of it.

JAY

You didn't love your life.

    [Silence.]

These are the people who made your life real, and they're right here.

RICK

I was real without other people.

JAY

Then you still are real.

    [Pause.]

RICK

I hate the New Age. I was an exception, I was aberrant burp in a hideous time....

JAY

Then wait until Doomsday, you're right…something will come along that deserves you.

RICK

Why do you think they've plunked me down next to you?

JAY

To punish me for accepting too much, this is the ultimate test: how much compassion and wisdom can you extend, here's a real stumper, go, Jay!

RICK

What did you do?

JAY

I was a stock analyst.

RICK

I wrote astrology charts.

JAY

Did you believe in it?

RICK

Oh, I believed in it the way one believes in whatever pays the bills, it was fun when I was an amateur, and then.…

JAY

Rick…?

RICK

Statler.

JAY

Oh my God! Your column was great.

RICK

Thanks.

JAY

It was so funny.

RICK

Thanks.

JAY

I read it every week, me and my lover.
[Pause.]

RICK

Thanks.

JAY

You were really famous.

RICK

Maybe you'll get your picture in the society pages now. Standing next to the ghost of Rick Statler is the once devastatingly handsome, but now rather hazy figure of Jay...?

JAY

Gilson.

RICK

Gilson. Jewish?
*[**JAY** nods.]*

JAY

You?
[Headshake.]
What did you—I mean, what were your beliefs?

RICK

I believed in the stars.
[Pause.]

JAY

Oh, listen, somebody brought their boom box.

RICK

I love this song.

JAY

Me, too.
>[**RICK** *listens, then starts to sing along.*]

RICK

Don't talk about love
Don't talk about a wedding ring
>[**JAY** *joins him.*]

BOTH MEN

We're here
Right here
Right now
And we need one thing....
I gotta have you tonight
I want—
>[**JAY** *keeps singing but* **RICK** *breaks off, seeing some-*
>*thing.*]

JAY

—to do it all
And scale every—
>[**JAY** *sees* **RICK** *staring.*]

What?
>[*He, too, looks at the unseen figures approaching.*]

You know one of those...?
>[*Pause.*]

Is that...? You know him?

RICK

Goddamit!

JAY

What?

RICK

You tricked me.

JAY

What?

RICK

You got me distracted.

JAY

I didn't.

RICK

I didn't want to see him.

JAY

God, he's...what a soul.
    *[**RICK** wails.]*
He can hear you, I swear he can....

RICK

He's so beautiful. Look at his nose, I could swallow it whole.

JAY

He does have a nice face, but I mean...look at those thoughts.

RICK

He's playing that fucking song....

JAY

Is—? I mean, is that some special song, or something?

RICK

That fucking asshole.

JAY

Oh, it's...he wants you to know he doesn't regret anything, from
the night you met till the morning you died.

RICK

Stop reading his mind, it's none of your business.

JAY

It's all of our business.
> *[Pause.]*

RICK

We should never ever have made love, I gave it to him, I GAVE IT TO HIM!

JAY

And he still doesn't regret it, that's the amazing thing.

RICK

I did it, I killed him.

JAY

Just love him and get over yourself. He's still alive.
> *[Pause.]*
He's rewinding it. He's going to play it again.

RICK

You should have been a simultaneous translator.
> *[Pause. **JAY** starts, moving his head to an unheard rhythm, then starts to sing.]*

JAY

I saw you there
You saw me here
Do we need to know more
I need you with me
Your hand in mine
And your clothes on my floor

RICK

[Overlapping.] Shut up, this isn't about you!
> *[Silence. **RICK** watches his invisible boyfriend and listens to the song. Jay is looking around. He sees a loved one.]*

JAY

There you are.

> [*He reaches up and touches an unseen face.* **RICK** *is lost
> in the vision of his love; he hums along with the song, then
> sings.*]

RICK

—*Tonight*
I want to do it all
And scale every height
I gotta have you tonight
Who cares about tomorrow
I gotta have you tonight
Slide up next to me—

> [**JAY**, *touching the body in front of him everywhere,
> kissing it, joins* **RICK**.]

BOTH MEN

Rub up against me
Feel my heat feel my need
I need your skin
I need your mouth
The beast in me must be freed
I gotta have you tonight
I want to do it all—

> [**RICK** *stops singing abruptly.*]

JAY

—*And scale ever*—

RICK

[*Overlapping, to his lover.*] Take me back! Bring me back! I'd do
it again, I'd die again if you'd kiss me again, please.

JAY

He hears you.

RICK

Please, baby…come on, do it…I want to be there.

JAY

You are.

RICK

I want to be there.

JAY

You are.
>   [**RICK** *is punching his unseen lover.*]
You fucking fucking bastard…I love you….

JAY

He hears.

RICK

I love you so.

>   [**End of play.**]

Angela Lam Turpin
The Clay Ring

On Ash Wednesday at the Joie de Vivre Café in Marseilles, France, you place a clay ring on my finger, reminding me I go back to earth soon. The doctors have saved me once, twice. And this time, the third time, I vow I am through. I ask, "Are you listening?"

You rub the tip of my finger, the finger with the ring on it. "I made it from earth and fire and water," you say. You smooth my hand with your fingers, caress my palm. Your tenderness arrests me.

Around us, the trees have lost their leaves. In spring, they will return. White and pink blossoms.

I remember the spring you left as my lover. Nearly ten years later, you return as my friend.

After lunch, we take the flowers you purchased from a sidewalk florist and pluck every petal off of each purple violet, each white rose. We gather them in handfuls and scatter the purple and white petals over the red tiles of the patio beside the waiter who frowns and swears at us in French.

This time you promise me forever. I smile and remind you, "Make only promises you can keep."

You unfold a letter from your breast pocket. I think it is a note from Clarissa, the young woman you fell in love with in Spain, the young woman who replaced me in your heart after that one night I replaced you with Carlos in my bed. It was so many years ago that I cannot remember the jealousy and pain we both endured.

Still, a pang of loneliness throbs in my chest. "Are you leaving me again for another?" I ask, though I know I shouldn't appear too needy, no matter how many hours I have left of this life.

You link my arm in the crook of your elbow and reassure me, "I am going nowhere. I picked this up at your former address. It is from Carlos."

The unfolded letter is covered in stilted letters, an angry, upright scrawl. It begins:

Dear Belinda, I am writing to tell you that I, too, have tested positive for the AIDS virus. I have all the symptoms: night sweats, tremors...

My fingers tremble. *That night, once, long ago. He made love like a feral cat. Lock your arms around my neck, he said. Thrust forward, quickly.* Suddenly, I am ashamed. "So, all this time, it was not you, but Carlos."

He originally told me: a rare blood disease.

"Anyway, this news cannot save me now." I hand you the letter. "I derailed myself somewhere back there." I toss my head toward Spain, toward the years we have spent together and apart. I imagine your concern as you stare into my eyes, your pupils contracting. "You know, I didn't do it willingly or unconsciously, but stupidly, blindly ruled by an insatiable curiosity, ignoring what you so generously considered my formidable intelligence." You pat my arm again as if to sympathize with my anger, my disappointment, my hopelessness, my inability to change anything whatsoever.

And, as we walk along the cobblestone road, I remember the acrobatics of it all: one darkened bedroom after another, one climax after the next, on the sienna tiles, on the clay earth, on the molten river, on the rocks. And I stare at the ring, the ring you made me with your own hands, hands of life, not death. I glance at your artist's fingers, long and self-defined, a masterpiece, each and every one, ten digits of perfection. I wonder, sadly, how long this moment will last.

"This is probably the last time I will visit you," you say. "It is too painful to watch you suffering. Sometimes—I hate to say it, but it's true—I'd much rather you were dead. At least then there would be peace."

Although I hear you, I am thinking of something else, the letter, what it indicates, implies. "If it was Carlos," I say it hesitatingly, slowly, as if to measure my words accurately, one tablespoonful at a time. "If it was him, then if I could go back to that one night and undo what I had done, we might have had twenty years of us together."

You sigh. We turn off the street and head toward the beach.

Again, I am rambling out loud. I do not care if you are listening. It is enough to hear my voice. "It took one touch to end up like this." I pull my arm away from your protective stance and roll up the sleeves of my sweater. My outstretched arms bleed with purple blotches: an incurable sarcoma. You glance away from my arms, from my death, hovering like an invisible alphabet over our heads. No words form. Your presence, the presence that comforted me so often, so long ago, leaves me lonely and distressed. I tug on your shirtsleeve. "Let's go," I say.

"No, not yet. Look at the sun."

It is blazing, on fire, against the water, igniting the white foamy waves with shimmering iridescence. The clouds drift pink and gold and red and orange. I imagine my ashes being scattered in the sea.

You could come back every winter to look for me. I'd be swirls of black particles in the glassy water. I'd suck away at your feet and then flood back in. The patterns of my disassembled body would disappear and change like abstract and instantaneous photographs, compositions of water and ashes, fleeting, but sharp and definite for the instance of coherence. You would be glad to be here to see them, for they would never recur. Except, maybe, in your dreams.

Again, I tug on your shirtsleeve. The sun saddens me. It is setting fast. "Let's go," I say.

You follow me back to the hotel where I spend my days when I am not at the hospital. There is no need for me to take out a lease. I have only moments left, not even days, hours, minutes. Just moments.

You remind me I'm talking as though I am already dead.

I am.

At the hotel, I am thirsty. You bring me a cup of water. A chalice. Silver bells. The choir and the altar servers. *Take this cup and drink from it. It is my blood. Contaminated blood. House of love. The greatest love of all. To lay down your life for a friend. You are my friend.*

"Lie down with me," I say.

We undress and spread ourselves on the clean, crisp cotton sheets. You stroke my hair.

The ultimate trust.

Carlos whispered, It is safe.

To let go in the dark.

You stroke my hair. Your tenderness arrests me. I whisper softly to you stories I have longed to share with anyone who would listen.

I tell you about the endless days in Chinatown when I worked for a Chinese restaurant. I used to envy every girl's hand any man held like a polished stone. The men talked about Picasso and Mozart and the theater. On the street, rain poured over a yellow taxi cab. I fell in love with the sound of a male's voice. Any male's voice. Alluring. Enduring. I imagined that is what love is all about: Picasso and Mozart and the theater, girls' hands like polished stones, rain, and yellow taxi cabs. I envied every single one of them. I was twenty-one then and vowed to reshape the world according to the dictates of my desire. I thought sex would redeem me, make me worthy of love, but if anything, it destroyed the only chance of happiness I might have had with you.

Outside, it is raining. Droplets splatter against the glass. I move closer to you. The warmth of your body heats through my skin. "I am sorry," I say.

You stroke my hair as I speak. A smile begins at the corners of my lips and spreads across my face. A soft smile. The smile of an angel before dawn.

My stories continue: I grew up reckless, a child of no restrictions, prohibitions, inhibitions. I did whatever I wanted, whenever I wanted, however I chose, wherever I happened to be, with whoever would join me.

That night, once, long ago.

He made love like a feral cat.

Lock your arms around my neck. Thrust forward, quickly.

I hide my face in the hairs of your chest. My body shivers. You wrap your arms around me, containing my brokenness.

All I ever wanted—

One night, once—

If only—

You breathe into my ear, "Tell me another story."

For a second, I am quiet as I think. Then it happens; swiftly the story unfolds:

In death begin possibilities. I become Madame Forget and you become Sir Forget-Me-Not. We are travelers on spaceships skirting the planets, searching for a constellation we have not yet sullied with the senselessness of our invincible lust. When we fall in love here, in this imaginary universe, it is like looking at our reflections: a completely seamless trust.

You fold me in your arms and whisper, "Let us go there now." I close my eyes. Darkness presses in on me. I twirl the clay ring on my finger and am reminded I go back to earth. Soon.

Aldo Alvarez
Property Values

I

There wasn't anything short of a shantytown shack that Claudia
Ferrier had not scouted as a property that could benefit from her
skills as a realtor. That some of these dwellings had people still living in them who had no intention of relocating was another matter
altogether. Such were her ambitions that, at a wake for an acquaintance's mother, she asked the bereaved if the departed's lovely four
bedroom house was going to be up for sale.

In that booming year of 1988, Claudia operated out of Mireya,
the medium-sized city that served as a hub to the west coast of Puerto Rico. Her mother rode shotgun as she drove around the nicer
neighborhoods of the area, and around neighborhoods with major
gentrification potential, often late into the night. They looked for
For Sale and For Rent signs the way some people look for guavas in
other people's backyards—with stealth and no intention to be neigh-
borly. Of course, she was all pulpy sweetness when she called the
phone numbers posted on oak or mahogany doors, or on the steel
grillwork that enclosed most self-respecting upper middle-class
porches. And people always took her calls. This was how she came
to represent other people's properties. Sometimes buyers contacted
her before she had a suitable property available. She would do her
field work and find them one.

Her wardrobe was never short of style or brand-name designers,
for this hustling of buyer and seller, in a seller's market, made for

more than a decent living. Especially since she charged a fee to both buyer and seller. Claudia Ferrier had not heard of any regulation of this practice in the Commonwealth of Puerto Rico and nobody had openly questioned her business methods. Before she swooped onto the scene, most people had handled real estate issues without a middleman. By the time she attempted to discourage Dean Rodriguez from acquiring a home, Claudia had gained a reputation among the *cognoscenti* of Mireya as a relatively harmless nuisance whose greed and malfeasance was tolerable. Harsher opinions saw her as the ambulance chaser of real estate agents.

II

The old-landed-gentry-turned-professional-money women's auxiliary—the *cognoscenti di tutti cognoscenti*, really—met for breakfast once a week. Three times a month, lavish breakfasts were held in the privacy of one of the social-club members' houses. Thick potato and onion omelettes, guava or mango jelly-filled confections dusted with the finest powdered sugar, crisp yet flaky pastry fingers filled with sweet cheese would accompany conversation whose intimacy and warmth belied the snobbery accorded to the group's members by the larger social whirl of the town. Gossip did pass between the ladies, of course, but it wasn't all frivolous. The group had a hand in all kinds of fund-raising for worthy causes, got involved in library drives and literacy campaigns, and took care of the housebound elderly and infirm who had no extended family to look after them. They played canasta with Spanish playing cards; they had an unspoken, ongoing "top-this!" competition involving breakfast comestibles. They wished their children to marry into one another's families, and always planned major social events around their core group. But they were, actually, very sweet and conscientious in a cautiously progressive way. They tried to better themselves and their town, and they were sincere.

Once a month, though, the breakfast club met in a restaurant or a coffee shop. Claudia, knowing that these people were the shapers of good taste and public opinion, desperately wanted to become a member of this elite. After all, the group included the wife of the town's most prestigious architect of luxurious houses and apartment buildings, the wife of the most reliable and well-liked appraiser of land value and property, the wife of the financier who approved most of the loans that went into the large-scale building of homes, besides the wives of doctors, lawyers and sundry professionals at the top of their fields, all of whom invested in real estate. A lot of business was done inside this group. Claudia wanted to be part of it. But she knew that a bald-faced request to be invited to the group would lack propriety. So, on Thursday mornings—their usual meeting time—she would check all the possible breakfast venues, hoping to casually pop in to say hi at the table, be invited to sit down, and stay in all morning. And then, pop in often enough to feel she had arrived and invite them to breakfast at her place the next week.

On this momentous morning, she finally found the group breakfasting at the coffee shop of the chichi department store in town, the place with the best teeny-tiny cupful of strong, bitter coffee.

"What a coincidence!" Claudia said, hovering over the table, to the few who looked up from the group to acknowledge her presence. "I was just coming over here for a quick bite to eat before showing a house to a very nice couple...and I find you all gathered here!"

"Well, it was just a matter of time," said Olivia, the wife of the reliable and well-liked appraiser. Claudia had had the opportunity to become acquainted with Olivia when her husband did a small appraisal job for her. "The world is a handkerchief, isn't it? How is your mother?"

"Fine, fine," Claudia said, still hovering, her hand suggestively holding onto the back of an unoccupied chair. "With her usual aches and pains. But she's such pleasant company, not a burden at all. She makes my life so much easier, truly. She really helps out with my business."

"Well, it's nice to hear your mother's doing well," Olivia said. "So nice of you to stop and say hello." Olivia smiled politely but not widely, and turned to speak to another member of the party.

Claudia hovered over the table, at last reaching the point where she could no longer bear the embarrassment of being ignored, when another voice rose up to her from the coop.

"Actually—Claudia, isn't it ?—maybe you could sit down for a bit and give me a little help with something."

Luisa, the doctor's wife…What an opportunity, what an opening! Claudia quickly swept to her side.

"How could I serve you?" Claudia asked.

"I've been looking for a house for my son, and I am at a loss as to how to help him."

"But you, you know so much about houses! Surely you don't need any help from an *arriviste* like myself!"

"Oh, but Dean is so fussy. He was a fussy eater as a child," Luisa said.

"Was he?" Claudia said. "Poor thing."

"You see, his tastes are…extravagant and specific, and I haven't been able to locate something he'd like. He's looking for a castle in the air, and I haven't been able to please him. And I'm going on a trip to Europe very shortly, and won't come back for two weeks or so, and Dean wants to move in before Christmas.…Could he call you for help? He doesn't like stucco. Everything I've seen has stucco."

III

"Something *must* be wrong," Claudia said to her mother while driving around in the middle of the night. They were driving through San Sebastián, a small town to the northeast of Mireya, on their hunt for signage. "Luisa could not possibly need any help from me. Luisa, the wife of the head surgeon of, at last count, three hospitals in the county, is a canny investor. She must make as a landlord at least as much as her husband. And she's sold locations downtown to fast-food concerns, and owns parking lots and houses on the best locations in town."

"Who gave you this information?" asked her mother.

"Town records, registered deeds and such," she said. "It's all written down in paper, if you care to find it. Anyway, I just don't get it. What would she need me for? All the signs indicate that I'm being taken advantage of."

"Maybe she's doing you a favor, out of kindness."

"Hah! I don't need her *noblesse oblige*," Claudia said. "But at least she's giving me business.…"

"That's all that matters, doesn't it—Stop!" her mother said. "I think I saw a sign."

They backed up.

The house had a few patches of faded paint which had once been a rather fetching kingfisher blue. A cement base held up a wooden structure, two floors high. The long, wide porch ran from the side of the house that opened to the side street and around a rounded corner to the side that faced the main thoroughfare of the town. The porch was framed by lovingly fluted columns and intricate, leaf-shaped lattice work, some of which had fallen sideways onto the floor. The front doors had wooden slats that opened and closed to let light and air in, and on the second floor the windows that faced the side street were made in a similar manner. The top story opened up to a small balcony above the porch. The roof was flat, like most roofs in the tropics, but the edges curved out slightly, embroidered with sinuous, florid arabesques, joining at the corner of the street to meet a horn of plenty that poured forbidden fruit.

There was no stucco on the house. No stucco whatsoever.

"What a trashy little house," Claudia said.

"Shall I write down the number?" her mother asked, pen and paper ready.

"No," she said. "Who'd want this? Only to tear it down. And who wants to live near the center of town anymore? To live near the transvestites who hang around the plaza at night? Forget it. This has no potential. Let's go near the mall, property values are higher there."

IV

The next morning, she got a call from Dean, Luisa's son.

"Thank you so much for taking my call," Dean said. "I don't want to impose on you and on your friendship with my mother, but

I need help finding a house for myself."

Claudia was properly flattered by the fact that he called her his mother's friend. All that worry for nothing! "I am here to serve you," she said. "Where are you calling from?"

"Upstate New York."

"Oh! Maybe you can help me improve my English. I've always wanted to be a polyglot. Shall we speak English?"

"Sure," Dean said, switching tongues.

"What an enchanting young man!"

"I'm not so young, Doña Claudia."

"Call me Claudia," she said. "Well, your mother tells me that you are looking for a home."

"Not just any home," Dean said. "I've driven Mom crazy. You see, I've made my living in antiques and collectibles, and I'm...retiring, so I want to keep some of the things I really like...and I can't just place all my things in a place that doesn't *go* with them. My mother sent me snapshots of these houses that, well...they're a bit *too* modern."

"Something traditional?"

"Not exactly. I'd love a townhouse with a turn-of-the-century feel. You know, classy yet exuberant. Like...how do I explain it to you? You know, like an Aubrey Beardsley illustration."

"I am not familiar with her."

"Him," Dean said, "I guess. Anyway...you know Art Nouveau? Toulouse Lautrec?"

"Oh, yes! I can see it now. Art Nouveau. Very decorative."

"That's it. I want a house with that feel."

"That's going to be difficult."

"But oh so worth it...I don't know, I'm very picky with details."

"It's going to be difficult to find a propriety like that."

"It's the kind of *property* I'm looking for. Price is no object. But I am a little short of time, and I'd like to move down to the island as soon as possible."

"A townhouse, though? Maybe it is too large a place for one person."

"Don't worry, I'm going to share it with someone. We both need lots of space. And I expect to have lots of houseguests over from the States, and have my family stay over for weekends…"

"Ooh, a friend? You have someone living with you?" What a piece of gossip! She hadn't heard that Luisa's son was living with someone. Maybe a wedding was in the offing? Surely she would be invited now.

"Well…yeah. My partner…He used to restore houses on the side, so if the house needs a lot of work, not to worry. Mark likes a challenge."

"Partner?" That killed the wedding idea.

"Yeah. We met when I was buying pieces for a house, and he was restoring it. We've been…business partners and friends since. He's gone back to the music business—he's a record producer—but he still does a little rebuilding work here and there. Me, I just buy things, but he makes them."

"Maybe your friend can do some work for me…for some of my clients. You maybe have not heard, but the Luna section of Mireya is being redeveloped. You know, it was once a nice neighborhood…well, the latest is, the wealthy young, they take these old house and remake them to their taste. So now it's becoming a nice neighborhood again, though, for *my* taste, it is too close to the university…"

"Maybe you can find me something of that sort?" Dean asked.

"Let's see what I can do," she said. "Anything else you have in mind?"

"I want a nice big porch, and please, no stucco!"

V

The first thing that Claudia noticed when she saw Dean was how thin and sickly he looked. Then she saw how tenderly Dean and Mark argued about who would carry a small piece of luggage out of the baggage claim area. And she noticed how they touched, casually flaunting their desire for each other.

As she stood by the Plexiglas divider which separated the arriving from the receiving, she decided to pretend she was waiting for someone else. Dean had homosexual AIDS! And he brought his fornicator with him! She didn't know how to hide herself and wished she could make herself invisible. However, she forced herself to continue smiling and looked at a young couple who had arrived on the same flight as if they were the ones she was waiting for. She kept looking at them while the plot came to her in a flash: Luisa was giving her what she herself did not want to deal with. A homosexual son! Of course, no one would like to sell or buy from degenerates. That's why Luisa dropped him on her. *She* wouldn't look like she approved or abetted him; her reputation would be clean. But Claudia wasn't about to do Luisa a favor that would dirty her reputation. Look: Claudia sells houses to degenerates. Look: Claudia brings down property values. Look: Claudia brings the horses of the apocalypse to your neighborhood—

"Doña Claudia?"

Claudia pretended not to hear.

"Excuse me, Doña Claudia?"

Claudia had never been put in such a situation. Yes, life had ugly things, but she thought she left them behind when she left South America.

"Doña Claudia, it's me, Dean."

"Call me Claudia," she said turning around, a wide toothy smile on her face.

Before her stood Dean, in a white long sleeved shirt, gray slacks, and wingtips. He held in the crook of his arm a winter jacket lined with the most amazing and unidentifiable fur. He looked as if a wind could lift him away. His friend Mark had the mien of yet another unremarkably cornstalk-tall American man: jeans, blue jersey shirt, Converse canvas shoes. And a ski jacket.

"It's me, Dean Rodriguez," he said, and he held a hand out in peace.

She shook it, practically trembling. She resisted the urge to wipe her hand in horror.

"This is Mark Piper," Dean said. Mark mumbled a hello and shook her hand coldly, keeping his scary grimace. "He's kinda shy," Dean whispered.

As if that mattered to her.

Now she faced the indignity of having to force herself to speak to the homosexuals while looking at them in the eye.

"Where did you get those shoes?" Claudia said.

"Schenectady," Mark said.

VI

Claudia had had a few properties in mind before their arrival. She did not show them to the couple. While she shifted her comfy seat cover to the shotgun seat, with the pretense of making Dean comfortable—she could burn the seat cover later and avoid contamination—she wondered what to do. She would subtly discourage the dregs from buying anything by showing them dregs. But where would she take them? This question did not remain unanswered for long, for Claudia had a prodigious memory for properties. She recalled the house in San Sebastián. Genius! she thought. Who'd buy that filthy thing? Meanwhile, there was the matter of preparing them for a disappointment.

"Oh, it was so hard to find something to suit you!" Claudia said, practicing her English. "I am afraid that houses like the ones you like have been torn down."

"What a pity," Dean said. "I've always wanted to live in one. My grandmother had one. When I was five years old, she hired someone to wreck it and build a cement thing in its place."

"Funny how your mother couldn't find you one," she said. "She buys so many houses…"

"Yeah," Dean said. "My mother collects houses like I collect cookie jars. But well, my mother's tastes run to the conventional, and I just couldn't live in something like that."

"If you pardon me asking," she said, "why do you wish to move to the island?"

"Can I speak with you in the strictest confidence?"

"Not at problem," she said. Her curiosity was stronger than her distaste. Besides, this would be great currency in the gossip exchange.

"Well, I'm going to pass away, so I hope to spend my last few years in my native land. Mark here agreed to take a year or two off and move here with me.... So it's a matter of finding the perfect place for me and all of my things."

"Oh, you are deadly sick?"

"Don't I look it?"

"Not at all! I just thought you were a vegetarian or something."

Mark, in the backseat, somehow found this awfully funny. Why, she was just being nice.

They drove by the main plaza of San Sebastián. It was a late Tuesday afternoon. Sadly, Claudia noted, there was no suggestion of the town loonies, drug addicts, drag queens and indigents that would congregate there at nightfall.

"Here we are," she said, with a slight sigh, as if this house was the best she could find. She stepped out of the car. Mark stepped out and opened the door for Dean. Now those two, Claudia thought with piercing irony, are perfect little gentlemen...

She stood in front of the house with absolute stillness and gravity, as if she were pondering a great injustice, noticing that the For Sale sign had fallen onto the floor of the porch. Mark and Dean soon joined her, looking at the house in silence.

A queer breeze flew through the shutters of the front door.

"It's perfect," Mark said.

What? She turned in shock to look at Mark smiling shyly, putting his arm around Dean.

"But...but...it is badly in need of disrepair!" she said.

"Mark likes a challenge," Dean said. "You should see what he did to our house in Ithaca. Shall we go in?"

Oh Sainted Mother, she did not have the keys. It wasn't even her house to represent. She did not know to whom the house belonged. Now her charade fell apart.

She made a show of looking through her purse. "My Lord, I forgot to bring the keys with me—"

"The door's open, I think," Mark said. "May we go in?"

"Ah, well, ah...why not?" Claudia smiled, rictus-like.

Mark and Dean climbed up the steps to the porch. With a slight push, Mark jostled the thin doors open. Inside, ceilings rose to great heights, wallpaper fell and folded over the floor, dust accumulated. Mark felt the walls and the beams of the house like a doctor palpating for unseemly bumps in glandular regions. Dean followed his own path into the house, going straight to the kitchen in the back. Claudia followed Dean, hoping to help him find something he didn't like. From the backyard there emanated the smell of guavas rotting on moist ground. In the bare and dirty cupboard, Dean found a ceramic cookie jar in the shape of a log cabin.

"An omen..." Dean said, inspecting the jar with an expert's eye. "You know they haven't made these in God knows how long. And this is in perfect shape. People just don't know what they're throwing away." He put the jar down, leaned on the countertop, and swept his eyes over the expanse of the kitchen.

"We'll take it," Dean said.

"I'll...I'll call you tomorrow to sign on the propriety," she said.

"Fabulous," Dean said. "Fabulous property."

"Property," she repeated. Fabulous, my foot.

Mark walked into the kitchen, an aw-gosh smile on his face, holding a player-piano roll in hand as if it were a treasure.

"Found this upstairs," Mark said, and showed it to Dean. "Does this mean something, or what?"

VII

Claudia started a bonfire in her backyard with her mother's help, and threw the car-seat comforter, and the coffee cup she offered to Dean out of social obligation, into the flames. How could have she missed those signs? "Partner"? "Antiques"? "Upstate New York"? Dead giveaways. It could have not been clearer. And she was so desperate for a sale that she did not listen to her reason and patch those pieces of information together to figure out that he was a pervert. She couldn't shake off the feeling of being violated somehow, even after scrubbing herself raw with a brush, à la Karen Silkwood, to make sure there was no risk of contamination. Maybe all he wanted was to move back home to torture his family with shame. Yes, revenge, the revenge of the perverse; now that he was sick with the filth of his desires he was rubbing it in the face of his family, and making them watch him die slowly. No wonder his mother couldn't find him a home! And Claudia was caught in the web of that family's intrigue.

But no, she would not embroil herself in this. She would not lower herself to help those two find a home in her adopted country. Or would she? Could she could find a way of selling them the house, and let Luisa and her clan suffer the indignity? What would other people say! Look: what a bad mother, she had a homosexual child. Look: how her child pays her for not raising him well. Look: now she brings death and decay to our tropical paradise—

But at what cost! Claudia's reputation would look even worse. No, she would not bother to call the owners of that ugly house. She would call the couple the next morning and say the deal could not go through. Better yet, that the owners had already accepted another offer. She would call Mark and Dean at the hotel where she'd dropped them off. The whole thing had so perturbed her that she had driven home with the fur-lined jacket on the backseat. She almost threw it in the fire with her things. But the fur, whose origin she couldn't place—was it fox? sable? degenerate, for sure—was too beautiful to throw into the purifying flames. She put on dishwashing gloves and stuffed it into the thickest plastic bag she could find. Maybe she would return it to Luisa as a sign that she washed—scrubbed, really—the whole dirty affair off her hands.

The next morning, Claudia called Dean with the terrible news.

"What a sad day!" she exhaled.

"So, are we closing the deal?" Dean asked.

"Ah, I am afraid that the people who own the house, well, they are already in negotiations to sell the house."

An odd silence occurred.

"Really." Dean sounded completely unconvinced.

"Yes," she said. "A fast food thing, you know, have been getting clearance to build there. And just yesterday they got a permit from town government."

Another, odder silence occurred.

"And there is nothing else available that I know of—to your taste, of course…" she added. "Maybe you could return home, and I could call you when I find something…"

Last night's bonfire still smoldered in the backyard. The bag stuffed with the jacket lay in a cupboard in her laundry room, near and dear to bottles of bleach.

Dean took a deep breath on the other side of the phone. "Can I tell you a quick story, Miss Claudia? It just so happens that I called my mother as soon as I got to the hotel. I told her I was delighted with the house. She told me she knew the house, that a family her family was friends with not long ago owned the house, and that a bachelor uncle of theirs lived there until he died forty years ago. And that nobody had been able to sell the house since then, that someone had said the house was jinxed, or that it had a ghost or something. Now, Mom keeps contact with everyone she's ever met, and she told me to call her friends and say hi for her."

"Heh, the world is a handkerchief," Claudia mumbled.

"I phoned them up. They were delighted that someone wanted the house, and that it was someone that they knew personally. You see, I had dinner at their table and played with their kids when we were very young. They said they had fond memories of me. They said they would be, to use the Spanish term, *encantados* to have me over for dinner tonight and sign the papers."

"How...?"

"The thing is—did I hallucinate this? Or are you lying? And if you are lying, let me tell you, I'm going to get the house no matter what."

Claudia was *incensed* that he should dare question her integrity. "The house is mine to sell, not for you to take from me!"

"By the way, I mentioned that you showed us the house, and they had absolutely no knowledge of your existence."

"It is not proper for you to go behind my back like this! The propriety is mine to sell!"

"Propriety is theft," Dean said.

Claudia heard the line go dead, and she was *furious*.

VIII

Claudia immediately called Olivia, the appraiser's wife, hoping to smear things up as much as she could with the high-grade dirt she had on Luisa's son. If she put Luisa in enough trouble, maybe she would be shamed into seclusion...and perhaps her place in the social order might need to be filled...

"Ay, Olivia," Claudia said. "I know something so terrible...so terrible...I cannot possibly keep it secret any longer. Oh, the shame..."

"What is it?"

"You know, the Rodriguezes' youngest son..."

"Dino?"

"He calls himself Dean now."

"I know."

"Well...He came over to do some business with me...and, well..."

"Yes?"

"Dean is homosexual. And he is sick with AIDS! Can you imagine, Luisa letting her son have a lifestyle like that! How could a mother let a child do that to himself?"

Today was evidently the day for odd silences.

"You heard?" Claudia said.

"No, no...I hadn't heard," Olivia said.

"Terrible, isn't it."

"Very sad," Olivia said. "Everyone embarks on a sad journey."

"Speaking of journeys, we must go on a shopping trip to the capital. I found the quaintest shoe store in the old city center. It's adorable; it's no bigger than a living room but their stock is imported and exclusive to the shop."

"That sounds very interesting. But right now I'm all set for shoes."

"We wouldn't just buy shoes. There's much we can talk about. Share. How about tomorrow?"

"Tomorrow we're having breakfast at my place."

"Really!"

"Yes. We're organizing a fund-raiser, and we're going to have an expert come in to help us out. He's raised funds for this cause before, and he's well known in the community, so we're looking forward to breakfasting with him."

"Has...has a chair been decided for this committee?" Claudia asked, the intricate machinery in her head spinning, spinning plots.

"Why, would you like to run it?"

"My organizational skills, if I may say so, could be an asset to the group."

"Perhaps you should offer your help tomorrow?"

"It would be my great pleasure!"

"Fabulous," Olivia said. "I'm sure you'll fit right in..."

IX

Within the idiom of casual daytime wear for the tropics, Claudia Ferrier dressed to impress at the breakfast. The outfit she wore cannot be fully described without naming a designer or two. It consisted of a blue-green silk blouse, the slacks that came along with it as a set, accessorized with a big dark blue belt with a silver buckle, matching shoes with not-too-high heels, silver-mounted aquamarine earrings and necklace (her emeralds would have been *too* flashy) and a tiny little handbag that hung and swung from her shoulder by a silver chainlet. Elegant yet colorful, composed yet casual, classy yet friendly, serious yet fun: why, the outfit stood for how she wanted to be seen. She showed up slightly late to make an entrance, and be noticed, and be introduced to everyone as the glittering new member of the family.

An entrance she sure did make. The room fell into silence as the group, one by one, turned to glare at her.

Dean sat on the center seat of the table, holding up a cheese pastry in the air, Mark leaning over and whispering into his ear.

How could she save this situation? Talk, quickly!

"Dean…" she said, running over to his side, "Dean…I am so sorry, you left your beautiful coat in my car…"

"And?" Dean asked.

"Ah…What brings you here?"

"I'm organizing an AIDS benefit. And you, what kind of mischief are you up to?"

Dean smiled, a wide, toothy smile. Mark looked at her like he was about to throttle her. Claudia looked around to see that all eyes were upon her.

"Oh, you know Dean, how pleasant," said Olivia, from her corner of the table. "I'm so sorry Luisa is not here to see you as well."

Claudia kept trying to ingratiate herself with Dean. "Uh… Uh…What kind of animal fur is your coat?" asked Claudia.

"It's cretin," said Mark.

Claudia visibly amused herself with Mark's remark. "Oh, what a funny American—"

"You have no power here," Dean said. "Begone, before a house falls on you too."

X

Claudia left the party soon after, bursting in tears and agony. What would she tell her mother?

David Messineo

Miss Manners Enters the 21st Century

I know the outside fork is for salad,
the inside for the meal,
and I never could figure out
that small spoon above the plate.
But there is a little etiquette issue
I've been meaning to ask:
Should I attend the impending funeral
of a friend I've known for years
whom I believe is dying with AIDS
and who won't tell me?
Is it a delicate thing
to view through cheesecloth,
handle with kid gloves?
IV hookups by evening,
extended absences from work,
vague answers from coworkers
when asked when he'll return:
This is not right.   Not right.
Should I be sympathetic
in spite of his silence,
or should I be insulted
that he apparently thinks
I'm stupid enough
not to have figured it out?
Come on, Miss Manners,
give me a policy.
Afternoon tea is 2:30 to 4
(or 2 to 4:30)
and a millennium change
means nothing to a disease
likely to kill half a million Americans
by 2001.
My friend may be one.
Should I attend the funeral
if I'm not part of the departure?
Should I light a candle,
read a Psalm?
Which Psalm?
What is the proper procedure?

William M. Hoffman
Riga

Characters:	**WOLF** Middle-aged, white
	Z In his thirties, African-American
	4 MEN AND 4 WOMEN, performing as an ensemble can play all the other characters. At least two of these men and one of these women should be African-American.
SET:	An empty stage in a theatre. It should be as bare as possible: a chair here, a bench there. The rest of the set can be projected. Good audio equipment is a must.
TIME:	We start off some time before 9/11, New York City, then off we go.

Act I, Scene V

WOLF

Z, sometimes when I hold you in my arms this is what I see.
> *[Z comes out of the shadows. He and WOLF wend their way through the dead bodies. It is late August or early September.]*

Z

... But that was over fifty years ago.
> *[More gently]*

You can't bring them back.
> *[DENNY steps forward from the shadows. Since he's only a figure in Z's mind, WOLF can't see him.]*

DENNY

It couldn't have begun more wretchedly.

Z

I can't bring Denny back.

DENNY

I slept through the alarm.

Z

You know, Denny's memorial was today.

WOLF

Shit, I forgot.

Z

It was your idea to come.

DENNY

Our plane was delayed in Chicago.

WOLF

Fuck.

Z

I didn't give a shit if you came until you made such thing about "being" there for me.

DENNY

The violinist had a sprained wrist.

WOLF

I can't believe I missed it. How did the chorus sound?

Z & DENNY

The mezzo had a strepped throat.

WOLF

Shit.

Z

You didn't have to attend.

DENNY

I'm so glad to be home.

Z

He was *my* lover.

WOLF

Sometimes I think he still is.
        [**DENNY** *goes back into the shadows.]*

Z

What's that?

WOLF

Nothing.

Z

All you think about is Jews.

WOLF

I'm sorry.

Z

What about blacks? What about people with AIDS?

WOLF

The world is getting ready for another Jew killing.

Z

Here we go again.

WOLF

The Nazis are rising again in Germany.

Z

It's the Christian fundamentalists in America who are after our asses, not the Nazis.

WOLF

In Riga they're selling swastikas.

Z

In Africa one out of five people has AIDS—that's your new holocaust.

WOLF

After the Bible, *The Protocols of the Learned Elders of Zion* is the
most popular book in the world.

Z

What are you talking about?

WOLF

The Protocols of the Learned Elders of Zion. It's a Czarist forgery
accusing the Jews of trying to take over the world, the banks, the
media, the politicians. Our very own Henry Ford distributed millions of copies.
    *[**WOLF** just happens to have a copy in his back pocket.]*

Z

Never heard of it.

WOLF

Sells better than chitlins in Chattanooga or sushi in Japan.

Z

Please, I'm so sick of the Jews.

WOLF

They're selling it on street corners in New York...

Z

Don't you get tired of it?

WOLF

...along with the incense...

Z

Yo, how about a little vacation?

WOLF

...and Million Man baseball caps...

Z

Put a li'l ol' cross around your neck?

WOLF

...and pro-Palestinian t-shirts.

Z

Have a nose job?

WOLF

...and Nation of Islam videotapes.

Z

[Feigning shock]
That cannot be!

WOLF

And books on how the Holocaust was a hoax!

Z

I'm absolutely thunderstruck with horror!

WOLF

Pirated from editions originally published in Germany.

Z

Is you suggestin' that us color' folk be anti-Semantic?

WOLF

The Semites be fine. It's the kikes they don't like.

MUHAMMED[4*]

[Wearing Nation of Islam bow-tie, very softly, sweetly]
We kill the women.

4*   Khalid Abdul Muhammed, speaking at Kean College, Union, N.J., on
November 29, 1993.

Z

After all the Jews did for the shvartzes.

MUHAMMED

We kill the babies.

WOLF

After all the shvartzes did for the Jews.

Z

After we marched—whites and blacks together, arm in arm—in Alabam.

MUHAMMED

We kill the blind.

WOLF

[Shoving The Protocols *in his face.]*
Have you ever read it?

Z

[Throwing the book away. Yiddish accent]
Oi-yoi-yoi!

MUHAMMED

We kill the faggot...

Z

Pogroms in Crown Heights!

WOLF

Look.

Z

Gas chambers in Brighton Beach!

MUHAMMED

The Lesbian.

WOLF

Listen.

Z

Soul Nazis run amuck in the Diamond District.

MUHAMMED

We kill them all.

WOLF

[Reading]

"The goyim are a flock of sheep, and Jews are the wolves."

Z

Please.

WOLF

"And you know what happens when wolves get hold of the flock."

Z

Stop it!

WOLF

It accuses Jews of plotting to take over the world!

Z

You're driving me away!

WOLF

Z!

Z

Everyone I know is Jewish! I'm tired of feeling guilty!

WOLF

I was mugged last night.

Z

What?

[Beat]

JOHANNA

If I were a man I would kill them.

MAX

I know you had a rough time in Berlin, but that was Germany.

WOLF

One more reason to leave New York.

JOHANNA

I would kill them.

CHARLES

Europe's on fire.

Z

Were you hurt?

WOLF

Killed the motherfucker.

Z

You what?

WOLF

Grabbed his knife and cut his throat.

MAX

This is Latvia.

WOLF

Kidding.

CHARLES

Your house is on fire.

Z

Fag bashing?

MAX

You think the Germans want a war now?

WOLF

Called me a kike.

CHARLES

You must leave.

WOLF

A blood-sucking Jew.

MAX

And go where?

Z

I'm sorry.

WOLF

It's not your fault.

Z

Were they black?
        [**WOLF** *nods. Beat*]
I'm sorry.

WOLF

Ditto. New York's really getting to me.

Z'S MOTHER

They're putting your brother on trial for murder.

Z

I have to go to L.A.

Z'S BROTHER

It was his own fault.

WOLF

What for?

Z

Thanksgiving.

Z'S MOTHER

You gotta help him.

Z'S BROTHER

The Ko-reans, they got Jewish blood. They bloodsuckers, ya know.

WOLF

I'll come with you if you want.

Z

No!...

[**WOLF** *is surprised at* **Z***'s vehemence.*]

Z'S MOTHER

*[To **Z**]*
But he's your brother.

Z'S BROTHER

He shouldn't a pulled out a piece.

Z

I mean you don't have to.

WOLF

I've never met your family...

Z'S MOTHER

Please come home, child.

Z

I'll be there for only a few days.

Z'S MOTHER

*[To **Z**]*
I don't care what he did, he's my child.

Z'S BROTHER

I was eating a fuckin' pear.

WOLF

I could "take" a meeting with an agent. The networks are desperate
for anything new.

Z'S BROTHER

He grabs my shirt and goes…
> *[Racist imitation of Korean grocer]*

"You get out my store, you no-pay mullahfucka."

WOLF

They actually pay you for work in L.A.

Z

Please!…

Z'S MOTHER

I never aksed you fuh nothin'.

WOLF

Come on, we've never traveled together.

Z

No!

Z'S BROTHER

> *[On telephone]*

A salaam aleykoom, my brother.

WOLF

Never mind.

Z'S BROTHER

I need your help, my brother.

Z

You don't understand.

Z'S BROTHER	Z'S MOTHER
You don't understan', I didn't mean to kill nobody.	Don't you understan'? I didn't raise my baby to kill nobody!

WOLF

I don't understand.

Z

Fuck it, I need some space!

Z'S BROTHER

A little help, thass all.

Z'S MOTHER

Please, child.

WOLF

[Leaving]
You can have all the space you want.

Z

No!

Z'S BROTHER

You're a white-ass faggot punk.

WOLF

Fucking "space"!

Z

Don't go!

WOLF

"Space."

Z'S BROTHER

Bent over and sold you pussy.

Z'S MOTHER

Help your brother.

Z

I've been upset.

WOLF

Is it Denny again?

Z'S BROTHER

How much your Jewboy leave you?

Z'S MOTHER

Blood is thicker than water.

Z

   [To **WOLF***]*
Wait! There's something you don't know.
   [To **MOTHER***]*
I can't—

Z'S MOTHER	**Z'S BROTHER**
Please, child?	Please? I'm sorry.

Z

…You see, my…

WOLF

What is it?

Z'S MOTHER	**Z'S BROTHER**
At least your brother's a man!	You sorry-ass faggot!

Z

No!
   *[***Z***'s* **MOTHER** *and* **BROTHER** *turn their backs on* **Z***.*
   Beat. **Z** *thinks better of telling* **WOLF** *about his family.]*

Z

I mean…the orchestra in Topeka has been getting threatening phone calls.

PHELPS

   [With a smile, leaving message]
God hates fags.
   *[***PHELPS*** hangs up.]*

Z

Phelps swore he would disrupt Denny's retrospective in the spring. They don't want music by a dead cocksucker.

WOLF

Bastard. Can't you get a lawyer?

PHELPS

First amendment.

Z

Phelps is a lawyer. His whole family are lawyers.

PHELPS

I'll say anything I please, you devil-worshipping sodomite.

WOLF	MUHAMMED
Kill him. Kill all the lawyers.	*[Quietly, under at first]*
Z	I kill the Jew. I kill the Jew behind the tree. I kill the faggot. I kill the lesbian. I kill the babies. I kill the women. I kill them. I kill them all…
Why didn't you kill the muggers?	
WOLF	
Why don't you kill Phelps?	

JOHANNA

If I were a man I would kill them.
[Beat]

WOLF

Let's move to LA. Make a new beginning.

Z'S MOTHER	JOHANNA
Please come home, child.	"Yes," I said.

WOLF

You could be near your family. Fuck the movies, I'll get a job-job. We could stay at Bill and David's. They have a pool…

Z

I hate LA! Every dirty palm tree. Every filthy piece of stucco.
Every greasy aqua swimming pool. Every sun-drenched dreck-
filled strip mall. Every network-approved buff-body white-toothed
blond-headed 12-Steppin' serial-fucking AIDS-burger. Every mile
after mile of cracked-out, smacked-out, maxed-out T.B.-racked
ticky-tack gun-totin' Crips and Bloods, hoods-and-thugs homeboy.
We should have burned LA to the ground while we had the chance!

WOLF

Seattle?

Z'S MOTHER

They're putting your brother on trial for murder.

Z

Look, I'm the executor of Denny's estate . . .

WOLF

I'm sorry for pushing you.

Z'S MOTHER

You got to help your brother.

JOHANNA

"Yes, I said.

Z

The taxes are due . . .

JOHANNA

That was all the English I knew.

WOLF

You just lost your lover . . .

DENNY

I'm so happy to be back.

Z

Topeka . . .

WOLF
*[Overlapping, to **Z** in audience]*
It went something like that, didn't it, Z? Then I said something and you said something and so forth, and then you said:

Z
I didn't know how much I loved Denny until he got ill. And then we moved in together. He was fine until he was…
*[**DENNY** coughs.]*
not so fine. How lucky I was to have lived with him for five years. No one understands that.
*[**DENNY** steps forward from the shadows]*

DENNY
The performance was pretty decent. We had only about an hour to rehearse, and the acoustics were all wrong, but we got a screaming, standing ovation.

WOLF
And then I touched your head…
*[He holds **Z**'s hand]*
…deeply moved, loving you for loving your lover…
[Strokes his face]
jealous of your dead man… hearing dead Jews in my brain all the time…

Chip Livingston
Anthology of a Spoon River AIDS Walk

Susan
I picked up Mason in Charleston.
It happened that I was there for a meeting.
          Good timing, Right.
Thank you Universal Forces of Love and Light.
I met Mason through Tim.
I'll walk with Mason in memory of Tim.
                    And for my father.

Douglas
I can't walk on Saturday.
I have a UYO workshop.
Understanding Yourself and Others.
I had already made these plans
and to change them would show a lack
in Integrity. Mason kids me
that it's a cult. We met at Wolfgang's
for lunch. Mason had organic greens
and smoked lots of cigarettes.

Mason
The first thing I said
When I walked into the Kelleys' house:
'Quit barking at me!'
To Sterling (Tim's dog)
To Patches (Mrs. K's)
Then I hugged Mrs. and Mr.
Sisters: Brady and Karen.
My lover died here.
I came back to walk in his memory.
I'll sleep in his old room.
Our old bed.

Brady
It means a lot to us
That Mason came back to walk.

That he changed his middle name to Kelley.
That he's part of our family.
But when he moved away
It felt like I lost another brother.

Karen
It was great to see Mason
and so many of Tim's friends
who came to walk
and for the dedication of the library.
My boyfriend couldn't get here from Columbia.
I'm driving back and we're leaving
for a Utah ski vacation right after this.

Chuck
I didn't make it up to Spoon River.
I've walked the last four years.
I had too much work this this time.
Karen and I are going skiing for a week.
I had a lot to work out before we left.
I hope Karen isn't late.

Brian
I feel ostracized
from the Kelley family.
I lived with Brady 3½ years.
Was there when her brother died.
She moved out in November
when she found out I was cheating.
Now I'm dating one of Tim's nurses.
I walked the course quickly. For Tim.
Then I left quickly and went back to work.

Christy
I was one of Tim's nurses.
I became very close to his family
during his hospital stays.
The first time I met Mason
He was in the hospital bed with Tim.

I thought he was Tim's brother.
I walked with the family
in the AIDS Walk this year,
Petrified they would find out
I'm sleeping with Brian

Mrs. Kelley
My son died of AIDS January 1, 1996.
          He was my life.
I don't know how I've survived
          without him.
I don't know if I am
          surviving.
I've kept in touch with most of his friends.
          I've organized a library
in his name at the AIDS Network.
          I stay busy, busy, busy.

Mr. Kelley
It is great to see all of Tim's friends.
Together we will raise money
and awareness and keep fighting
until AIDS is cured, and fighting
ignorance and prejudice against
People With AIDS.
I planted a Magnolia tree at the hospital
where Tim spent so much time.
We took Mason by to see it
before we drove him to the airport.
Hopefully it will bloom this year.

Pam
I rented a car to get to Spoon River.
I came to see my son Mason. And to walk
in the memory of his friend, Tim.
Tim's dog barked at me every time I moved
or spoke. I met some very nice guys during the walk
Most of whom were gay.
Some of whom were sick.

Hudson

My wife drove down to Spoon River
for the AIDS Walk.
Our son's friend died from the disease.
I had to stay in Charlotte with the other kids.
I coach baseball.

Jason

I came in to town to see my ex-lover.
I ran into Mr. and Mrs. Kelley at the store.
I told them I would be walking
but I was too hungover on Saturday.
Tim was my boyfriend once   long ago.
Eight. Nine years back.
I slept with Mason a few times too.

Maria

I only met Tim once.
He was beautiful. He was with Mason
at a benefit. I knew he was sick
but he was so gorgeous. You couldn't tell
(at all). Mrs. Kelley asked me to
paint something for his quilt panel.
I'm an artist. But I couldn't take any money.
I never knew anyone with AIDS before.
I walked this year with his family, in his memory.

JT

I never actually met Tim.
I work with Maria in Personnel.
I slept with Mason last year after Tim died.
I had no idea at the time.
I spoke with Mason's mother
most of the walk. Tim's mother too.
They were so cool. I can't picture my mother
ever doing anything like that.
I wonder if Mason will sleep with me again.
He was drunk the first time.

Jan
I work with Karen.
We do PR for the University.
I
secretly
write
Po   etry
and want to talk to Mason
about writing.
He had a photo from Thanksgiving
of "The Poet Why."

Monica
It was so good to see Mason.
He came by the office
where we worked together.
I gave him $10 for the AIDS Walk.
He's as cute as ever.
I asked him if he knew JT
who works here now.
I said he reminded me of Mason.
Mason said it was a "gay thing."

Angel
I used to be Mason's supervisor in Personnel.
A friend with AIDS died
in my arms a few years ago.

My husband died of Cancer
in my arms a few years before that.

I sponsored Mason for $25.

Bob
I worked with Mason several years ago.
I was his supervisor's supervisor.
He and Tim went to the same church
as my wife and I. I only had six dollars
in my wallet to give him for the walk.
Mason always said funny things like "Word up."

Carl

Mason was my secretary, at the Library, he corrected my writing, that was always all over the place,   Commas, in the wrong places, and such, I knew, he was coming to town but, I was in a meeting, when he came by, I'm producing movies now, Thats right Right here in Spoon River.

Jody

Mason is like a spirit brother.
We worked together in the library.
We used to send porn to each other
on the Internet. I left early
the day he was coming by.
For some reason I like e-mail
but I didn't want to see him in person.
I told him I would walk
but changed my mind.

Renee

I drove up with my fiancé.
I'm glad his family waited
to dedicate the library
until all his friends could be here.
I gave Tim his first lizard in 1989.
He named it Timex. He had 33 lizards
when he died. Mason hated living
with all those lizards,
but he loved living with Tim.
I teach Special Ed and have an iguana
in my classroom. I'm afraid to touch it
but I can't let it go.

Sam

I came up with my fiancé from Edisto.
Renee and I were with Tim and Mason
the first time I got drunk. Tim took me
to all the stores in SR that sold comic books.

Peggy
I run the head agency for federal Ryan White funds.
Mason and Tim were on the Board of Directors.
They got involved to advocate for client services.
Made some great changes in funding for alternative therapies.
Tim was among three other board members who died this year.
Mason looked good. Seemed to be holding up. I gave him a
    strawberry.

Rick
I made the walk and the dedication
of the Tim Kelley Memorial Library.
I can't believe it's been a year since Tim died.
Mason amazes me. He's like a cat. Always
lands on his feet. He looks exactly the same
as he did eleven years ago when I met him.
I met his mom—he looks just like her—same
dark skin. My mom would freak if I came out.
Mason had two mothers walking with him.

Thomas
I love Mason.
I can't believe he was here
and I didn't get to see him.
I got too fucked up
to make it to the walk.
My phone's disconnected.
I wanted to party with him.

Tom Girl
I used to live with Tim in Columbia
I wanted to come up but I just couldn't
I wanted to see Mason and the Kelleys
It's too hard
I can't deal with it
I wonder how many people
will wear shirts and walk for me
I still feel great but Tim went so quick

John
I won a trip to Hawaii
for outstanding sales
the same week as the Walk.
I loved Tim more than anything.
He was my best friend. Roommate.
I used to hate Mason. Until I fell in love
and realized what he and Tim felt for each other.
Mason and I share the same birthday.
We're friends now but we were way
too much alike back then.

Mike
John and I went to Hawaii instead of the AIDS Walk.
I wish we could have made it
but it was a free trip. To Hawaii.
We sponsored Angela for $100.
We'll go visit the Kelleys when we get back.
We hope to visit Mason this summer.

Angela
I cry every time I think of Tim.
I didn't want to drive up by myself.
Luckily Gordy decided the night before
to go with me. Also all my friends
who bailed felt guilty and sponsored me
with big donations. Gordy walked
with Mason's mom most of the time.
They talked about teaching.
We drove back to Columbia after.
There was a big party I couldn't miss.
A Big Party.

Copper
I loved Tim.
I loved Mason.
They took care of me
when I got drunk and showed my tits,
when I got drunk and showed my ass.

I saw Mason at the walk.
Nobody noticed that I have lost 20 pounds.

Patrick
I walked with Copper
but had to go to work right after.
I didn't make it to the library.
The last time I went out with Tim,
he, Copper and I went to Roger's Slut Party.
Mason was in Atlanta.
Tim talked us in to going to the Bluebird Theatre
—a very hetero nightclub—in our gold lamé hotpants.
People called us Fags and Tim just laughed
and waved to them.

Gordan
Tim used to hate me.
He liked me until John and I broke up.
Until I slept with Mason.
He was dating Tad at the time but still
Mason was OFF LIMITS.
To everyone. One time he called
when I was there. I felt really bad.
I walked with Mason's mom most of the walk.
She was really cool. Mason didn't say very much.

James
Tim was one of my best friends.
He was the first person I came out to.
I was dating Renee but Tim knew
I was gay. He was dating Jason. Then Ryan.
This was a long time ago obviously.
Tim said I should take my time.
It was no hurry.
He and Jason walked in on me having sex with Renee.
They were coming in from sex
on the beach. It was Spring Break.
We were all sharing a motel in Pawley's Island.

Donald
I only knew Tim through David.
We've been together four years
and Tim was always really great to me.
He made me feel included.
I always thought he was beautiful
and that Mason was really lucky.

Nancy
I was Tim's home healthcare nurse.
He always cheered me up
when I went to his house to check on him,
to change his portacath, to take his blood.

He had a house full of lizards.
And the most wonderful family.
His mother read a letter she wrote
when I received Nurse of the Year.

Timothy was the kind of beautiful person.
who makes my work worthwhile.

Cathryn
Tim was my roommate in college.
Well, I dated his roommate and practically
lived with him and Randy. I married Randy.
Tim moved away. I was the nurse
for Dr. Young when Tim was diagnosed
and moved back to Spoon River.
I've seen hundreds of AIDS patients
and none were as well-informed as Tim.
He knew as much as the doctors.
He made Dr. Young laugh
which no other patient has ever done.
He talked Dr. Young into getting acupuncture
—just to check it out. I've never seen
a family more supportive or a lover more
loving than the Kelleys and Mason.
I try to keep in touch with them. I left a poem

on Tim's grave last month.
Mrs. Kelley called and thanked me.

Randy

I'm not gay but I loved another man.
I loved Tim Kelley.
He was the best friend I ever had.
He would've made a helluva social worker.
  his major.
He was the kindest man I ever knew.

David

I'm the Walk Coordinator
for the Spoon River AIDS Network.
The Kelley family and friends:
  "We're Walking for Tim"
made up 1/8 of the total walkers.
They had over 50 people registered
and wearing T-shirts with Tim's picture.
They raised more than $3,000
  —their group alone.
They're a great benefit to our community.
But I'm glad they didn't bring their dogs this year.

Scott

I met Tim when he came to the Network.
I talked him and Mason into running for the Board
for the Ryan White Consortium.
Mason gave a speech that made everyone cry.
We were all used to death and dying
but they were so young and scared.
They got more votes than anyone.
I felt so sorry for Mason. So happy
and sorry too. I'm also an AIDS widow.
I hate he had to go through the same thing.
I didn't walk this year. I saw Mason at the dedication
of the Tim Kelley Library.
I'm leaving Spoon River and this whole AIDS business.
I'm moving to California. Starting my life over.
I've been here too long.

Roger

I've known Tim forever.
Since we all started SRCC.
He and Mason came to my first Slut Party
back in 1990. They got in a huge fight.
Mason made an ass of himself. Tim left
with someone else. They both moved away
a short time after that. To different places.
Then they showed up together at the next party in '91.
Shocked the hell out of everybody.
Tim apologized for Mason's behavior.
They dressed really slutty. We didn't
give out awards yet then, but they would've won.
They left the next morning for Georgia.

Linda

Mason came to town for the AIDS Walk.
My husband Joey and my baby Kaitlin
and I walked too. Joey wanted Kaitlin
to meet Mason. Mason was the first friend
I made when we moved here from Barbados.
I walked into the office where he worked
and he caught my spirit. I loved Tim
before I ever met him. Because I loved Mason
and Mason loved Tim so much.
They were beautiful together. They lived
across the street from Joey, Kaitlin, and me.
Mason and I used to sneak cigarettes.
Our husbands didn't like us to smoke.

Jessica

My brother Kevin is gay.
My parents, Kevin and I walked
in the AIDS Walk for Tim.
I hope my brother never gets AIDS.

June

My son Kevin is gay.
I live in fear that he will die
like Tim did.

I worry about the kind of friends he has.
There were actually a lot of really
nice homosexuals at the walk.
I didn't know there were so many.

Kevin

I only met Tim once at church.
His mom and my mom are good friends
and Mrs. Kelley really helped my mom deal
with my coming out. I was in the hospital
the same time Tim was. I had an overdose.
I O.D.'d. Accidentally. I wasn't supposed to
come out of the coma. I'm still addicted
to drugs but I'm in rehab. I got to meet Mason
at the walk. So did my mom. It was good for her
to see that all fags aren't fucked up. Mason said
I could call him if I ever needed to talk.
Mason's mom came all the way from Charlotte
to be with him and to walk for Tim.

Danny

I am a Methodist pastor.
Sharon Kelley worked as my secretary
at the church. She had to quit when Tim got so sick
it required all her time.
I never knew a gay couple before Tim and Mason.
Through Sharon, the Lord opened my eyes.
I led the service at Tim's funeral.
I gazed out at a full church.
A congregation of young men,
young women, old men, and old women.
All colors. All shapes and sizes.
I saw the diverse group of people
this young man touched. I looked
out at the weeping faces and saw a bridge
of love. Tim Kelley built a bridge
in my heart to a population I judged.
I had to rethink my whole belief system.
This young man had a great effect on
my life and my ministry.

Tiger

The fifth AIDS Walk for me.
The first for me alone.
My lover Gene died last November.
My previous lover died six years ago.
Tim was a friend and inspiration
to the entire community.
It was awkward seeing Mason
who is grieving like I am.
We have so much in common
and I had no idea what to say.

Ed

I'm scared to death—I mean
I'm scared to *LIFE* that this will
be my last AIDS Walk. I know
I have to think positive but I'm scared.
I have CMV now. That's what Tim died of.
I helped my lover kill himself
three years ago. I never thought I'd live this long.
I'm only 27 but I feel so old. So tired.
I hardly recognize myself.

Clay

This was my last AIDS Walk.
I had to ride a scooter.
I'm too weak
I'm too sick.
I tried to kill myself last month.
I wrecked my car and ended up
killing someone else instead.
My mother will take care of my son
and daughter when I die.
I hope they live to see the end of AIDS.
I heard Gene say that Tim and Danny
came to him before he died.
Stood at the foot of his hospital bed.
I hope they'll be there to meet me too.
I really miss them.

Bonnie ZoBell
Massage

"You can turn over now," Nell, the masseuse, told me. The padded table had comfortable contours for your face and the back of your head, depending on which side of your body was being worked on. My therapist had suggested the sessions might help, but the whole idea had seemed awkward at first.

Soon I was lying face up. Nell adjusted the towels in such a way that only the part of me being massaged was exposed.

Despite my initial resistance, during my first appointment I'd started weeping uncontrollably. The therapist, who I'd started seeing earlier that year in 1984, said it was because I wasn't getting enough human touch. Sometimes I wanted to have sex with Joe, even though he was so thin, but I never suggested it because I knew he didn't feel well and wouldn't want to and then we'd have to be uncomfortable.

"Don't worry about it, kid," Nell had said. "I'm sure. Do you think you're the first person who's ever cried on my table? Have a good cry."

Since then, I'd been going to her once a week, though it seemed kind of decadent. Today was my sixth visit.

Nell, short and too young to have gone completely gray as early as she had, wore her hair down with bangs across the front and seemed young anyway. She was round and had a sweet but intelligent face that reacted expressively to whatever you said. Sometimes she smiled innocently; other times she put her chin down and looked at you from the tops of her eyes—teasing playfully. Her skin was smooth and white. I thought she was beautiful, though I doubted men found her attractive.

"I got a new roommate," she told me today, working with lotion on my right calf.

"What's she like?"

"She's a painter and teaches at the community college," Nell said. "And she's gay."

"Hmmm." I often wondered what Nell did when she wasn't working. Now I wondered whether she was attracted to the roommate. Did they touch each other at night, lie opposite each other, mirror images?

"Anyway, she seems nice," Nell said. "She doesn't mind my piano playing."

"I'll bet you're a great piano player."

"Naw—it's just for fun. Here, relax your leg a little."

When she touched my leg again, a hot stab of electricity ran up and down my body, ending in my groin.

§

That weekend I went to a baby shower given for Joe's sister, Alicia, by one of her co-workers at the 7-11. It was hard to believe Alicia Logan was pregnant—after all those years when *she* was the baby. I should have been the one to throw the party; until recently we'd been such close friends. But there was something that knocked the wind right out of me about her pregnancy.

Joe and I hadn't talked about babies since he'd been diagnosed. I'd about convinced myself I didn't want one anyway. What did I need with babies, I asked myself, trying to downplay the enormity of what had been stolen from me: the sweet milky breath of a little body clutching mine, the face a gorgeous and permanent reminder of the bond between Joe and me—permanent in a way it was increasingly clear Joe wouldn't be—a baby whose gentle dependence, whose life-giving rhythms, would always be mingled with my own, who would smile and cause me to smile just because we each knew the other was in the room. No, I told myself, I didn't need babies when I had the animals at my business, Zoo Dog Training, as well as a houseful of pets. Even before we'd gotten married, though, Joe had been very clear about wanting children, so clear it frightened me.

"Why?" I'd asked. "We're in our thirties; we've done okay this far. You've got the kids at work." Joe was a favorite at Rainbow House—he managed a home for teenage boys—because of his own boyishness.

We were sitting outdoors at an Italian restaurant. We'd had a few glasses of wine. Joe, still robust at the time, was wearing worn jeans, worn tennis shoes, a golf shirt.

"But now that we're together, aren't you dying to have one?" he said, teetering back on his chair, his eyes twinkling. When he saw I wasn't smiling, he shrugged and added, "Since we've been together, now I know I definitely want my own kids."

"Men feel more masculine if they leave offspring behind. Especially if they're boys."

"That isn't true," he said.

I touched his knee, laughed. "I can't see you home baby-sitting all the time, and I wouldn't be happy without the Zoo. Some people should never have kids. Like my parents."

Joe shook his head. "But that's exactly why I do want them, because I'd be much better at it." Our eyes caught, and he let the front legs of his chair fall to the floor. "Especially since I love you so much."

When he said things like that, so far advanced from the Neanderthal Joe I grew up with, I loved him most. That's when I felt bad about the things that spilled out of me, like my comment about men wanting progeny. I became convinced that now that his wild oats were sown, he'd have made a good father. He'd help me to understand more about families and togetherness. And so eventually we'd agreed to have a child.

His diagnosis had changed all that, though.

§

The girls at Alicia's baby shower seemed so much younger than Alicia. They were like a different species from me, a species able to reproduce. Nearly all of them had either just given birth, already had children, or were pregnant.

After we introduced ourselves, many asked, "What about you? Are you going to have kids?" like our parents asked and our parents' friends, our co-workers and our neighbors.

The girls seemed innocent enough, unaware of how hard things could be. But then I reminded myself that they, too, were doing their bit of hard work, propagating the species.

Alicia's stomach was enormous, stretched full with an eight-month-old baby. Her fluids fed it, her breasts seemed ready to burst with milk to provide for it the minute it arrived. She was assisted through doors, helped up from low seats or had to rock herself back and forth for momentum. Her clothes were huge, her face glowed, her skin was dewy.

"Can I touch it?" I said tentatively, already cupping my hand to her swollen belly, finding it miraculously squishy and hard at the same time. I'd heard pregnant women disliked people coming up and touching whenever they liked, but *I* wasn't people. I was practically Alicia's sister. Or had been. Though I'd grown up down the street from Alicia and Joe, babysat Alicia so much we'd become best friends, once Joe had vaguely confessed he was terminally ill to his father and his brother, Pete, the news had quickly reached Alicia, who'd first thought it was going to be as easy as asking me what was wrong. She and her father continued to corner me at various family gatherings, trying to make me fill in the details, and so I'd had to distance myself even further from them, explain that it was Joe's body, that they would have to ask him.

"You don't tell us, babe, he ain't going to tell us," Max Logan said at some potluck or other, his eyes watering up. "Always thought he took after his mama, and she died of the cancer, you know." Alicia ended up hurt I wouldn't tell her, and the family saw even less of Pete than they usually did after he got the news about his brother.

Despite all this, living vicariously through Alicia's pregnancy was as close as I was ever going to get. If I'd had the nerve, I'd have asked to see her naked body. After all, hadn't I practically raised her? She was my only hope of ever truly knowing what happened to a woman's body during this time—how her immense belly made the loop back from the extended naval area to the pubic bone, what the belly button looked like, how the vulva expanded in preparation for birth, whether you could actually see the glands that would bring forth the milk.

"'Course you can touch, silly," Alicia said, giggling along with her friends at the party. She pressed my hand harder on her stomach. My face burned, my eyes got wider. I had never felt anything so wonderful—the firm orb of the mother's belly nurturing along this human tadpole, knowing just what to do. I had never wanted to have a baby so badly in my life.

The next day I called every clinic in San Diego associated with AIDS and asked: Is there a safe way of being impregnated by someone who is HIV positive? "Wow—no one's ever asked before," a clerk told me. I didn't fit the profile of the usual caller at the AIDS clinics. I explained, answered questions, was transferred to other departments, referred to other agencies. I was put on hold, accidentally cut off, told to call back later. "Good question," said an aide at a university hospital with an immunology department that treated AIDS. "I'll talk to a couple of doctors and get back to you." Finally she did and reported that, no, as far as she knew there was no known process by which the sperm of someone with the AIDS virus could be washed or sterilized and then inseminated.

I cried in bitter disappointment, but was also tremendously relieved: I'd done everything within my power. The matter was now closed. It crossed my mind that I could be inseminated by someone in Joe's family, maybe his brother. But did I want his brother's baby? I thought of nursing an infant, trying to raise it while caring for a dying man. Did I want to have just anybody's baby? I decided I wasn't sure I did. Sometimes I already felt like I was in over my head.

§

Nell's fingers pressed deeply into my back several months later. The muscles hurt when she leaned so hard against them, but hurt in a pleasurable way—a deep-down-to-the core way, a way that made them give up the strain they were usually fighting against and let go. I'd learned to do this now that I'd been coming to Nell for a while. My face, along with the rest of my body, had grown so relaxed during the massage that now saliva slipped from my mouth and onto the towel covering the padded table.

Usually I wore a bra and panties during the massages. Nell had explained at my first appointment that I could either leave them on or take them off. Today I'd taken them off. At first I'd felt self-conscious, hyper aware of being naked underneath all the towels that she expertly shifted from limb to limb, from shoulder to back, as she worked various body parts. Maybe she doesn't notice, I tried to convince myself. But of course she noticed—there were no straps or lines of elastic cutting into various parts of my flesh. And then I felt foolish that I was focused on such trivial details of the massage, details that a professional like Nell had no doubt been taking in stride for years. Finally I settled down and became so comfortable that the whole concern floated off onto another plane.

"Okay," she said, "you can turn over on your back now."

And then I got prudish all over again—holding towels to myself while she discreetly turned around for more lotion. I settled in quickly, tried to relax, though my front hadn't been done yet. What was the matter with me?

While I'd never told Joe anything about calling all the clinics about babies, I'd told Nell everything, every last detail—what different nurses had said, the questions I'd asked, how I'd cried when I got the answer. Somehow it was okay to talk about babies here. It was safe.

"Maybe you'll have one later," she said today, kneading my right arm. "You never know. You could get married again someday, have kids then."

"I don't think so. What this is all about is me realizing I'm never going to have any."

Nell nodded, and I was glad she didn't go on about adoption and artificial insemination like some women might, suggesting that if you didn't have children somehow your life wasn't complete. "So then, you're okay with it?"

I nodded, and she covered up my right arm, moved to the other side to work on the left. "And what about Joe? Is he doing okay? Any more problems?"

I shook my head, dreamily now that I'd stopped worrying. "You know, he's going to die, no matter how hard it is to say. It's only a question of time. No point in focusing on babies."

"Hmmm."

"What about you? You want kids?" I asked.

One of her eyebrows arched slyly, and I thought she really was very attractive, in a sexy rather than a beautiful way. Her face took on a knowing smirk, a small smile creeping out across her lips. "Oh, I'll never meet anyone. Maybe I'll just become gay like my roommate."

Her hands reached to the muscle under my shoulder blade, and she lifted. I felt such a confusion of sensations: pain and relief. Pent-up stress and release. Aching and yearning.

"How's that?" she said.

"Fine," I mumbled.

"So it's awkward to feel aroused on a massage table," my thera-pist said a few days later.

"I didn't say I was *aroused*."

"What would you call it?"

I squirmed in my seat. "I really like her."

She nodded. After we were both silent a few minutes, I added, "I guess I might be a little attracted to her."

"Isn't that okay?"

"I don't know."

"You're needy right now, Caitlin, and it isn't your fault. You're in a difficult situation. There may be some things you can no longer expect from Joe, especially now that he actually has AIDS."

"I wish my life could be normal."

"Is it more frightening because it's a woman?"

I tried to look unconcerned.

"It's okay to have those feelings, to remember you can have them."

"We talked about going to a movie together. We could go to a movie and be friends."

She nodded.

"I just want someone to hug me and take care of me and tell me all this other stuff is going to be okay."

§

People were always cornering me about Joe these days, trying to get more information. Alicia was the most frequent. It was hard to keep avoiding her, especially right after she had the baby, when I knew she needed me. Her mother-in-law was around, but Mrs. Logan had died when Alicia, Joe, and I were kids. Though I didn't know anything about babies, I'd always been there for Alicia when she needed me.

One day I was over at her and Wings' condo in Solana Beach. I was holding the baby in their living room, and I was astounded, really, that Alicia and Wings had made this tiny living thing. It was a little girl, Juanita, and she'd come out perfectly. Despite being such a small human being, she had ten pudgy little fingers, ten toes. When I held her—maybe twelve pounds now—it was hard to believe that dumb animal instinct could produce something so perfect, that nature could deliver again and again such a wonderful package. I handed her back to Alicia as soon as I could since Juanita broke my heart. I both loved her and was devastated by her.

Perplexed, Alicia said, "What's the matter? Why did you want to get rid of her so fast?"

I smiled, flipped through zillions of baby pictures she and Wings were constantly taking.

"I mean, I thought you kind of loved her." Alicia gazed down at Juanita in her arms, then at me again. Backing up to the dining room table, I said, "Oh, I do, Alicia. She's absolutely beautiful." Tears formed in my eyes. Could Joe and I have made something so wonderful?

Alicia nodded, but also wrinkled her brow. She knew me better than that, that I didn't go around sniffling because I thought people's babies were beautiful. "Joe's okay?"

"Sure," I said, working to keep my voice steady. My mind raced. "Does it ever scare you," I asked, nodding at little Juanita, "to be responsible for something so small?"

Alicia sat beside me. "Of course it does. Everything about her scares me. Sometimes I worry maybe she'll get sick, or have eyes like Pete's kid, and I won't know how to handle it."

"Have they found out any more about that?" I said, relieved to be off the subject.

"They had him tested. He seems okay except his eyes."

We shook our heads gravely, stared down at Juanita.

§

Joe and I were having an argument. On the one hand I was livid with him, on the other I wondered how in the world I could be so reckless as to waste any of the time he had left on arguing.

"I'm not going to be a godparent," he said. He was reading the newspaper at the breakfast table before work. I was feeding the animals. I was due to teach a puppy class in an hour.

"How can you say that to Alicia?" I asked Joe. The longer he was ill, the more edgy he got, the less apparent any sense of humor. His reddish-brown hair had dulled some; his eyes rarely sparkled. His clothes were so baggy they looked like they belonged to somebody else.

"I say it because it's true. I'm not going to be a godparent for Alicia's kids. It would be a promise to pass along all that Catholic junk."

I slammed the cereal down on the kitchen table, turned to face him. "We're their family. What it means is we're telling Wings and

Alicia that if anything should ever happen, we'll take care of their kids. We can't tell them no, Joe."

"I just said it. *No*. End of discussion."

I felt my mother's genes bubbling over in me as I searched for a plate, a bowl, anything that would make a lot of noise, go crashing against the floor or wall. I watched Joe scratch his arm, his leg, his back—reacting to the skin problem the doctors now called folliculitis. They hadn't been able to control it yet. Even though the light treatments three times a week at the dermatologist's helped, I didn't know how he could stand it. He was always scratching. *I* could hardly stand it. I wondered how long I'd be able to manage all this—the injections he had to give himself at home, the three-hour transfusions at the clinic, the medications that completely covered the bathroom counter we shared. Sometimes it seemed like it might be better if it ended sooner rather than later.

"Besides, Caitlin," Joe was saying when I managed to tune back in, "I have no idea how long I'm going to live. I can't take on somebody else's kids. It wouldn't be fair."

And then, after he said that, I felt like such an idiot. Sometimes I had to forget about his health or I wouldn't have been able to function, but when I remembered it was so shocking.

"Why don't you come here and eat something?" he said. I glanced over, and he reminded me so much of the handsome teenager I'd had a crush on—sitting there working on his cereal, some coffee, wearing a denim jacket like he'd had in high school, his legs stretched out long and lanky in front of him.

"I will," I said, but I kept rinsing out the sponge, trying to scrub away years' worth of stained grout, wiping cabinets clean.

Soon he was leaning against the counter beside me, holding me, and I thought he must get tired of seeing me in such horrible shape, though he never said a word.

"Things will work out," he said, but we both knew this was utterly untrue. In reality, not so long from now I wouldn't even have him to hold me when I got like this.

We didn't say anything more about the godparent situation when we finally sat down. It hurt him, too, that we couldn't have kids. Joe refused antidepressants, not wanting to add more medication to all of what he was already forced to take. I, on the other hand, had been able to rise out of bed without as much effort once my doctor had started prescribing them for me. I'd been able to go on with my life rather than sinking into the sadness quite so often.

"I'm so sorry, Alicia," I told her a few days later, giving her a watered-down version of Joe's refusal to be a godparent based on religious grounds.

She shrugged, looked me over. "Joe seems thinner these days. You sure you don't want to tell me about it?"

§

I was watching Juanita so Alicia could shower, pick up the house. Afterward, the three of us went to the grocery store. Alicia had been distant since the godparent episode, but Joe was her brother, and I could tell she was trying. It was Wings—good old mild-mannered Wings—who'd stopped speaking to Joe. "He doesn't like me getting my feelings hurt," Alicia said, smiling. "He doesn't see why Joe had to pick this thing to take a stand on when it meant so much to me."

"Joe is just so…stubborn." I wasn't quite sure how to finish the sentence.

Alicia and I smiled at each other, like the old days.

In the produce section, I held Juanita while Alicia shopped. A baby suddenly wailed across the aisle. He could hardly catch his breath. "Darn!" Alicia said as two wet spots appeared on her blouse over her breasts.

"What happened?" I said.

"It's that baby." She pulled her jacket across her front.

"You mean its crying made your breasts leak?"

Alicia nodded. "It's called weeping."

"How can that be?"

But Alicia shrugged and went on with her shopping, and I was left feeling again like there was a whole human phenomenon, an animal response, that I would never know anything about.

"The Teen Sexuality group I'm running at work seems to be turning into an AIDS group," Joe told me that evening.

"What do you mean?"

"I've been pushing the kids to talk about being at risk, and a couple of them suddenly admitted to the group they were HIV positive. Then a few talked about friends who were."

"That's wonderful, Joe," I said. But he moved away when I went over to hug him, wouldn't look at me. "What's the matter?" I asked.

"Just not in the mood." He made a lot of fuss in the kitchen, went from cabinet to cabinet without really getting anything done, finally sat down at the table with his head in his hands. "My head hurts. The pain…it just won't go away."

§

I was lying on Nell's table. It was my fourth or fifth time back after not being here for a while. All she'd done was hug me when we finally saw each other again, smiled that cherubic smile under her playful gray hair. "It's great to see you!" she'd said, and she was right—it *was* great. She never asked where I'd been, why I'd stopped scheduling, if there was some reason she should know about. Instead, she picked up where we left off. Today she worked my shoulders in deep, round motions, making them hurt in a necessary sort of way, a way I needed to feel now so I'd be okay later. I felt her sweep my hair over to one side of my neck, then the other. As if she were playing with it. In fact, after she'd done it several times, I didn't know what else she could be doing.

Then I felt her own hair whisk by, tickling my back. Could this really be considered part of the massage? It had to be my imagination. But then it happened again: her hair brushing across me. Quickly I lifted my head and looked. That's when I saw her bent over to adjust the angle of the table, reaching underneath to turn a knob, her hair falling over both me and the padded leather.

"Everything okay?" she asked, her brows raised in concern when she saw me facing her.

"Oh, sure," I said, lying back down.

She winked, teasing. "Good."

Finally a towel was pushed over my shoulders. Lying there, I waited for one to be replaced over my torso, too. My breasts tingled with the unaccustomed feel of open air, of being exposed in front of another person, though it was only the sides of my breasts since I was lying face down. Finally, after a lag, the towel was replaced.

Next, she removed the towels draped over my legs. They, too, felt prickly and bare. Had I shaved? Did Nell shave? Somehow I imagined that she didn't, that she left the downy hairs to grow naturally, like everything else about her.

She rubbed the backs of my legs in deep, full motions. Difficult, incisive motions in which she somehow knew just where there was a jangle of nerves, a knotted muscle that needed prodding, stroking. She worked up from my ankles, and I tried to make my mind a blank, an empty screen, full of nothing but nothing. She worked my calves, the back of my knees where it tickled, my thighs. Higher and higher, and then she stopped, and I didn't know what she was doing. I longed to glance over my shoulder again, but lying in a stupor of sensuality allowed me to imagine I was only half aware of what was going on, and so I waited. I knew her hands better than I'd ever known anyone's, even my own, and it was taking too long to feel them again.

Then one of her hands lightly touched my inner thigh. I trembled involuntarily. I felt the towel being draped over my legs again, patted down in a friendly way. "Okay," she said softly. "Relax a minute, and we'll get you turned over."

It was all in my imagination, I knew it was. I was just some poor woman having trouble dealing with the fact her husband was dying.

My face burned. Strands of damp hair stuck to it as I began to think about pushing myself up. I wasn't wearing anything underneath. I hadn't since I'd returned. I swiveled my hips around just as Nell walked around the table. Our heads banged together like some stupid cartoon, only we didn't move apart but stayed there, our faces in close proximity for longer than they should have been. Finally I lay down, this time on my back. A warm flush crossed my face and chest.

A few moments of strained silence passed. I didn't know whether either of us would ever speak again, how I would ever get out of the room. "How's your roommate working out?" I asked.

"She's fine. She and her girlfriend are always off doing stuff, though."

"She has a girlfriend?"

"Right."

Nell's hands worked my arms; she pushed my hands straight up like I was stopping traffic, pulled my fingers. I lay there waiting. For what, I didn't know, but something had changed. Something had not righted itself since our heads collided.

"Still playing the piano?" I said.

"Still playing."

She started on my shoulders again, but I knew the routine— we'd already done my shoulders. Would I say anything? What did not saying anything imply?

Her hands played over my neck, the back of my head, my temples. I kept my eyes closed. The sheet drifted as far down my belly as it could go without revealing anything that was normally covered. Her hands worked my neck, my pectorals, the tender underside of my arms.

"You have such pretty hair," she said, and I felt her hold some strands of it away from my head, draw it out as far as it would go, then drop it down onto the towel. "So soft and blond," she said.

Without speaking, Nell ran her fingers through my hair. My scalp tingled, like it had never been touched before. I opened my eyes, and she was there, our faces inches apart. Was it really me reaching up to touch her hair, too? That's when I discovered the gray was smooth and young, just as I had known it would be. Soft. I held onto it, and I didn't let go. We seemed frozen there—each holding onto the other. I put the back of my fingers against her cheek, lightly rubbed the down that grew there; her hand mirrored mine. The look on her face was one of intensity. My mind was jumpy, blurred. I imagined reaching for her, taking her in my arms, being taken into hers. I imagined our mouths circling each others' and then touching, soft and warm and sweet. It would be so easy for her to climb up onto the table with me or for me to climb down, get dressed, leave with her. Her home would be white and peaceful, lack stress of any kind. We would lie on her bed, on a white feather comforter, and talk, really talk. Eventually our mouths would meet up again, and we would kiss there, first, and then explore, tasting gently, warmly. We'd wander over each other's bodies, finding things, touching them, going slowly at first, then hurrying because it would all feel so good, all of it, until we were finished.

"Caitlin?" I heard Nell say, seemingly far away.

Abruptly, I sat up on the padded table, swung my legs over the side—the side opposite from where Nell stood. Towels dropped from my body so that after all my modesty, finally I was standing in front of her naked. I picked up my clothes, dressed as fast as I could. "I have to leave," I told her.

"Is something wrong?" she asked, seeming genuinely puzzled.

"I forgot I had a meeting." I could see out of the corner of my eye that she was watching me curiously while she picked up towels, cleaning the table.

"Okay."

"I'll have to call you about our next appointment."

"Sure."

I opened her office door so rigorously the knob slammed against the inside wall, but by then I was already halfway down the hall, nearly out the front door.

Joe Jiménez
Inevitable

I wasn't home the day Chuy got out. If he'd written or phoned to inform us of his release, no one had told me. Parole wasn't something we had hoped for; understandably, we'd stopped hoping the second time he got denied. Ama let herself down after that second denial, stopped praying, stopped her promesa, stopped hoping.

"Pa' que?" she said, scissors in hand, hope a twisted dead floorboard knot at her feet. "Siempre nos chinga la vida." For what? Life always fucks us over.

My sisters, myself, we believe it.

Nothing could have prepared me for the day Chuy got out. I guess it was best that no one told me anything, if, of course, they knew anything at all about his release. 6 p.m. and our house was packed, overflowing with music and voices and laughter, relatives spilling in and out, too much food filling our countertops, the face of our table, our plates.

In some sick silly way it reminded me of the day Papi died—the mixing smells of familia y comida, the ripple in people's breathing. It was celebratory, no doubt about that, the air around my house, and I was eager to know what was going on, leaving the keys in the ignition, and unexpectedly meeting my older brother's face and breath and maloso arms around me, holding me tight like air in his lungs, at the door.

"I told you I'd get out." His words were flat and whispered and wrapped around my ear like a mouth, the smooth eel sound of his thin cholo voice.

"Simón. It's good to see you, too." My voice cracked and I counted years, months in my head, and came to seven ... seven years, seven months. I stood there in disbelief; puro shock, a candy rock in my heart. I stood there and my tongue was still and I was sweating, smelling, searching for something to say, something to feel, to focus on other than the thick dick vein pounding in his throat, my ear, my eye.

"I can't believe this. I don't believe it, man. How?"

"I know," he said. He pressed his face in my neck and hummed. "Es la verdad."

I'm not one to put faith in dreams. My sister Letty buys these books, the kind that are supposed to tell you what your dreams mean, like translate or interpret them for you and shit. Homegirl devours that kinda shit, but me, I don't buy it. I'm not about all that Dionne Warwick Psychic Friends bullshit. And no matter how many times I watch *La Bamba*, I don't think some TJ curandero can give me a bone-feather-rattlesnake necklace that'll take my nightmares away, and if it did, then what would I have to keep me company in the middle of the night, to pull me outta my sleep each madrugada?

Letty would die to read my dreams. She is always prying, trying to get a peak inside my head or my heart, one or the other. I don't let people know they aren't connected.

My mother says I should speak to a priest.

My ex called me a freak because of these dreams, in a sweet, cariño, let me make fun of you then suck your dick kinda way.

They're my dreams, though, and so I plead the fifth.

He found out in the pen, Chuy said.

May 24, 199-.

He'd suspected it for about a year, mas o menos. The sore throats, the sweats, the undying colds and the rash, a simple collective indication that something was wrong.

"It was coming to me," he said. "I was totally expecting it, ey. And I was right. So one day when the health department lady was there I took one of the tests and then I waited and I prayed, guey, I prayed, and replanned my life and then when the ten days were up I just walked in there and told her, 'Ey, I got it, right?' And she nodded and she told me I needed to sit down and she took my hand and started goin' off about how this wasn't the end and what I should do next and whatever. I wasn't really listening to her too much 'cause all that my head was thinking was fuck, fuck, fuck...I got AIDS."

He tells me this in my car. We're driving to an ASO to meet with his case manager, so he could get in the system and see a doctor and get his meds. His appointment is at nine but we left home at seven because I promised him tacos and are just cruising around after eating, charlando. I'm showing him how the city has changed and how it has not, and we are trying to make sense of how fucked up and silly our lives have been for the last seven years and seven months. We park by the bay and he wants to walk. We stop, give some time to Selena's memorial. He asks about the movie.

"Loli has the tape at home," I say.

"Yup. She tried to show it to me yesterday," he says.

We listen to the breeze. He sips his coffee. In minutes, Chuy gets quiet, steps back from the small talk. He asks me about school, if I ever think of going back.

"Maybe," I say, hesitant, not wanting to shut down the idea, thinking maybe he wants to go back, not wanting to discourage him. "And you?"

"Naw. Doubt it." Chuy shakes his head. He sighs, lets go. Tells me he's full-blown. Not just HIV, but full-blown. It's a quick disclosure, and I hurt for him, for myself, for our family. My bones ache and my fingers massage his shoulder, the upper part of his arm, the small of his back.

"I feel like shit. You know, I look fine, but I feel like shit and I'm afraid of fuckin dying like this in front of Ama." He tenses, holds his breath, and I hold him.

He tells me he was a user. I tell him I like vatos. He tells me has 183 Tcells, and I tell him I shoulda been a dad two years ago but Marisol and I decided it wasn't the right time. Out of respect I don't pry about the pinta. He asks me about guys. I tell him about Juan. He tells me he wants to stay clean, start over, and I tell him it's hard, I'm trying, but it's good, all good, and I'm so glad he's back.

We look at my pager, and it's a quarter after nine.

In addition to HIV, Chuy has contracted Hep B, which is better than C, the nurse a white-haired lady with visible dentures, powdery gloves, and a white lab coat explains.

"What medications have you been taking?" she asks.

"None."

"And who was your previous physician?"

"Didn't have one. I was in…" he pauses. "Incarcerated."

"And how long have you known about your condition?" She stares at the scripted tattoos on his inner arm and neck, the small cross fixed between his right thumb and forefinger.

"And have you contacted your previous sexual and/or drug partners?" She eyes the small circular scar at the inner bend of his arm and jots something down.

"And do you have insurance?" She looks at me. The pen moves before he even answers.

"And are you aware of any other sexually transmitted diseases you may be carrying?"

"And at which lab did you say you had your last CD4 and viral load counts done? And what date were those tests administered?"

"And what are the reasons you haven't been taking medications again?"

She ends her interrogation, removes her gloves, exits the room. I watch as disillusionment and distrust contort my brother's face. It's no wonder Chuy asked me to sit-in on his visit. I wonder how it will be for me.

Like Chuy, I wasn't surprised for shit. I expected it. I know my story. I know what I risk. I know protecting myself with a strip of latex is nothing like protection I've known in my life. I know things might've been different, but like alotta other things in this life, some of us are set-up for shit. Alcoholics, wife-beaters, gang statistics, murder rates. It's inherited. And unnatural. An unnatural mother-fucking disaster, as my ex, Mr. Raza himself, put it.

"Our primo David had it, tambien," Chuy says, as if stating this common known but unspoken fact could offer me comfort.

"I know. I just hope we don't go the way he did. Alone. Sick. All fuckin alone."

This is our late night conversation. Two, three a.m. He nudges me when he wants to talk. For the sake of solitude and not waking anyone up, we keep our voices soft, firm, but unmistakably tight, the way tones and inflections couple when voices, experiences, and memories connect. This way—soft-spoken, bodily, open like breath—we discuss disclosure, our deaths, his meds and side-effects, my decision to wait to take any drugs, the drama of doing our genealogies, or the precise tracing of who we think infected us, whom we might've infected. This is not our luxury.

"You're lucky, ey," he tells me. "You have me to go through this with. I didn't have nobody. Solito. Yo lo 'guante solito."

I agree with him, wrap my arms about his waist, pull him to me. "But you have me now, ey."

Eyes shut, he smiles, leans back, places a hand on my wrist. I comply and place a simple soft, closed-lipped kiss on the left side of his neck. He hums, and I can taste his vein, again, pounding in the center of my throat. I don't tell him I've dreamed this kinda inevitable air before.

Ron Mohring
Activism

Carol and Eddie pace before the administration building.
It is twenty-seven degrees and the wind is fierce.
The university's Board of Regents has just voted
not to withdraw their South African holdings.

Carol and Eddie hold hand-lettered placards:
QUEERS AGAINST RACISM: DIVEST NOW. In ten years,
organizations will have reclaimed the word—queer love,
Queer Nation—but today Carol and Eddie march alone.

In five years the Board will reverse its decision.
In six years Carol will die in a Los Angeles freeway
collapse. Eddie will not attend her funeral, will not
remember her name: wasted beyond recognition,

he will die of infections brought on by a complex
virus that will enter his body tonight, four hours
after leaving the campus, two years before the virus
is named, five years before Eddie will learn

he is infected. He will become the seven hundredth
reported case in his metropolitan region. Eddie stamps
his feet; they tingle in the cold. A campus reporter snaps
photographs. *I'm scared,* Carol hisses. *What if*

my boss finds out? What if she sees our picture?
—Too late, Eddie says. *Hey, nobody's gonna fuck*
with two butch queers like us. Give the man
that mean dyke stare. Come on, girl. Say cheese.

Steven Riel

Places We Have Never Been
(remembering Scott, with AIDS)

Unblinking, unwavering,
though clearly it's a struggle, you stand
as if the soles of your feet were glued
within a gun-barrel, a gleaming tube
that guarantees death will find you,
& soon. Aware you're a target,
you're also taking aim:
you look me in the eye,
& though sallow skin twitches over your temples,
you / tell / me / why / you / like / me,
& I make myself meet your steely stare.

We're standing in the center
of a braided rug that is
mostly blue at the going-away
party of our friend. It's an affair to savor:
with Burkina Fasoian chutney, Buffalo wings,
delectable dill bread from Moosewood, &
a few gay comrades among the crush.
Earlier, a sense of how delicious life can taste
rushed through me when I rediscovered
maybe there *were* other people on this earth's crust
I could talk with: one guy actually wanted to chat
about Dorothea pacing down that row of limes
in *Middlemarch*, as she wondered, in shock,
How did it ever come to this?

                              Of course
you've already spat that question
at your midnight mirror. That was just
the beginning. With how many sobs,
involuntary punches against your mattress
you have come to this
focused truth-telling, I do not know.

I know fatigue shadows the nooks of your face;
that beneath your sideburns, your jaw looks clenched;
that this is probably our last encounter.
As you speak, out of the corner of my eye,
I glimpse the span of that gun-barrel's ring
like some metallic halo above you
that majestically widens & brightens into
the calm blue of a hurricane's eye,
ushering in a shaft of silence
amid all the glorious buffet banter
—& I think, *We are always going*
places we have never been

—or where we've failed before.
Scott, I've stood just outside a gun-barrel,
with another comrade I oh so dearly loved—
though he'd be crucified on crosshairs,
I spoke of love but not the bullet;
about the bullet I told white lies,

& so, I'm rigid before you,
unfortunately can't hear much else but my own
regrets ricocheting
only centimeters from this ballistic cylinder
you accept as your final home,
a chillingly tiny, vast circumference
where you show me
one / chosen / word / at / a / time
there can be comfort in honesty.

Rachel S. Thomas-Medwid
Where Are All the Juliets?

From page one Haley has placed herself in the perfect story. A peach of a doctor meets the cream of the writers, they marry and produce an evenly blended swirl: an ice cream cone of a child. Sam, Sammy Jr., and Haley are a Fisher-Price family, complete with a jack-up garage, the plastic baseball hats, and the keylime car.

They schedule. That's how it works in suburbia: schedule sex, schedule baby to emerge in the appropriate season, schedule spice time to flavor the sex when the dishwater dulls set in. They order brown-bagged parcels from dirty catalogs, fumble with the toys, and bang on their synthetic walls in search of a compromise. It is not between Haley and Sam, this mediation, but between those monsters of expectation and reality.

This is life in America.

This is life until Belize.

It is a work trip, a story assignment for a travel magazine, that rips a slit into Haley's careful packaging. There is talk of a family trip, yet their respective date books demand the week be marked solo for the purpose of efficiency. It is the first time Haley has been away from Sammy for two years and the idea of solitude is both frightening and exotic, a mirage shimmering just beyond her reach. Her editor wants a story on the "largely undiscovered paradise," a title Haley does not fully swallow. Alone in the puddle jumper to Caye Ambergris, Haley sketches an outline for her article, her words ripe and premature. Drawn to the buzz of the plane window, she finds the barrier reef she has read about below, carving a criminal smile up at her.

As the propeller plane conquers the stubby landing strip of San Pedro, she momentarily loses her preconceptions. The town is only speckled with tourism, the houses humble, fishy, crooked. Their friends in the suburbs would call it *rustic charm*, gloating over their dry Chardonnay and pâté de foie gras. There is sand everywhere, babbling uncontrollably, whitening the smell of poverty. Later Haley discovers it on the floors of the restaurants, the bars, her bed.

After exploring the resort, taking notes, Haley retreats to the beach café. She drinks excessive Belikan beers under the prickly wig of the thatch roof, roosting the bottles on the table like collector's items. In the flapping of unaccustomed alcohol consumption something shifts in her perspective. When a man approaches her table, a native, she is accepting of his presence, grateful almost, for his attention. Foreign in her unattached body, the world is tinted a new color.

His name is Jerome, his voice like syrup. She picks and chooses from his decipherable words, edits his language for sense. He tells her that he has always lived on the island, that he is one of thirty-eight kids. She laughs at his joke until she sees it is not one.

"My dad had four wives." His lips wrap around the top of his beer bottle.

"Is that legal here?" Haley asks, stunned by the beer, the air.

"They are not married," he says, and she understands that wives are women with babies, the successful sperm receptacles. Jerome is twenty with one baby already, another on the way with a different "wife." It is a bragging right, a flag of fertility. With its waving, the games have begun, the unpeeling of the sexes. Haley feels a bulb flick on in the vicinity of her pelvis.

The bartender, Ruby, overhears their conversation and strikes a warning with the next Belikan.

"The men are all Romeos on this island, girl. Watch out for the Romeos."

But where are the Juliets? There is no sign of their presence; only the Romeos, walking the walk. What went wrong in the succession of the story that allows the men to keep going without her? Breathing. Mating.

After more beer, more layers unhinged, Haley tells Jerome of Sam, moving the vacant bottles back and laying down the truth. There is a shift in Jerome, but he does not move. He leaves it up to her. When she walks away, determined in her intoxication, his eyes snuggle the back of her kneecaps. She knows her thighs are too wide, wifey. Extraordinarily white. In the moment Haley takes the first step, the pattern of her life is temporarily delayed. Without her date book, without the milky state of her hormones, she can no longer follow the straight path of her habits. Jerome's presence is inspiration not for Haley's article but other concepts tucked neatly in the folds of her starched marital protocol.

Whatever is rioting between her legs stops its dance back in her room. The phone brings Haley back to her boys, the play station of life in the United States. Her body stiffens like a popsicle at the sound of their conventional voices. Relieved, she wallows in the air conditioning until her flesh splinters into spider veins of propriety. It is only then that Haley lets in the wet tongue of tropical air, just to see how it feels against her temporarily paralyzed principles.

§

In the morning Haley finds Jerome down by the dive shop, ready to take a boat out to stingray alley. In their brief encounter, she hands him her ticket and waits with fishy breath for him to punch it. When he asks to see her the next day, she releases the stored oxygen one air bubble at a time. Haley has landed below the reef, surrounded by bathtub-colored fish, jewel-toothed barracudas, and hammerheads. She feels the cold hand of anticipation down her back as if Sammy, a mischievous boy, has dropped an ice cube down her bathing suit. Her skin is both delighted and rebellious, fighting against itself in a battle sure to be unwon by either contender.

§

In her roller coaster fantasies of Jerome, disease never occurs to Haley. She lives, after all, in a plastic house with Everlast protection. Her existence was built strictly for safety and any life form not indigenous is sure to expire. Viruses, warts, boils, sores, murderous cells, she believes, will all be shot down by her upbringing.

Haley, generous, open-minded, does not believe those inflicted with the virus deserve such a sentence. Haley, liberal and eager to donate to color causes—pink ribbons, blank arm bands, the Red Ribbon—is intelligent enough to know that it can sneak its way into anyone's life. Yet she simply believes that its distance, its adherence to stereotypical lifestyles, its maliciousness, will choose someone other than her.

Until she meets Jerome's child.

Until she is faced with a Caribbean replica of her own.

Jerome brings him to the café at breakfast, parting the waves of sleep faster than her thick coffee. The wisps of sexual musing are puffed away, clouds, at the sight of his boy. Oneil is Sammy's size, the sweet color of chocolate milk, his eyes two pennies watching her.

Jerome speaks to the boy, chewing leaves, words Haley cannot digest. They are speaking something beautiful, buttery, Creole, she believes. Then he switches to English.

"Oneil was born during Mitch."

"Mitch?"

"Hurricane," he says. "Mitch the bitch. It was a curse. It is what is wrong with Oneil."

"He doesn't look like a curse to me. He looks like my son." She doesn't ask what is wrong. Doesn't imagine.

But he tells her anyway.

"Oneil has the virus."

The virus with a capital V. The HI-Virus. Hello, HI there, Here I am. Just try to get rid of me, try to kill me, strangle me to oblivion. Just try. The sickness that is spelled so high, towering like the Empire State Building above other ailments. Oneil, this baby so like hers, will eventually be taken by AIDS. This information tumbles the space of Haley's head, spinning, in the dry cycle. Still damp, she doesn't know where to hang it.

"I'm sorry Jerome," she fumbles with her coffee cup. "What about you?"

"It's his mother." He leaves himself out of the equation.

Haley realizes she has an article topic, an unexpected twist of lemon. Sour but potent.

"I need your help." He asks, snipping the words from her mouth.

"Me? What is there for me to do?"

"Your husband. You said he was a doctor."

"Yes, but there's nothing yet. Nothing that works."

Jerome looks at Haley like there is *something.* Like in her lap sits hope simply because she resides in the good old U.S. of A. Yet what Jerome cannot see is the boundaries, the fact that they are non-existence. Departure waits at the end of the train ride, the drop off of the tracks. Gap-toothed and thin-limbed, death might be a welcome face after aspirations are bounced back insistently like a racquetball in play. Bruising until the skin is uniform, defeated, the color of the ground in wintertime.

"But what about the drugs?"

"There have been advances. Antiviral drugs. The cocktails. They can slow down the process, but they don't save you Jerome." She sounds like she is speaking of a new computer program, malfunctioning that is inconsequential. Haley doesn't actually know what she is talking about, only reciting the world daily news verbatim.

"Oneil needs something. He can't just go like this. You can help."

"What about the doctors here? Can't they do anything?"

"There's no care here. No means. You have the means."

"No one has the means. Yet."

And she sees him latch onto this three-letter word, wrap it around Oneil's neck like a scarf in frigid weather. There is a keyhole it leaves behind and she takes the opportunity to stick her way in.

"What would you think about an article on you? Your wife maybe. Maybe you could talk to her."

"We're not a case study, Haley."

Oneil is watching her hands like they are his breakfast.

"But it might help."

"We don't need that kind of help."

When he gets up to leave, towing Oneil like a tender piece of luggage, Jerome turns one time before the landscape sketches him into the scene. "Why don't you do a story on Mitch. The bitch did lasting damage, but at least everyone survived. Even the babies."

Haley watches as they cut a line in her view, receding in their own time.

How did she avoid the misfire when the small sheaf of this child stepped straight into it?

In her premarriage days, she flew the sexual landscape of college like a caped hero. Superwoman, above the lash of tainted sperm and blood that shoots bullets. It wasn't the confidence, the Wonderbread white girl attitude, that kept her untouched, even though she believed in the power of it at the time. Like a religion. Watching Oneil totter down the beach, those gods scatter like they are playing kick the can. All of them running, out of breath, sidestepping without even the courtesy of an explanation.

§

Haley calls her husband after breakfast, caffeine running the bases of her body. She tells him the story strategically, professionally leaving herself out of the plot.

"Is there anything you can do, Sam? Can you send the drugs down here?"

"It's illegal, Haley. I can't administer these drugs without seeing the patient. We need to monitor blood levels consistently. It could do more harm than good if he doesn't get the care."

"But he's getting nothing here. Isn't the chance that they could help enough to do it? Isn't fifty-fifty odds better than zero?"

There is silence in which she hears her husband's ethical whip crack. Haley's stomach turns at the sound.

"Please Sam." She doesn't say, *what if it was Sammy*, because she cannot play pawn with her own child. Yet Sam hears the shuffling of pieces.

"I'll see what I can do."

The next day, an overnight package arrives in her room miraculously. Haley sees in the box a model of her family, wrapped brightly in purple and orange. She does not want to open it for fear the three of them will run loose, take their own trails, fleeing until footsteps are lost in sand. Without them, her path back is erased.

But of course Haley opens it.

And Sam has provided, as she knew he would.

In the box is Sustiva, generic name efavirenz, along with extensive instructions for ingestion. The names sound like wild child girls, like forbidden towns. She handles the pills like babies, like they will crack their skulls and spill their guts in the heat.

With them she walks down to the dive shop to find Jerome.

"Cocktail." She says, presenting them as a gift while feeling something contrary. Who is she doing this for? This ghost of her own child, Jerome, some code of enforced decency? She is bound in a gender straightjacket, the image of the female provider, when what she really wants to do is *take* and the urge is indescribable, unforgivable. Despite the unruly facts laid out like land mines, she knows the only way to complete the taking is to fuck Jerome. And she knows, standing with chance in her hands, that she will do just that.

When Haley notices the sun, rising above the slit of the water, she swears it is falling. A coin into the back of the great sea piggy bank that she wants to grab and save. But by the time it legs itself fully into the sky, saving its own life, Haley finds her arm still by her side, unmoved and useless, attached it seems, to someone else's body.

§

Her desire pokes at her like insistent thumbtacks. She is the cork-board, spongy, dry, hung up for display. Jerome's agreement to do the story has jackknifed Haley's angle. She realizes there are no words she can pilfer from Oneil. Instead she takes his picture, at a church that is curled up between two half-abandoned hotels. The structure is concrete, solid on the transient beach. Yet through the lens it appears to be crumbling, disintegrating like unearthed artifacts from a lost civilization. Oneil sits on the steps like a statue, resistant to Haley's camera. Here is he unlike Sammy, unwilling to whap his smile against the giant eye with the innocent expertise of her son.

Despite Haley's intentions, she feels herself walk away with something of Oneil. Her camera weighted against her shoulder, she brings him back to Jerome at the dive shop. He is sitting on the dock, gutting a fish with his bare hands, and Haley feels the unexpected twist of lust when he wrenches the fish head free.

"You go for a drink with me now? A cocktail." He asks.

She looks for the irony in his words, on the pink snail of his tongue, but does not find it. Haley nods, watching the eyes of the fish as the head swings, unencumbered, to meet the ocean bottom with a succinct explosion of sand.

"I'm going to bring Oneil back to his mother first. You can come if you want. Ask questions."

"Are you sure? I don't want to intrude."

"It's what you want."

She is shot with his directness, not sure if it is what she wants, but she goes. The three of them walk through town, hints of Haley's husband and child reflected in the extraneous shadows of her compassions. The houses remind her of Nepal, their last trip before conceiving Sammy. There, Haley had been turned to patient, her diarrhea, her projectile vomiting making her resentful of Sam as a doctor. The scent of her weakness lingers in the back of her nasal passages now; how can Jerome not smell it? How can he crave her when he should want to tuck her against his gums like tobacco and spit the waste of her out?

Suddenly Haley questions her editorial skills; is she using them correctly in this scenario? She is aware that life and stories never quite match, that it is her who dictates the Y in the street where they separate. But here, where does the difference lie between the sick and well, the poor and the wealthy? Where does the road begin to fork?

When they get to the house, the first yield sign is apparent. The stairs are wobbling, the house leaning into the air as if expecting its support. In the chipping paint, Haley sees unexpected faces, grimaces and grins.

Inside there is only one room the walls red and womblike. Jerome's "wife" lies in bed in the corner, her legs like thin gods beneath the sheets, separate beasts from her body. On the bedside table, the truth sits out like a piece of bread, waiting for anyone's taking and tearing. Here, in what her suburbia friends would call *paradisio*, reality is stale and ugly and undisguised.

Haley finds herself wanting to cover up, as if it is her in the bed. She is cold in her inherent whiteness and remote ideas of AIDS. The shame rises to the surface, covering her face like the sores on this woman. They blend into her dark skin like patches of jelly, and with the sight of them Haley's trustworthy skill of interviewing hides its head in the panic of her perspiring armpits.

The installation of home is pulled back, the walls stripped of their paper. The headline news, medical reports and breakthroughs that never quite make it under the covers of their Laura Ashley bedding, is watching her with two moons for eyes.

"Haley, this is Marina. Oneil's mother."

Haley keeps her hand to herself, biting the inside of her cheek for this indecency. She knows how she should respond. How she could rest her head against the tidal wave of this woman's breasts and be unharmed, how she could kiss her, wrap her arms around the branches of her legs, tongue lash her, and walk away the same woman. Oneil goes to his mother, as if he senses Haley's insult, and latches onto her hand.

"Nice to meet you Marina."

"You come to ask me questions?" Her voice is chunky, swollen with sorrow.

Betrayal wraps around Haley's wrists like handcuffs. Here is this woman, dying, her child on a leash behind her, and not only does she want to squeeze work from her, she wants to wring her man dry. Haley's own husband is remote, like a black and white photograph of an ancestor hung on the wall, lifeless. Sammy is there, somewhere, creeping around the base of the bed, but his back is to her. All of Haley's energy is placed into Marina's bed, wriggling beneath the staleness of it. There is no way to extract what she needs when she does not understand what it is anymore.

"No, that's okay. I really just came to meet you. Oneil is beautiful. He reminds me of my child."

Neither of them thank her, as is apropos in suburbia, and the eggshell of Haley's face cracks. When Jerome steers her from the room, her uncertainty is guzzled by anger, the words in her mind solidifying beyond recognition. The sight of Marina had made her want to give, to take back her taking. She could have, but instead she stood and stared and took something unspeakable from her.

The shelter Haley lives in, her American passport, kept her again from the storm. Even with the door in her chalky palms, she had left it closed. Walking from the crooked house, the shifty stairs, she understands Jerome and Marina's living each day as a balancing act of survival. The house is them as is her own. Descending the steps off center, Haley tilts with its wave, hoping that it will skew her until she can no longer see from where she stands.

§

On the beach with Jerome recognition of herself is left completely behind. Until this moment Haley could always picture it, a head shot, a full page ad in a magazine. In the wet stomach of the tropics—in the wave of her impending adultery, the incurable dis-

ease that whooshes consistently in the surf of her ears—she has become a fashion victim. There is a black band over her eyes, turning
her to a nameless, misshapen bandit. When Jerome wraps his arms
around her like an octopus, suctioning, her own are taken. With each
sucker, part of Haley is erased, the sand beneath them her infidelity
sheet. With Jerome's tongue on her belly, her Sammy scar, the birth
of her own child becomes someone else's. She is the woman in the
bed. She is already lost.

They use no protection. Haley wants nothing between her and
her newfound greed.

When Jerome enters her, she hears something fracturing. What
could that be? Surely not her body, in its orange Play-Doh state.
Surely not her wedding vows that have already been vacuumed up
by their biweekly maid service. No, it is her house itself, the fort that
kept the world behind the gates. She is breaking the code of their
alarm system. As Haley moves toward her own pleasure, the moon
over the water turns to the bulb she had felt upon meeting Jerome. It
brightens with her, winks, and manages to hang by its fingernails in
the sky when she falls.

The fall, of course, is inevitable. The return of her family, of
Jerome's. But the only guilt lies in the predominance of Oneil over
Sammy, Marina over Sam. Haley has broken the walls between
them, erased the boundaries that weren't ever there. She knows they
will never be safe again.

She tells Jerome she will send the drugs. Packages of plastic
hope. And she will do it, for years. After, in all probability, they are
not needed. Haley does not attach Marina and Oneil to this duty,
only adds the task as part of her chore schedule.

In the end she leaves them all out of her magazine story. Haley writes a fluff piece, folding the corners of her article until it is an impeccable paper airplane, flown crisply to her editor. She kisses her husband and child at the airport like they are survivors of a plane crash. The guts she acquired to sleep with a stranger are left in the temperate sand along with the waste of their coupling. She dreams of it occasionally, the curve of the sperm, the expression on the tiny heads one of malice. She wakes up in a reef of sweat.

The first test is negative.

In the six months that follow, Haley, criminal, allows her husband to touch her in familiar ways, latex free, hoping that the marriage sex will unearth the lost version of herself. But she knows that it will never be found. Not because of what she did, but what she saw standing in that bedroom in Belize.

The six-month test hands her an undeserved gift. Haley, in her bound world, can continue as the inviolate Mommy package. She is tied with a bow and put under the Christmas tree. She tucks away her memories of Belize, all of them, behind Sammy's outgrown crib in the attic. Haley develops the film without checking the results, inserting them snugly beneath the mattress of the crib.

They schedule. Time walks straight along their plans, begins jogging down the years, the road signs blurry with speed. Sam has saved lives. Haley has filled some with words that pose as ideas. Sammy has grown into one of his very own. It is only then that Haley takes out the trip again. Behind the crib, pink fiberglass below her feet, the cold air of the attic pressing her neck, she lets herself go back.

Haley unearths the pictures hesitantly, as if they will bite. There is the water, that illegal color of her occasional dreams. On the one taken from the plane, a pulpy Band-Aid of a cloud covers the coral, turning it to snake skin. There is nothing of Jerome and she has forgotten his face. She remembers Marina as perfectly as a mind can, slim and beautiful in her bed, but it is not that she wants to see. Haley recognizes the hand of expectation down her spine, tickling, teasing her. When she gets to the picture of Oneil she understands that is what she has been waiting for. Flipping through each one Haley believes she will find it, the white clam shells of Oneil's teeth glittering against the church steps.

Yet there is nothing but his modest body, leaning against the solid backrest of the structure, a pillow disguised as faith. Haley keeps looking, checking the pews visible through the open door, the sand curled around the chocolate of his perfect toes, for some sign of his smile. When she does not find it, she puts Oneil back where he is safe. In the space between the mattress and the bars, not smiling ever, but surviving. Existing somewhere in the dusty folds of a life already lived.

Mark Moody
Mrs. Ong

Her skin is strong
and supple for her age,
the veins easy to see and find.
She's not really afraid of the pain,
but closes her eyes
and sucks in her breath
when the needle comes near.
She endures the stick
with a stiffened posture.

Later when the vein swells up
she rings her bell for the nurse.
"Too much blood," she says laughing,
pointing to the embolism,
"too much blood."

Yesterday's units have returned her color,
but maybe they gave too much.
She puffs out her cheeks
like she's been overinflated,
her eyes a playful umlaut over the joke.
She shakes her head
as the nurse prepares a new needle.

All this fuss.

Later the nurse tells me
that Mrs. Ong designed
and made the hat that she wears,
and was once a famous designer in Peking.
She escaped China with her husband,
a famous movie director.
Now she lives in the Sunset,
comes up the hill for infusions
just like I do.

Today we sat together,
reduced to being patient
with our suffering, ringing bells
about our needs.
I silently agree with her:
it's not the pain people are afraid of,
but the idea of it.
It's not the blood,
it's getting too much.

2001–2005

2001 At a UN Special Session, the world's leaders sit down formally for the first time to discuss the gravity of the AIDS situation and to set long-term objectives for dealing with the crisis.

2002 A rapid HIV-1 test is approved by FDA. • The Global Fund is established to begin a coordinated global response to the AIDS, TB and malaria crises. • An HIV-positive Muppet joins *Sesame Street*.

2003 October 1 is declared the First National Latino AIDS Awareness Day. • The "3 by 5" campaign is launched to expedite greater access to AIDS treatments and better healthcare in developing countries.

2004 Erasure's lead singer, Andy Bell, announces he is HIV-positive. • *Green Arrow* becomes the first major comic book to feature an HIV-positive character. • America launches a major anti-AIDS initiative called PEPFAR, which is politicized by right-wing religious organizations who tie AIDS funding to abstinence in many parts of Africa. • Housing Works' Keith Cylar dies.

2005 May 19 is declared the 1st National Asian and Pacific Islander HIV/Awareness Day. • South African film *Yesterday* scores an Oscar nomination.

John Medeiros
Eulogy: For Agustin "Eddy" Jeudy

To think you've taken the two corners of the world
and pieced them together and folded them before you
like a flag
that once waved over stateless people.

The Atlantic became the Pacific
and Haiti was a small town in New England.

And you adapted
like a native,
your tropical smile slit open like the seam
of a bedroom pillow.
Your eyes like firecrackers on parade.
Your voice full of fables and Guy de Maupassant.

My friend, I have not seen you since
you left the world for Port-au-Prince.

Since your wrote,
I'll be on your way again.
At that moment I believed in voodoo,
the forbidden magical remedies and shaking leaves.

But now we drink another toast,
not to red, white and blue weddings,
but rather to dusk.
Faded purple spilling across the sky like a wine stain.
Purple is the color of death,
the color of dried flowers and tired hearts.

Do you know that I would walk all the way from Providence
speaking my finest Creole
if I could once again touch the veins that flowed compassion into
your hands
like little rivers to the rhythm of the compas?

My friend, I have not seen you since
you left the world for Port-au-Prince.

Alex Cigale

The Teacher's Curse
for Mark T. Rifkin

The word of first impression was "neat, trim,"
a female student put it "well-preserved,"
in his own words "a smiling public man."

A colleague ascribed "religion up his ass,"
his mantra "Oo boom!", answerless questions.
He taught us "How a Poem Means": pause,

pivotal line stop, a tragedy in miniature,
the shark-tooth-charted progress of emotion.
I loved that vibrant voice, his proud posture.

In my high school yearbook he wrote: "Let me not
to the marriage of true minds admit impediments.
I know your sincerity, sensitivity, and insight,

but always wanted MORE! The teacher's curse
I guess." And signed it "Mark T. Shakespeare (sic)."
I heard he was depressed, his illness serious.

This morning my kid brother called and said,
"He is dead," and "Did you know he was gay?"
Those who say you died of AIDS lie. The sad

ones like us succumb to disappointment.

Peter Schmitt
Asking For It

It was already late when he wandered in.
He could have chosen the gurney-wide front door
in that dorm that had been an infirmary,
an electric and I-V socket open-

mouthed, halfway up the wall. He came, instead,
without knocking, through the adjoining bathroom
from the small party next door. I was still
at my desk despite the music and voices,

and though he looked familiar I did not know
his name till he slipped into the recliner
and started to talk. I put my pen down.
It *was* late, after all; I could pick it up

tomorrow. His need for conversation—
with a stranger, even—seemed more pressing
than whatever filled the paper at my hand.
I don't remember what we talked about—

his friend, my neighbor, no doubt, but a couple
hours passed, while I wondered when he might
be returning next door, the stereo
now lower, the voices fewer. But on

he stayed, merely smiling when I yawned and looked
at the bed. He asked if couldn't he just sleep
right there, in the chair. Though puzzled by now,
I assured him that the tattered La Z Boy

was famous for early morning rescues:
friends too frathouse drunk to find their own beds,
or my own resort to chivalry when dates
had missed their rides. So, with borrowed blanket,

radiator banging at winter's chill,
he stretched out, twisting and turning a bit
as I quickly undressed, stopping this time
at t-shirt and underwear, before hurtling

beneath the electric blanket with a book.
The other blanket kept moving. At last
he said he thought he'd try the floor, the throw rug
in some abstract Aztec pattern on the cold,

black hospital tile. For maybe a chapter
or more he lasted there, still shifting, squirming,
but the real story never occurred to me
until he asked, conceding that chilled air sinks,

if I would terribly mind his sharing
my single bed—small-framed, he pointed out
what little room he'd take—and then exactly
what I said I don't recall, something about

how restless I could be, how I wouldn't want
to disturb *his* sleep...But the message must have
finally sunk in, for with no further word
he climbed back in the chair and nodded off.

Thus ended an exchange that surely ranks
among the most polite in all the annals
of come-ons and rejections. Yet of my friends,
who among us, more times than he might admit,

had not tried every rhetorical means
for one night of speechless gratification—
but with a *woman*. That this unlikely source
lay dreaming, as it were, of my underclothes

as a white cotton flag to be hoisted
above the fortress, did I see something
of myself in his method? By morning
he had vanished, the blanket neatly folded,

and I never heard his name again until,
a few years after, late one night on the phone
with my old neighbor, with whom I'd kept up:
he mentioned that his friend (did I remember?)

had caught the virus and would soon be gone...
Could he have been infected even then,
I wondered, and heard confirmed what I had
only imagined: that basic scene replayed,

and not always with identical results,
a hundred, five hundred times, in different
bedrooms, other parties. Here, near the end,
my friend was saying, as the brain itself

fell open to attack, the fat cells there
were busy dumping stored-up LSD
and these last days passed in a bath of acid
flashbacks. What could one wish him but a good trip...

But now, from this distance that we call safe,
if in some eyes he was asking for it,
the one promise in promiscuity,
how can I not feel, were he asking for

anything, staring up at me so early
one morning from an icy infirmary
floor, that it was, finally, for nothing
that I—nothing anybody—could give him.

Marc Elihu Hofstadter

Medford, Oregon, 2000
for Nicholas Follansbee and Drew Giambrone

Morning sun burnishes ragged hills of spiky pines
with a golden sheen.
Your log cabin, deep in shaggy woods,
seems a world apart.
We've barbecued juicy burgers,
played with the dogs Auggie, Stella, Blanche,
listened to Mozart and Madonna,
talked half the night.
Since sunrise I've sat here in a rickety wooden rocker,
my feet on straw and chocolate earth,
trees and flowers growing like lamps,
birds singing their hearts out,
air dancing with gnats and dust.

Mary Jo Mahoney
Figures Less Than Greek

Streetcar lights filter through the treated glass of picture windows. Their bone and yellow manes trifle around the tables. We
meander through them. I think the management aims to cloister its
patrons early in the evening. Ray says this is because we are only
twenty years and spitting distance from the Stonewall Bar.

A brass and cinnamon horseshoe bar sits in the heart of the
building. Poinsettias reach up from half-walls and sofa tables. Their
suede leaves hold the aspect of open hands in wonder and praise.
We are looking for seats with elbowroom. Four men sing at a piano.
They look cheap and luscious like a gay line-up in a police station.
Two men at the piano stand with their body weight more amply cast
on one leg. One man has his weight shifted high and thrown back.
He is open and ready with song. The third man, small and square,
bats his thighs in tempo. I think they look like incarnates of a 1986
erotica calendar that still hangs in the nurses' bathroom in the AIDS
treatment center, where Ray and I met three years ago, on the south
wing of the fifteenth floor of Saint Vincent's Hospital.

During my job interview, Ray, the assistant head nurse, asked
me in all truth, "You want to work here?" "It's important," I said
hesitantly. I felt one brow beginning to rise. He chortled a little to
the head nurse, Peg Malady, a gritty nasal sound from the upper part
of his larynx. They both knew I had worked for five years in the
intensive care unit. Peg was as familiar to me as I was to her. Our
orbits crossed often enough in the hospital lobby where Peg stood

morning fresh in a pressed lab coat talking to administrators and I'd pass her on my way out to the revolving doors.

Some mornings I would stop to say a quick "He's bathing now. See you tonight," to Diana Landry, Alan's wife, who slept beneath her wool coat in a hard resin chair in the lobby. Alan had a private room on the AIDS floor full of boxes of magazines, wedding photos, mail-order booster-vitamins and stock portfolios. He even had his own refrigerator. I knew him from the ICU. He would arrive from the AIDS floor to the ICU with pneumonia every few weeks, with an entourage of helpers who wheeled his estate with him on steel carts.

I may have sounded smug answering Ray, so I considered new words, more intelligible ones. "I've seen the silent hate about this epidemic," I said, but Ray was already out the door, with the kick of one leg back into the office as if he were riding a scooter.

Minutes later, he slid back into the office. He stood against the wall and listened calmly as Peg and I talked about Alan. Ray held two white ceramic cups of cappuccino, large as a grapefruit cut in two. When Peg finished speaking, he pushed one cup into my hands. "Bless you," he said.

§

Ray and I clink wineglasses to the firm tushes in the barroom. Our vision has adjusted to the dimness. Our speech has adjusted to the hubbub of chatter and drinks. Ray says he can barely handle the heterosexual blinders that he faces daily. When he goes out, he cannot bring himself to spend an evening in a sports bar full of straight assumptions. He is showing me his life tonight: here in the diocese of the body, over drinks, and later at the assumption of the soul: after dinner, we are going to Carnegie Hall to see the Gay Men's Christmas Choir.

At the bar, I am eager to laugh with him. He is careful to hang close. He is too honorable to say he knows I may be construed as a fag-hag here more so than an aboveboard friend though I feel this evening is by far better than those spent being mocked as "spacey" by straight men. I am comfortable here. Ray and I are both between lovers. We appreciate each other's company.

"Spacious maybe," I protest.

"Look at you!" Ray says laughing.

"And look at this," he rebuts, changing the subject, grinning as he reaches into the interior pocket of his coat. He pulls out just the green and white box top of a disposable enema and drops it back into his pocket. Ray still has sex between lovers while I do not. I am overly afraid of strangers. "You stole that!" I laugh. Ray and I have a ritual of shocking and sanctioning each other. This binds our differences within a larger alliance.

"Borrowed," he amends, and so smiling, we size up the singers at the cherry grand piano. I like the first man who leans mostly on his leg. Ray likes the one who could walk without hesitancy into a blaze. We sample more of the house white. At 33, Ray looks like a praying mantis. He wears an evergreen turtleneck he has given himself early for Christmas. I am the 27-year-old woman who never went to her prom, at a time when British punk music was too tangled an interest for a suburban girl to still seem pretty to a suburban boy. I look like the woman who, ten years later, still cannot disregard it.

§

I discovered the gay pinup in the bathroom on my first night of work at the treatment center. "Ladies first," Ray said to me, shutting me out of the single unisex toilet. I stood in the hallway eager for my turn to pee. In room 20 my patient rested on his bed waiting for me with a white towel draped lengthwise from his nipples to thighs. Through the bathroom door, I heard Ray sing "My Funny Valentine" from start to finish to the row of men on the calendar. He was testing me, to see if I had tenacity, a characteristic of nurses who proved to be proficient. I squatted against the wall in my scrub pants until the fluorescent bathroom light caught me crouching, my hands squeezing my hamstrings as one might do playing dodge ball. Ray hung in the door light, singing to his pointer finger, turning the finger to each of the male models for October. "You're my favorite work of art," he crooned to the shirtless one in jeans. He bowed slowly from the center of the light to a phantom audience. He bowed as if the north and south of a faint hallway of a hospital floor at midnight were really eaves painted by a stage crew, as if the art of a nurse was really theater, as if he provided a chance for the men in towels to take flight while their nurses left them.

"You dick," I said and ducked under his crescendo. And so we are friends.

We both took tonight off to paint the town pink. "I have never been to the Gay Men's Choir," I say at the bar, into my sleeve nearest Ray. Down to his maroon duck shoes he believes I need to find my inner child. I smirk at him as I light a cigarette. He closes his eyes, disgusted again by the thought that, just after nursing school, I became a Deadhead for a little while.

You are so sad, his face says. "Please. I was nineteen," I vouch, turning my cigarette on the lip of the square glass ashtray. Ray pats my perm, feigning compassion and hopelessness. Not long ago, Ray had had his heart cut into pieces by a doctor, which comes to mind again, and I look right back at him about the inexperienced wit of this. The wine glasses hang over the brass and steel taps. A mirror doubles the matronly hips of liqueur bottles. Our bills and coins stick to the bar. I have known a room to go away. I have set a needle into winter flesh. I am the princess of ambivalence lately.

I come back around and say, "Let's play illness."

§

Two men stand across from us. One man eyes the lemons and cherries in the condiment tray. The other man's hands shake against a brandy glass. He wears a blue pinpoint shirt that is too big for him. One sleeve is spotted with a patch of soft threads matted neatly with iron-on tape. His face is easy though he shakes. He seems relieved by distraction, glad indeed to cradle a festive glass of young, amber wine and grateful just now to be swallowed by waves of mirth that cascade down the bar, the glee of three transsexuals in reunion.

I want to transform unwillingness, I should have said at the interview.

"Girl?" Ray says. He slips down from the red wood barstool to do a body shimmy. Ray thinks we can forget ourselves. He pretends to be a cliché in order to forget. I pardon him, and me, and the public, and the entire anonymous carnival around us, a relief we are, a testimony to our humanness that we are all so imperfect, though I worry about how we pitch around bodies of words carelessly. Most days, I think we cannot help ourselves. When I am tired, I think too few of us feel accountable to try to clean ourselves up. Most nights though, Ray and I choose to clean it up, soak it up, our wide human failing of compassion, wipe it down with soap or bleach it clean. Sometimes we even revive a heart, but thereafter we toss and turn our words like restless bodies to lampoon it.

"Here's to the black leather ass third from left," Ray emends with silly hand gestures. Ray has down the tragedy of a comedian, and the moves of an artisan who trembles beneath his merriment. I think I know what he means. We drink because the world cannot help itself. Silently. Like this, in a bar of gay men, some of whom pretend a jubilation for singing with friends, some of whom carol out of fantasy, willingly, still young enough to hook their hopes on naiveté. One blond boy, barely of age, sings with the full trust of this prophecy, a vessel for a carol about a girl named after a snowflake who gets to wear an evening gown. Do straight girls learn this lesson, the one about letting go of fantasy, earlier than gay boys, I wonder?

When Ray sees me, he says, "Oh honey, let me teach you a thing or two about men."

§

Playing illness is like playing scavenger hunt, except you cannot appear to be looking for anything. Ray and I do this so we can pretend we're careless. "Rosie, weight loss to the left," he says. I look left. Ray is right. A cadaver arm leans down on the bar next to a highball glass of orange juice and ice. The too-thin man is wearing a black wool vest over a long-sleeved thermal undershirt that fans in the air. "One for Ray," I say. I lift off the stool, raise my left hand deep into the evening, near the inverted wineglasses, and scratch a single line up and down. Ray knows that I will keep a fair tally.

Behind the lime poinsettia a heavyset man wears gold cufflinks, each one a cube carved into the head of a panther, each with fangs and ruby eyes. A monogram stitched on his breast pocket rises and falls with his sandbag chest, but his nail beds are chalky and opaque. He is lonely, sick and rich, and I am taken with his quandary. I blow smoke down by the legs of my stool. I harness my curls and drop them. I adjust the weight of my hair in order to right my back so that I can say under my breath, "Nail rot. Primary symptom."

Ray is beautifully suburban as he looks over to the right side of the room. Hale, but not vain. His hair, a horseshoe of stubble, is velvet-short and very brown. His arms are not too hard and not too soft because our work is so physical. Ray is always prepared for the weather.

"I win," I say. We lock eyes and look down. I shut mine to make the room turn black until my queen says, "You win" and pushes me. I grab for my cigarettes before opening my eyes. The blackness rushes. When it moves away I see the likes of a bar again. Ray is pinching the roll of belly that hangs like a planetary ring on the waistline of my jeans.

"Jump a little lighter Rosie," he says, and I know he is right so I say, "Okay, okay, you win."

§

Rosie is not my name.

An elderly woman in a vintage car coat holds a yellow umbrella by its pleated trunk. She stands by the curb of Greenwich Avenue waggling the umbrella at the night. The ribbon hops up and down and fastens to her gloved fingers. A taxi hooks over to her from the center lane. The air is brisk and dry. We are happy again, chewing gum and famished. A scaffold runs the length of the block. Plyboards on the building are pasted with fliers, scuffed by shoes and boots, dusty with bus exhaust. A newspaper puffs out of the mesh trashcan. A few pages hold in the crease between the sidewalk and the boards. A younger woman coaches a beagle to relieve itself on a sheet of newspaper. Overcome, it cowers and begins to cough like a goose.

We are walking up nine streets to La Mer. I wave one finger in circles at a sky blue flier on the plywood. I touch my finger to the titties of Sheila Alexander, a female impersonator and cabaret singer. "Too hot honey!" I say and blow on my finger as if it were a match. I take Ray's wool derby and put it on my head, crudely tucking my hair beneath it. Ray tells me Sheila wears chandelier crystals from her pierced nipples. I become myself immediately, occupied that he is familiar with her. My hair falls down like snakes from beneath his hat. I say, "That would hurt." To which Ray says, "So? The crystals swing slower." I have a pair of black stone earrings that look like licorice teardrops. I say to Ray that they swing heavy too and must be why I like to wear them when I am in love. Ray pats me on top of the hat. I do not smile and give him back his hat. We begin to walk briskly in step, and silence, to the restaurant. I am unsure about feeling irritated with him as my Irish can rise up when I have been drinking.

The maitre d' at La Mer seats us in the galley where a kerosene lamp casts shadows that jump across a white linen tablecloth in a booth against a wall of wainscoting. The restaurant smells of fish and garlic. We order wine before we are seated. A rope net drapes down from the ceiling. Without a word, I duck exaggeratedly beneath it. He taps me on the arm and has his cheeks sucked in. His mouth is a pucker. He flaps his hands by his ears like fins. We take off our coats and settle in.

§

A platter of paella is lowered on the table by two hands that place it down, tipping one end to touch the table then easing the other end to meets the table plane. There is no noise or spill. The yellow rice is specked with orange threads, saffron surely, and the seafood medley is motley. Red and white lobster meat, pearly scallops and nearly candy cane shrimp, but in the flickering light, the blue mussels appear to be moving. Silverware clinks on plates. Roy Orbison sings for the lonely. We drink and talk shop.

Ray continues, "It was the saddest fucking one, Rosie." When Ray is sad he speaks barely above a whisper. The waiters, like seadivers, run coolness over us as they swim past our table. Our sentences diffuse in the current. We cast words back and forth across the table. Everything moves slower under water.

"Jesus," I say, sad for Ray, and he continues, "Howard was standing at the foot of the bed holding him by the ankles. When I

shut off the machine, Howard made a noise that was not human."
Ray is being sincere. I am a little nervous. We eat the bread and rice.

"It scared me," he admits.

"The way he cried?" I ask.

"The way he howled, Rosie," he corrects me. He corrects himself, "It was the saddest fucking one." I toss back what is left in my glass because I cannot stand it. I stand accused for talking shop when there is no reason for it. We do this kind of work almost every night. Who else is going to help us? I light a cigarette from the flame of the kerosene lamp.

§

Carnegie Hall is all gold and red velvet. I push my back against the grain of the velvet on my regal chair. The whimsy of the caroling makes me feel lighter. On the rim in front of the right stage box is where Ray leans. His hands are perched on the ledge. His head is well over his arms. He may swan dive right down to the five tiers of risers. The chorus sings a third encore. Ray leans happy-go-lucky over them. Eight of the singers sit on stools. Frail from disease, they cannot stand for the length of a song. They move their knees in little circles keeping time. Ray looks weightless as he tilts into the cathedral space before us. I reach and hold the back flap of his wool sport coat. I sit back and close my eyes. I believe I am wearing diamonds and that I am a politician's wife.

§

The cabbie yells at me to come back in from the open window. Cars hedge and stop. The vehicle staccato and the pedestrians walking make a wealth of noise. Ray holds the back of my green loden coat. I am playing air guitar to the southbound cars on Broadway. I am overcome with Bruce Springsteen which is why Ray calls me Rosie. "I broke a string," I yell back to Ray over my shoulder, who leans heavy on me by the window. I think I point a black and silver Stratocaster at each driver who will look at me. Almost every driver will. I look at a blonde woman driving her Jaguar. My ringlets fly in the wind. Some fly into my mouth. She rolls down her dark blue window and looks at me.

"You have the power to lower the night sky," I yell at her. Ray pulls harder on my coattails. He knows that I might scare her. Ray's free hand comes out the window of the cab. He pats my face with a handkerchief. He is trying to put it in my mouth. As our yellow cab proceeds, Ray and I jerk forward. We fall against the casing of the passenger door. His handkerchief tangles with my hair, and I rise up through the open window. He holds on. There is no one else accountable on these streets. A woman walks alone wrapped in a cape. A grocery worker drapes a blanket on plastic bottles of cider. I point the neck of my guitar to the North Star, the only heavenly body evident to me from here, and sing a fierce song about desire.

Mary Kathryn Vernon
Visit IV

On the skirted porch
that flanks two sides of the house,
on a wicker table,
kept in place by rocks,
two stacks of mail wait,
one for me, and one for you.

There's nothing important for me—
a few flyers are all.
For you there are cards
wishing you well,
arriving the day after your passing.
One small card, handmade,
with a heart carefully drawn,
says, "Get well soon!"

Across the street,
Mr. Davis pushes his mower,
which makes a pleasant whirring sound.
Standing, leaning with my hands on the table,
I listen.

Wayne Scheer
Three Friends

Ricardo knew Felicia would arrive late, offering a fury of apologies and explanations. Still, he chose to arrive at the restaurant early to get a table by the window overlooking Virginia Highlands, home to Atlanta's hip galleries and bookstores. He enjoyed people-watching, and he enjoyed being seen.

Tall and thin, with carefully trimmed blond hair graying at the sides, he wore a yellow and gray shirt with white slacks and no socks. The top three buttons of his shirt were open. A gold necklace, matching the gold stud in his left ear, glittered in the fluorescent light of the café. He frowned as he recalled Felicia once saying he looked like a man wearing amulets to ward off the evil spirits of middle age.

After ordering a Compari and soda, he assured the waiter, whom he knew as Andre, that his friend would soon join him. He watched as Andre, clad in tight jeans, turned towards the bar.

Felicia strode into the restaurant just after he finished his first drink and ordered another. He watched her wind her way through the crowd. She walked with a sense of authority, her heels clicking as if she were much taller than her five-feet two-inches. Heads turned, not because she was beautiful, but because her confidence made her sexy. Her face opened to a full smile when she spotted her friend.

"Sorry I'm late," she said. "I'm terrible, I know, but I refuse to

pay for parking in the afternoon. I found a spot three blocks away."
She may have lost some of her New York accent, Ricardo thought,
but she certainly kept the attitude.

"So to save three dollars, you left your dearest friend waiting. I
should be angry with you." Ricardo stood up and held out his arms.
"Instead, I demand a hug and a kiss." She balanced on her toes and
Ricardo bent at the waist in a well-practiced greeting.

As soon as she sat down, he told her to order a drink and a lunch
entrée under fifteen dollars. "I sold a painting this morning, but
I'm still not rich enough to afford you." They laughed comfortably.
"What's it been? A month? You must catch me up on everything.
Derek tells me you have a new love in your life. Is his name really
Larry? Not even Laurence? Or Lorenzo? How drab."

Ricardo saw her confident gaze transform for an instant to a nervous stare. "It was good talking with Derek. He sounded upbeat."

"Don't change the subject now, girl. Tell me all the dirty details." He was determined to keep conversation light.

Felicia talked about Larry. "This time it's real," she said. "I can
feel it." As she spoke, Ricardo tried to recall how many times he'd
heard her say those same words since her divorce three years earlier.

She stopped talking long enough to order a shrimp salad and an
iced tea. Ricardo ordered a hummus wrap, but showed considerably
more interest in another Compari.

"You should have at least three drinks with lunch," he told her.
"Helps keep things in perspective by desensitizing you for the rest
of the day."

She laughed a bit too much and avoided his eyes.

Ricardo needed to talk, but he was afraid of what he might say. Until recently, he and Derek routinely invited Felicia to their home for dinner. This time, with Derek in the hospital, Ricardo suggested lunch at a crowded restaurant. It was a way to protect themselves and each other. They both understood this without either uttering a word.

The food arrived, and she continued where she had left off. "He's everything I'm looking for. He's fun, he's smart and he's wonderful in bed. What more is there?"

"Not much." Making a mental note to return to Larry's third attribute, Ricardo added as straight-faced as possible, "But you have to ask yourself one question: how does he make you feel?"

Ricardo stared into Felicia's deep brown eyes. He had never met anyone with eyes like hers, so dark and mysterious. They sucked in poor, unsuspecting men and refused to let go of them. He recalled the brief fling they had in college. He knew he wasn't attracted to her as a woman, yet he felt compelled to try. There was no conversion, they laughed afterwards, but more chemistry than either of them cared to admit.

"I'm waiting for an answer." The long pauses when he spoke with Felicia drove Ricardo crazy. She'd stare into space with a slight smile on her face, as if she had to journey to another dimension for an answer. "How does he make you feel? Like a little girl or like his mother?" He finally asked impatiently.

She narrowed her eyes. "Like a little girl, I guess."

"Conviction. I need conviction." Ricardo was speaking too loud for the small restaurant. An elderly woman seated next to them gave Ricardo a disapproving look. A broccoli sprout dangled from his bottom lip and Felicia instinctively reached and brushed it aside.

"OK, he makes me feel like a little girl. The way he..."

"Wrong."

"What do you mean 'wrong?'"

"He should make you feel like a little girl AND like his mother. My goodness, do I have to teach you everything?"

Now it was Felicia's turn to act annoyed. "Don't give me your fag bullshit. Explain yourself, Little Ricky."

"The name is Ricardo. Act nice or I won't impart my wisdom or let you share my dessert."

"I'm sorry, Ri-car-do, although it says Richard on your driver's license. I'll be nice."

"That's a little better," he said, acting hurt by closing his eyes and wetting his lips. "Now, as I was saying, if you truly loved him you'd let him to take care of you and you'd want to take care of him."

"That almost makes sense."

"Of course it does, girl. I heard it on *Oprah*!"

They both laughed. "Look," Ricardo said in his let-me-momen-tarily-step-out-of-character voice. "There's no way of knowing if this is the one or not. It takes time. You'll just have to wait like the rest of us."

"But waiting is a bitch."

"Tell me about it." He felt his voice break and his eyes glaze.

Felicia squeezed his hand.

After a moment, he leaned forward. "Now's the time to tell me about Mr. Larry's sexual prowess."

Before Felicia could speak, the waiter cleared their plates and asked if they were interested in dessert. Like a hungry dog suddenly shown his food bowl, Ricardo almost panted as he ordered a chocolate éclair. "With two forks, please." Whispering, he turned to Felicia. "The éclairs are to die for, but I'll look like Marlon Brando's younger brother if you don't help me out."

She readily agreed.

"Now, let's see. Where were we? Oh, yes. Your boudoir."

Ricardo knew how comfortably Felicia would share the most intimate details of her sex life with him. In the old days, he would do the same, but lately both of them found it difficult to talk about what they really needed to say. Derek's illness created an invisible wall between them. As close as they were, they remained separated and separate.

"Last night, I had three orgasms in a row. That hasn't happened since...since before Aaron and I married." Pausing, Felicia added, "but Larry has this annoying habit of asking if it was good afterwards."

"Oh, I hate that."

"I know. I mean couldn't he tell?" They laughed. "I'm sprawled out on the bed, drained, and he wants to know if it was all right."

"Men," Ricardo said. "Anxieties and insecurities, seasoned with testosterone. They're all the same. But utterly delicious." They giggled like two schoolchildren making fun of their teacher.

Suddenly, Ricardo grew serious. "You are using protection, aren't you?"

"Of course."

"I've lost too many friends."

"I know." Felicia reached out once more. Lowering her eyes, she asked, "And how is Derek? Really."

"He has his good days, still able to joke. He says the hospital food is the worst part of dying." Ricardo appeared about to say more, but changed his mind, swallowing hard. "He sends his love. He enjoyed talking to you on the phone the other day."

She spoke quickly. "I'll stop by to visit one of these evenings, I promise."

She continued talking, but his mind wandered to old times when she and Aaron, and he and Derek would go out together. She used to get so angry when people stared at them, but Derek would laugh. "Hey, they're probably admiring your stamina being with three studs like us."

Ricardo looked at his friend. Although she was saying something about her job, her eyes gave her away. She was deep inside her own head

"You're wandering again, Felicia." He snapped his fingers as if trying to break a trance.

"I was just..."

"I know where you were. Don't go there. It only hurts more, believe me."

He felt a tear tickle his cheek. She reached across the table to wipe it away.

The waiter appeared carrying dessert. The two friends grabbed their forks and submerged themselves in chocolate and cream. Once again, they were joking and laughing.

When the bill arrived, Felicia asked, "Should we get another éclair for Derek?"

Ricardo's face turned red. "He can't eat chocolate anymore." He felt his body shiver. He could no longer control his tears. Felicia took his hand.

"Enough." Ricardo took out his wallet and paid the bill. Felicia left the tip.

"I'll pay next time," she said.

"You certainly will," he responded.

As they left the restaurant, Felicia turned and said, "You know I love you."

"And I love you."

"And I love Derek, too. Please give him my best." She hugged her friend. "I know I should visit him. It's not the same as a phone call. I . . . I just can't."

"I understand and Derek understands." He tried holding back what he needed to say, but the words tumbled out as if they had been stored in an overstuffed closet. "He misses you, Felicia. He misses hugs. His own mother is afraid to touch him."

Felicia closed her eyes.

After a moment, Ricardo said, "Let me walk you to your car and then you can drive me to the hospital."

"Sure, but I have to get back to work."

"Of course."

They walked down Highland Avenue to St. Charles where Felicia parked her car. Ricardo took her hand in his and squeezed it reassuringly. She quickened her pace, her heels clicking on the pavement.

"Maybe there's time for a quick visit," she said.

2006–2011

2006 FDA approves for sale the first effective one-a-day pill (Truvada) for the treatment of HIV infection. • The Gates Foundation—the world's largest private funding source for AIDS prevention and science—receives a promised gift of $31 billion over ten years from financial wizard Warren Buffet.

2007 March 21 is declared the 1st National Natives HIV/AIDS Awareness Day. • (RED) Campaign is launched. • A promising vaccine fails to deliver.

2008 The Berlin Patient is functionally cured of AIDS. • The United States' PEPFAR funding program is renewed on July 30th. • Mbeki resigns, bringing to an end an era of denialism in sub-Saharan Africa. • Music legend Annie Lennox launches the SING campaign.

2009 Building on the work of President George W. Bush and Congresswoman Barbara Lee, President Obama lifts the U.S. ban on HIV-positive immigrants and visitors (paving the way for the first U.S. hosting in decades of the XIX International AIDS Conference in 2012 in Washington, D.C.). • 4 million people in developing nations are on ARVs, while 9.5 million people in those same countries are without any treatment. • Scientists decode the structure of an entire HIV genome.

2010 AIDS Drug Assistance Programs (ADAPs) in over a dozen states face significant shortfalls. • Results from the iPrEx trial shows a significant reduction in HIV infection among men who have sex with men. • The United States, South Korea, China, and Namibia lift travel bans for people living with HIV. • Obama launches the National AIDS Strategy.

2011 Elizabeth Taylor, patron saint of AIDS, dies of congestive heart failure. • New York City Mayor Michael Bloomberg cuts funding for AIDS housing and nutritional services. • Known as the godfather of rap, Gil Scott-Heron dies.

Treasure Shields Redmond
matthew

"none but the righteous, none but the righteous, none but the
righteous shall see god."

it was five years past the first wave
of the michael jackson phenomenon
you were still wearing
your red and black thriller jacket
your high water pants
over white socks that were too thick
for your penny loafers
a husky football player said
hey michael
your reply: *just beat it*
you could quip and quote niggas
into submission
like the time we was in class
and some boy told me to suck his dick
and you said
that's the line i'd like to be in
all he could do is fall out of your eyes
pack up his untried manhood
and sit the fuck down
that is why, when you called me on the phone
to tell me what i had hoped to never hear
i put a practical face on my voice
listening at the right bend in
the revelation
and offering advice at the cul de sac of it
but when we said bye
and *i love you foolish*
i dropped the phone
as if it had grown tentacles
screaming to somewhere inside your biology
no

i was transported to a place where
we had all seroconverted
where the disease had become so common and benign
that it was just like the comedian said

old folks was complaining about their sciatica
and their aids acting up
but for now when we talk
i tell you
maybe you should take that trip to hot springs
and maybe you should forgive your daddy
and maybe . . .

at night the cures give to me in feverish dreams
tell me that i must make a gift of some of my t-cells
offer you a drink of some of my amniotic fluid
pepper your face with kisses
or let my newborn put his head on your chest
i wonder if i am up to the challenge
that when you go home to our small mississippi town to die
will i come down
bring you your favorite dish of my grandmama's peach cobbler
sit by your bed and spoon feed you
shhhh you don't have to say a word
will i then tuck you into thin sheets
and tip toe out
so as not to wake you
will your satisfied spirit
brush past me on the way out
light itself on my hood for a short way
just long enough to see me go in my house
and then grow so big that
the earth cannot contain it

Charneice Fox Richardson
For My Brothers Who Walk In Positives

He lived in positives,
always thinking before he spoke
he shied away from the negative
preferring yoga tree-like stance
he watched the world through the weeping willows
swaying. Perfected their ability to hang low
and stand tall. Simultaneously.
Protecting himself when the winds blew north,
he prepared for winter as the leaves fall,
as the tears fall. He lived in the positive
always thinking before he spoke
he shied away from the negative,
founding solace in Buddha, Jesus, Allah,
the rock of Gibraltar combined.
He stood tall, upright as the blood
traveled through his veins
he lived in the positive,
with flawless yoga tree-like stance,
he shied away from the negative
energy and became virtuous,
even in his afflictions
he walked through the valley of the shadows,
facing death persecuted for lack of knowledge
he shied away from the negative
energy standing tall like the willow
who weeps and hangs low
Standing tall.
he lived in positives
and he lived.

Jéanpaul Ferro
Young Brother

They all want to make him
a hero for his deadly disease,

but it is I who swam with him,
gave the gift of him,

the glint of bodies, naked,
down by the old Scituate reservoir,

growing up together,
not our religion, not our color,
not in the field where we were born,
not even our experiences together,

only the ghost of his life that begins
to waver in my arms; and him as he's
whispering to me:

I've been waiting for you.
I've been waiting for you.
I've been waiting for you
for so long, brother.

Montgomery Maxton

Haunting

You will someday die
from a cause attributed to that
bogeyman in your young blood;
acquired one night in the
only city that existed at that time—
Sit back, Michael; just ride out the storm
you say, casually,
over breakfast at Fisherman's Wharf
while touching my hand from across the table—
between the flutes of juice, goblets of water;
plates of poached yokes, seeded morning buns;
among the clatter of bone china, voices.

Baby, you don't understand,
I hate the way it rains in this city,
the way the thunder can roll in off of the
Pacific mystery unannounced and vulgar,
and how the lightning can strike you into a
pile of ash,
ash that after making love last night in
the safety mode of latex and dental dams
you ask me to mix into paint
and masterpiece it onto a canvas;
hang it above the cold bed

and fall asleep with you on top of me.

Lester Strong
Anagrams

There are times when a sharp emotion pierces through us, unexpected, uninvited. A stab of longing, regret, joy, or guilt, and suddenly we're transported to a different point in our lives, one until that moment veiled by the accepted and unremarkable round of our daily activities.

Midautumn, midafternoon, midway through that most prosaic of activities: pedaling a stationary bicycle. One second I'm sweating and trying to concentrate on the page of print before me I'm reading in an ever less successful attempt to ward off a dreary boredom. The next I'm hearing in memory the voice of a woman speaking over the phone—and once again reading anagrams from a scrawled note on a loose sheet of paper.

First the voice: "Is this L—? Yes? Well, this is John T—'s mother. We haven't spoken together in many years but"—a sob— "I wanted to let you know that last Wednesday John jumped off a bridge and"—another sob—"killed himself."

Stop the reading, stop the boredom. Instantly I'm transported back I time—not just to the phone call from John's mother six months before, but further back, much further, over thirty years to the early 1960s and the night John and I met. The night we fell in love.

This is upset, confusion and upset. A numbness I haven't recognized until this moment lifts abruptly and feelings beyond the shock I was aware of after that phone conversation in March reveal themselves with a startling clarity. Although, curiously, the pedaling and sweating continue unabated.

John and I met in the early fall of our senior year in high school. I use "met" with a peculiar emphasis because we'd known each other for two years before that, sharing classrooms and teachers of music and German. But until that revelatory meeting our senior year at the home of a mutual friend, there had been nothing more. My own awareness of John had been at best casual. He later admitted to more than a casual interest in the books he'd noticed I always seemed to carry with me. D. H. Lawrence's *The Rainbow* and *Women in Love*, Lawrence Durrell's *Alexandria Quartet*, Rimbaud's *A Season in Hell*, Dostoyevsky's novels—there were more, and he could name most of them. But until our meeting at the home of our friend, we'd never spoken personally. I doubt we'd ever spoken impersonally. I can't remember.

The night we met, though, we spoke. We spoke and spoke. I don't know what our mutual friend or his family thought, but we didn't stop. When it was too late to stay at our friend's any longer, we left, drove our parents' cars a block away and parked, then huddled in my parents' car talking until early morning. Finally we had to go our separate ways. John was assertive enough to ask for my phone number before driving off, so that a few hours later, around eight o'clock, he called. I gave him directions to my house, and we talked the rest of that day also.

Revelation, truly. Our high school was in turmoil that year— we the baby-boom generation had arrived in force and there were too many students, too few classrooms, not enough teachers. There were also many very simple multiple-choice tests, and that was fortunate because I don't remember studying much from then on. I just remember being in love, stunningly, overwhelmingly, never-a-moment-to-lose being in love.

First love. I was gay—in those days I would have said homosexual—and keenly aware of it. And knowing I was gay, I longed for a—longed for—Well, from the night we met I longed for John. Slim, fair-skinned, of medium height, with longish dark hair spilling over green eyes, he represented for me a kind of physical perfection. His clothes weren't of the skin-tight variety, but his jeans fit perfectly over a rounded rump whose smooth nakedness, I learned in the course of time, had the textured whiteness of mother-of-pearl. He also had a nervous energy about him that all but exploded in his every move. Very attractive, that energy. Very. And in its explosiveness perhaps a harbinger of things to come.

First love. Our falling in love was a mutual event, and when I pushed, John acquiesced after a fashion in our having sex together. Anyway in our trying to have sex. Twice. I still remember the intense excitement I felt on first taking his cock into my mouth—and I remember how he gasped in surprise. Even our first kiss is etched in my memory. Two men with lips touching, tongues attached, is still a potent erotic image for me, one whose sudden welling up in the midst of workaday life signals the rebirth of sexual need after a previous satedness.

But if our falling in love was mutual, the sex between us was not. John's surprise at the acts I wanted to engage in turned to frowns, then rejection. In short order he pulled away from that part of our being together, and I have no doubt his discomfort over our sex helped precipitate his own direct move into heterosexual experiences a short time afterward.

Abruptly, with a great deal of pain, I learned a defining truth: John was not gay. Clearly.

Still, from the first evening we met, and lasting far beyond the short length of our unsuccessful physical affair, there was between us a tie more important than sex: a longed-for intermingling, an attempted merging of our two persons into one. The "need" we dubbed it, and it cut deeply into both of us. It was an acknowledged bond neither of us was willing to relinquish for years, despite other friendships, other loves, even John's subsequent marriage and two children. It started with Rimbaud's *A Season in Hell*, then moved on to Jack Kerouac's *On the Road* and *The Dharma Bums*, which we read obsessively together. In those days the Beats were still cultural royalty, and we imagined ourselves the new Kerouac-Cassady. One person, not two. Of course we were the ones joining our names in a way probably never contemplated by Jack Kerouac and Neal Cassady. But we dreamed of writing a new literature together that would be post-Beat, that would say something new, do something big.

We dreamed, anyway. And above all, I suspect, we hoped our dreams would lift us out of our limping selfhoods into a rarified realm of feeling-good, feeling-whole—and definitely feeling removed from our parents' workaday world and the seemingly quite ordinary and mundane life of the small western city we found ourselves confronting each day. We never stopped to ask precisely just what we wanted. But it apparently had to do with movement: We drove around that town obsessively during the free afternoons our half-day schedule at a crowded high school blessedly provided us with, as obsessively as we read the Beats or Rimbaud. Only it went nowhere. The same for the writing: impossible feelings, impossible good, impossible wholeness. I can see that now. Looking back, the fantasies were pompous, ludicrous, typically adolescent. Certainly no literature came of them. But their hold had the clench of steel, so that moving beyond them was for me very difficult indeed. And for John? According to his mother: "He talked about you all the time. He said he wanted to get back to writing." The clench of steel. Yes.

Also from his mother: "John was diagnosed as schizophrenic. He lived in a half-way house, and was on medication which"—a sob—"didn't stop the voices he heard all the time telling him what to do, what to feel."

Schizophrenia. Perhaps I heard its echoes early on in our involvement. Because if John's and my need to merge was obsessive, the rifts between us were just as powerful. The first rift, of course, arose from our differences over sex, bridged through the "need" that bound us together with a greater strength. The second rift seemed less important at first, but proved ultimately more divisive. That was drugs. Pot, hash, acid, speed—the names today whiz through my memory almost as dizzily as the substances themselves rushed into John's life. That was in our college days, the "need" having driven us to enter the same school. By the mid-sixties everyone was trying pot, but John tried everything. And at least for a number of years didn't quit. I'll never know all the drugs he took; I'll never know how often or how long he took them. I didn't want to know at the time because it frightened me. Here if anywhere lay the seeds of the end of our merging. Through drugs John moved into a world I was too fearful to enter myself, and little by little our lives drifted apart.

Did the drugs contribute to John's schizophrenia? I can't speak as a medical expert. But I remember the letters I received from him over the years, which from the early seventies on became ever more perplexing, then frightening, in their incomprehensibility. This was after I had moved east, and he had moved further west and north, to Tacoma where his parents now lived. There was one last meeting between us in person, in the mid-seventies, and he was as incomprehensible in person as he had become in writing. But it is the letters that remain the most vivid in memory, or at least my reaction to them. Crazy, rambling letters. After the first few I stopped reading them; then I stopped saving them; finally in a frenzy of upset, I tore them all up and felt only relief. Over the years I've felt some regret at that ripping, but not much. Keeping them was too painful.

The letters were the third and almost final rift between us. But there was one more: his calls over the phone. Those started in the late seventies or early eighties, only once or twice a year, invariably from Tacoma. At first he called collect, but that stopped when I stopped accepting the charges. Then he found access to other people's phones—most likely his parents'—and the calls resumed.

His phone conversations were marginally less incomprehensible than his letters, but also invariably nostalgic: descriptions of threats he claimed he was receiving from people whose names I didn't recognize or of chaotic trips he'd taken up and down the West Coast, then talk about how he wanted to come east, how we'd have a cup of coffee together, how it would feel like old times. Of course it wouldn't have been old times. It would have been something I no longer wanted, no longer could tolerate. I came to dread those calls, but if I could turn down requests to reverse charges, once we started talking I couldn't stop the conversations themselves. I spoke minimally, but I listened, transfixed.

The truth was that over the years I'd made a life apart from John happier than anything I'd ever known with him. It might sometimes involve tedium—riding an exercise bicycle—but it also involved new ties, new love, new ways of relating more satisfying than John's and my ill-starred attempt to merge our disparate personalities.

A deeper truth: This satisfying life had no place for John. I could sense his loneliness and pain, but could do nothing to assuage them. Could do nothing even to attempt assuaging them.

A still deeper truth, one not apparent to me until that instant on the bicycle when I recalled his mother's phone call: I carried some part of John's and my old dependency into my new life. For years I could tear up letters unread and say no to accepting reverse phone charges, but I listened transfixed to his calls. I could not hang up on that voice. Somewhere within myself I was still listening to old needs, old satisfactions. To old love.

A last remembered comment from John's mother over the phone: "I called because we knew he kept in touch with you and saw from our telephone bill that he phoned you just a couple of weeks ago. Did he"—a sob—"say anything, give any hint, that he was thinking of—planning to—?"

Which brings me to the anagrams and scrawled note.

John's mother couldn't finish her question, but I could truthfully answer no—no hint he was planning to do anything. Not a word. Nothing. Then two days after her call, I received in the mail an envelope—no return address, its postage affixed to the wrong side, the cancellation date smeared and unreadable, the word Tacoma just legible. On the sheet inside were the following words scrawled in block letters:

Acquire
I ACQU?IRE
I ACQUIRED
YES I DID

we two
YES WE TWO

ARTHUR PAUL
IT AILS US
DO WE
SEE

SEE
I
DO NOT
Acquire?

AIDS. SIDA. Anagrams. One last message from John, clearly. This one neither torn up nor thrown away, but still in my possession.

There are many routes to AIDS: drugs, needles, transfusions, the varieties of sex. I had managed to miss them all, through new ties, new love, new ways of relating more satisfying than John's and my attempts to merge—and no doubt through a good deal of luck. But had John traveled one of them?

A sharp emotion pierces through us, unexpected, uninvited, and suddenly we're transported back to a different point in our lives. It's no longer the same precise moment, we're no longer precisely our old selves. But we are pierced: as if the intervening years have failed to intervene.

I've looked up the passage I was reading that fall day on the stationary bicycle when the thought of John flashed into memory: "Who knows, my God," Kerouac cries, "but that the universe is not one vast sea of compassion actually, the veritable holy honey, beneath all this show of personality and cruelty. . . . Live your lives out? Naw, love your lives out."

Kerouac. Vintage Kerouac. And a vintage message. Almost anachronistic. After all, this is the age of AIDS, of safer sex, of exercise bicycles that must be pedaled no matter what the upset. It's not the age of dharma bums.

And yet.

John wasn't gay. Clearly.

In my mind I hear the echo of his voice over the phone, clearly.

I don't want to hang up. I don't want to forget.

Perhaps in the age of AIDS Kerouac's message isn't so anachronistic after all.

"Love your lives out."

Clearly.

Michael Montlack
Black Book

At the end of the 80s,
he threw away his phone book;
everyone in it was dead.

Now strolling Christopher Street
to brunch and therapy,
he gazes into familiar doorwells,
remembering leaning figures, handlebar mustaches
curling, like fingers through denim belt loops:
those five o'clock shadows in the shadows.

He's 66, paunchy and gray
but they still wink at him from the grave:
cool invitations
to the piers, the truckyard,
back to their place.

Crossing the cobblestones,
he's still too stunned to be amazed
by all those faded one-nighters
lined up and waiting
for him to come.

Louie Clay

In the Name of the Father, the Son, and the Mother Spirit

Negative, Jesus, five times now,   but still
not sure.   I'll test again in six more months
since John has likely been exposed.   He'll spill
his fears to no one, nor even hint he hunts
beyond our bed.   I'm sure he'd never use
a condom—least of all with me, his wife.
He's too afraid the two of us will lose
our golden reputation.
                    Secret life?
Why can't he see I guessed it anyway?
I want only him, not what people think;
I've always known that part of him is gay.
So what?   Should that alone make him shrink
from me, not share his need?
                    Our need's not sin!
From isolation save us, God.   AMEN

Jennifer Su

Learning the Love Song

A girl leaves behind her beloved island, to seek the cure, riding a
poem over the Pacific, like a lifeboat full of mermaids.
With heavy debt to T.S. Eliot.

I. Taiwan

There's Death Rattle.
What word for final ardor?
The Dinner Guest checks his reflection in steak knife,
swallows girl. Arrange limbs
on gold-rimmed plate. No word to date.
Second wind?
Drag aluminum chair
outside Southern Taiwan storefront.
Envision Long Life Mountain on horizon,
blocked by concrete-block high rise.
The neighborhood's alive.
Tent-restaurant serves up Hot Pot.
Glass bottles clink, formaldehyde-laced
Taiwan beer. Shouts of, "Dry cup! Drink up!"
Corner bowling alley,
balls slide buffed lanes. Barber shop,
euphemism for Whore House.
Next-door, Goat Proprietor hawks goat soup,
stewed-goat on rice and goat-fried noodles.
My neighbors, intimate acquaintances.
Sound, smell, base desires, strange faces.
'The women come and go, talking of
Michelangelo,' to passing mopeds,
taxis, dark sedans
steered by 'lonely men' in black suits
'leaning out of' tinted 'windows.'
'Pinned and wriggling'
across that cross-section of capitalism,
Kaohsiung City. "Were you once pretty?"

I'll learn a poem tonight,
'I am no Prince Hamlet.'
My paltry life depends on this heroic effort.
Night sweats arrive punctual.
I am 'The Wasteland.' Twenty-one pounds
gone in a month. Tropical night,
thick with forfeited
flesh. I suck air.
The man begs, "Darling come inside."
Wave him away, and wanting to want to eat,
devour 'Prufrock.'
Autumn, Dr. David Ho, made in
Taiwan, my Cover Girl.
I peruse his cocktails in
"Time," furtively,
check whether strangers
notice my pulse quicken
with hope. Home,
floss my teeth,
first time in years. We talk
Aaron Diamond, on First Avenue
in New York. I'll fly there,
throw myself on the mercy of
a cold city. Was I once pretty?
I stay up with Taiwan the night
before my flight, long after the
night markets kill the lights,
muttering 'Prufrock' over and over,
disturbing goat patrons,
ranting 'from a farther room,'
hacking cough.
'So how should I presume?'
'Human voices wake us,' in lung fluid,
'we drown.' Good-bye, Taiwan,
my Love, won't be seeing you again.
I'm on a blacklist of undesirables,
won't slip back in.

II. New York

'April is the cruelest month.'
Only it's February in merciful New York.
Come alone to hospital.
Blind beggar in temple,
wash my 'feet' in snow and 'soda water.'
Visit clinic,
sleek Indian Doctor, with
Oxford accent—might I be
that woman 'talking of Michelangelo' in his well-appointed
rooms—such rooms I'll never know.
In snow, he hails my taxi to Saint Vincent's.
Driver covers mouth,
takes my fare with tissue,
like he's seen his head,
'brought in upon a platter.'
And let me say, in ER, one scared girl 'is no great matter.'
Wheel me to gurney-lined room.
Patients scrape Wasteland, near in proximity,
no anonymity. Proselytizer gives me
Jehovah's Witness pamphlet, on slipping past
Saint Peter's Gate. "You need this more than I,"
she says. "No, no. I am 'Lazarus come back from
the dead, come back to tell you all.'"
In the hall, Chinese girl explains
her assault, in Mandarin.
"We need a translator." I rise like
Lazarus from my mantle, tell them her characters—
radicals and all—they push me down the hall, roll my gurney
towards some 'overwhelming question…
O, do not ask what is it,
Let us go and make our visit.'
To quarantine.
May be contagious with tuberculosis
(part of April's cruelty is coming alive again,
the lilacs rising from the 'dead land,
a little life with dried tubers').
They poke skin for tubers of TB,

extract oceans of lung fluid to test for
PCP. Lucky quarantine. Most indigents
don't board alone
to vomit night away,
until two Columbia medical students arrive,
punctual, probe for capillary blood.
Think I'm an addict,
inured to needles, but I'd
'seen the moment of my greatness flicker,
and in short
I was afraid.'
My Dinner Guest etched poetry
in hysterical memory, with his steak knife,
dignity in bas relief.
They think I'm crazy.
Black med student, my Lady,
convinces her cohort to quit.
Indigent should let him play with her capillaries.
They keep me seven days
on Great City's tab.
I eat well, watch T.V.,
guard capillaries.
Strangers come and go.
I recite 'Prufrock.'
No one tries to make small
talk with a lunatic like me.

III. Coda

Medical-men release me,
with clean bill,
two weeks of cocktail.
Don't know why,
I defy
gravity,
rewind the decline,
when Thirty Million and Rising fall behind.
How many still without medicine?

I take my refund in pill box.
Disguised in silk scarf, as normal girl,
I pass, tuning ears to mermaids,
though 'they do not sing for me.'
Under water
under breath
chanting to that god,
Dr. David Ho,
whose island
the crowd, the crush
floated me life just long enough.

Bruce Ward

Lazarus Syndrome (An Excerpt)

Cast of Characters: **ELLIOTT**, mid-40s
                           STEPHEN, his partner, early 30s
                           JAKE, his father, early 70s
                           NEIL, his brother, early 40s

"No matter how bad things get,
you've got to go on living,
even if it kills you"
        —Sholom Aleichem

JAKE
So, here. Take it. The music. The heirlooms. Our history.

ELLIOTT
And what am I supposed to do with all these things, dad?

JAKE
Take them out, let them breathe. The music, play. Keep it alive.
The other things, that's up to you. Just don't keep it all sitting
there, stuffed up under the sofa. It's yours now. All of it.

ELLIOTT
No. It's not time yet. I don't want all these things now. Why do I
have to have them now?
        [putting the music, watches, etc. back into the case]
Put it back. It's from the dead. Watches, music. Dead people from
a long time ago. They don't matter now. Nothing matters. Time
marches on. Memories fade. Crumbs. Just . . . crumbs.

STEPHEN
Elliott . . .

ELLIOTT
[pushing him away]
History? There is too much history.

JAKE
Too much history?

ELLIOTT
It's the past. It's dead. I'm sick of the past. I want a future. I want a now.

JAKE
There is never too much history. If your mother weren't dead, this would kill her.

ELLIOTT
Well, she is dead, isn't she? The matriarch is absent. Not here.

JAKE
Your mother is everywhere! She's in the chicken soup, she's in the latkes!

ELLIOTT
Oh, really?
[lifting up lid to chicken soup pot]
You in there, Ma?

JAKE
She is in YOU!

NEIL
Jesus, Elliott...

ELLIOTT
Jesus has nothing to do with it. Or does he? He raised a dead person from the grave. But did Lazarus want to be raised? And what happened to him after? Did they give him his job back? Were his friends afraid of him now? Was he able to just pop back into society where he left off? Or was he treated as a pariah, some strange,

ghostly figure the townsfolk would retreat from in fear and dread? And what if all of his closest friends also died—and *didn't* come back? And why him? Why him? Why was he chosen for such a dubious honor?

   [pause]

Lazarus Syndrome. That's an actual medical term. For all of us who rebounded, who bounced back, mere inches from the edge of the precipice. Those of us who spent a decade hanging on, some-how, for the thing we really never thought would happen, to be saved by a handful of pills. All those little pills. And the others are gone now, they're all gone. Including those people who fought for the thing that keeps me alive. And I take the big blue pills and the little white pills and the fat red pills, and magically I'm supposed to pick up right where I left off. I am Lazarus, brought back from the dead! I'm the Phoenix, risen from the ashes. I'm the cat with nine lives, the sole plane crash survivor, the last man standing. I'm on a tiny raft, and every moment I'm floating further and further away from the ship, from land, from people. And I'm waving and shouting, "I'm here! I'm here! Don't leave me behind!" But they're having a party and no one can hear me. "Let me come back," I'm shouting. And they sail past me, leaving me there, alone, on this raft, at sea. And I just...don't know...what to do with it anymore. With all of this...loss.

Emanuel Xavier
Walking With Angels
for Lindsay

AIDS
knows the condom wrapped penetration
of strangers and lovers, deep inside
only a tear away from risk

knows bare minimum t-cell level counts,
replacing intoxicating cocktails
with jagged little pills

knows how to avoid a cure thanks to war
how to keep pharmaceutical corporations
and doctors in business

AIDS
knows the weight loss desired by supermodels,
knows the fearless meaning
of a friends genuine kiss or hug
converts non-believers to religion and spirituality

comprehends loneliness
values the support of luminaries
smiles at the solidarity of single red ribbons

knows to dim the lights to elude detection
how to shame someone into hiding
from the rest of the world
to be grateful for the gift of clothing and shelter,
to remain silent,
holding back the anger and frustration

AIDS
knows that time on earth is limited for all of us
that using lemons to make lemonade is better than drinking the
Kool-Aid

but no matter how much you drink
you are always left dehydrated

knows working extensive hours
to pay hospital bills, the choice of survival
or taking pleasure in what is left of life

knows the solid white walls
you want to crash through and tear down
the thoughts of suicide in the back of your head

AIDS
knows the prosperous could be doing more
with their wealth
and that everyone still thinks it is a deserving fate—
for gays, drug addicts, prostitutes,
and the unfortunate children of such
born into a merciless world
of posh handbags and designer jewelry

knows how to be used as another percentage
to profit politicians
knows it doesn't only affect humans but animals too, without bias
-providing fodder for art
and something to be left behind

if there is a God
he has disregarded our prayers
left his angels behind to journey along with us
-none of us knowing exactly where we are headed

Brent Calderwood
Disclosure

I really did cry over spilt milk.
Sobbing at breakfast, napkin in hand,
the broken glass,
the blue skim slick
spread thin as my mother's money.
And when I slipped and skinned my knee, I cried
about the pants, ripped too large for patches.

When even my husky boys' jeans un-
snapped, I tried elastic waistbands.
No loops for the Cub Scout belt
that didn't fit anyway.
Each meeting, the Scouts got to watch
push-ups, my penalty for the incomplete uniform.

When my bike tire got caught in cable car tracks,
I flew forward onto the cracked asphalt
and a homeless man asked, *Are you alright?*
—*Yes, I'm fine.*
I walked my mangled bike back home. Gravel
in my legs for two years,
scaly and bumped beneath the surface.
A doctor told me,
When a foreign substance enters the body,
the body expels it or surrounds it in tissue;
it's called envagination.

This is all to say, I have a bad habit of apologizing for accidents.
Ejaculating almost feels that way.
Alone, I'll drowse, then stumble to the shower.

With visitors it is more formal.

I gently clean their bellies with warm facecloths.

Here, I say, wiping quickly, as if the stuff had the power to kill.

David-Matthew Barnes
Don't Mention It

Cast of Characters: **STELLA**, 60s: an eternal optimist; a
                        woman with a kind heart; a believer in
                        true love.
                        MADELINE, 60s: a sassy cynic; flippant
                        and often indignant; challenging.

Time: A Wednesday afternoon. The last week of September.

Place: The Port Washington stop on the Long Island Rail Road
near a section of Queens, New York.

[*At rise,* **MADELINE** *is anxious and pacing. She is carrying a glamorous train case and a purse that looks much
too heavy for her. A woman with an obsession for all things
crocheted, she is wearing a pale pink beret that she has
made herself. Her hair color, make up and presence are
extreme.*

MADELINE *checks a compartment in her purse to make
sure that something is still there.*

STELLA *enters from the opposite side of the stage. She
is carrying an overstuffed book bag, a gift from a library.
Her movements are slow. She seems stunned, dazed. At
first glance, it is obvious that* **STELLA** *is simpler and
more subdued than* **MADELINE***. She looks to the train
tracks, the horizon, the city as if she is seeing them for the
first time—or perhaps from a new perspective. She approaches* **MADELINE***.*

*Both women have been born and raised in Queens. This is
evident in their words.*]

MADELINE
Didn't I tell ya, Stella? I knew you would be late.

STELLA

Am I?

MADELINE

No, ya never are. But I would have left without ya. To teach ya a lesson. I swear I woulda.

STELLA

Maddie…I'm sorry.

MADELINE

Is it too much to ask? I mean, really? You coulda brought me an ice cream cone. You know I need it when I'm nervous.

STELLA

Where are we going again?

MADELINE

To my audition. For the opera. I've been preparing for this moment for my entire life.

> [**MADELINE** *starts to warm up her voice. In truth, her singing voice is awful.*]

STELLA

That's right. The opera.

> [**MADELINE** *opens the compartment in her purse again. She pulls out two train tickets.*]

I bought your train ticket for ya already. Ya can thank me later.

STELLA

I'll pay ya back.

MADELINE

Don't bother. I still owe ya for the hotel room in Atlantic City.

STELLA

Atlantic City?

MADELINE

Two years ago. Remember? What's the matter with you today?

STELLA

I forgot about Atlantic City.

MADELINE

Ya forgot about it? Stella, how could ya? It was our first vacation in twenty years and the last one we'll probably ever take if my ungrateful children have anything to say about it.

STELLA

Jimmy was going to go with us. He wanted to meet us there. I remember now. He was going to drive and meet us in Atlantic City. But there was that snow storm.

MADELINE

You spend too much with your grandson, if ya ask me.

STELLA

Maddie, you know what his mother's like.

MADELINE

She's Catholic. That's what's wrong with her. By the way, I'm giving up pinochle.

STELLA

[More to herself:] You're giving up?

MADELINE

Only because Elsa Feinstein is a backstabbing Yenta. She would sell her half-Irish mother to potato farmers just to win a game of pinochle.

STELLA

I won't give up.

MADELINE

What are ya talking about? You don't even play pinochle. You spend all your time volunteering at that library. You should make those bastards pay you for re-shelving all of those old books. And I still don't understand why ya never like to crochet. It's very relaxing. See how calm I am. Have ya noticed, yeah?

STELLA

I can't go with you, Maddie.

MADELINE

I didn't ask ya to. Elsa lives in Hicksville. I wouldn't dream of asking ya to make the trip with me. Since I know ya get nauseous and car sick and throw up all over yourself even on trains. You should see a doctor about that. It's just not normal. A girl's gotta drink more than club soda, Stella.

STELLA

[Suddenly; panicked:] Here. Take my ticket. I need to go.
          [**STELLA** *hands* **MADELINE** *back the ticket.]*

MADELINE

What are ya doing to me here? This could be my shot. You promised.

STELLA

I need to find Jimmy.

MADELINE

It's two o'clock in the afternoon. Jimmy's probably at work. Come on. Come with me to the audition. Then after we'll get a double scoop of mint chocolate chip at that ice cream place by The Garden then I'll go witcha to Jimmy's office. He's still working on Fifth Avenue making those funny computer commercials?

STELLA

No. Not today.

MADELINE

What? Is he home sick? It's probably that mother of his.

STELLA

She doesn't know yet. Only me.

MADELINE

[Realizing:] You're hiding something from me.

STELLA

The train—

MADELINE

It's not here yet, so talk. Something's happened, Stella.

STELLA

Jimmy's sick.

MADELINE

What? Like a cold? I've got an excellent recipe from Rebbetzin Farber. She's the one with hormonal problem so she has a beard but her recipes always work. I swear by it.

[**STELLA** *sits on a nearby bench.*]

STELLA

Maddie, Jimmy doesn't have a cold. *[Beat.]* He's got something much worse.
[**MADELINE** *sits next to her.*]

MADELINE

It's bad?

STELLA

It's real bad. *[Beat.]* Jimmy called me up this morning and said he needed to see me. He said it was important. I could hear it in his voice. This nervousness. It made me feel strange. Like he had to say something to me that would change everything for us. Of course I went to his apartment.

MADELINE

Of course.
STELLA

I knew the minute I saw him, Maddie. He was standing there in the doorway and he said, "Bubby, I knew you would come." Something about the way he looked at me—it chilled my blood. I haven't been able to catch my breath since.

*[**MADELINE** starts to search insider her train case for a remedy.]*

MADELINE
Maybe I should get you something—

STELLA
[Still in the moment, the memory:] I reached up. I touched his face. And the boy broke into a million tears. He cried harder then I've ever seen someone do. He said, "I'm real sick. I need you to know." I thought it was cancer. Maybe leukemia. I said, "Jimmy, tell me what's wrong."

MADELINE
Stella, what did he say?

STELLA
He said, "I have AIDS."

MADELINE
Oi, gevald.

STELLA
I just stood there and I had no idea what to say. No words would come to me, even though I was praying for them to. He said, "Please say something to me. Anything."

MADELINE
What did you do?
*[**STELLA** stands, walks to the edge of the tracks.]*

STELLA
I turned around and walked away.
MADELINE
Please tell me that you're lying. For once in your life.

STELLA
I wish I were. I came straight here. I walked all the way.

MADELINE

Jimmy's apartment is at least three miles from here.

STELLA

I had all of these memories of him. I walked and I remembered.
When he was young. I thought about how he used to love that
cereal that would turn his milk into chocolate. And how he was
the fastest jump roper on the block. That he used to love animals.
Especially ducks. He always asked me for a duck.

MADELINE

You could have stolen one for him. There's plenty of those bastards
in the park.

STELLA

My son doesn't know yet.

MADELINE

Jimmy hasn't told his father?

STELLA

I think I'm the first person in the family to know. Jimmy said
as much as I walked out the door. He was begging me, "Please!
Please don't tell my father."

MADELINE

But you have to.

STELLA

Do I?

MADELINE

What else can you do?

STELLA

I'm his grandmother.

MADELINE

Come on, Stella. You're more than that to Jimmy and you know it.
The two of you are like Siamese twins.

STELLA

Then how could I just walk away?

MADELINE

The kid dropped a ton of bricks on ya.

STELLA

I should be with him.

MADELINE

Go on then.

STELLA

You'll forgive me?

MADELINE

This is the first time you've let me down in forty years. I think I'll
live.

STELLA

I'll make it up to ya.

MADELINE

Yeah, well I'll save ya a seat in the front row at the opera.

STELLA

[After a moment:] I'm not sure about this, Maddie. I don't know if
I can handle something like this. I mean, with Walter—it happened
so fast. You know, boom. A heart attack. But this…I might not
know what to do. That boy…he's my heart and soul.

> *[After a moment,* **MADELINE** *puts both train tickets back
> into her purse.]*

MADELINE

I'll make you a deal.

STELLA

I'm listening.

MADELINE

Just so you don't screw up and say the wrong thing, I'll go witcha.

STELLA

But the audition. The opera.

MADELINE

Stella, I love you to death, but let's be honest here. I might be a good looking woman, but I'm no Beverly Sills.

STELLA

I wasn't going to say anything but—

MADELINE

But you think I stink?

STELLA

I like your hat. Will you make me one?

MADELINE

You betcha.

STELLA

Maybe you can sing for Jimmy. He's always loved you so.

MADELINE

Jimmy has a heart of gold. Just like you.

STELLA

That's why I need to be there, to take care of him.

MADELINE

You won't be alone.

STELLA

I know.

> *[The two women share a look that speaks volumes about their friendship.]*

MADELINE

Now...I think we should stop by the park and grab a duck. It'll probably fit in my purse.

STELLA

Do you really think this is the time to bring Jimmy a pet?

MADELINE

There will be plenty of time for tears later, Stella. Right now, Jimmy needs to laugh...and a double scoop of mint chocolate chip.

STELLA

I think that's possible.
[They start to exit.]

MADELINE

Don't think I didn't notice how ya changed the subject on me.

STELLA

Maddie, not every one can be an opera star. *[Beat.]* Or a grandmother.

MADELINE

No...not everybody.

[Lights fade to black.]

CURTAIN

Phillip Brian Williams

Erosion

As you die, a withering
monument, I gather you pore
by pore into my arms.
Collect you and rock the crown
of your offering—night sweats, your
thinning frame, you slipping
through my fingers like battered clay.

I count clusters of onyx petals
inking your flesh,
recumbent roses of night. I soothe
your scoured creases, seams
of skin once soaked
by my spiral tongue

Tomorrow-touch my palm
Map out a path through
valences of silence outlined
in your clairvoyant hands
I will cradle your evicting
house, trembling in its own
crevasse of winter

To barely recognize you by memory alone (body
too quietly disfigured to recollect what once was)
must be suffered through bushel by piercing
bushel, the thorny foliage of failure un-evidenced
in Time's passage. This hospice allows nothing
private. Not your awakening nor your dreams

of insipid lovers, siblings to
your embattlement. Imperfect
vessels thoroughly wrapped
in secrecy. Had words extended
between lovers like stable batons perhaps

this visit would be innocuous speech
suspended from your earlobe. But regret
is a spoiled child, taffied fingers perched
in his mouth, rotten.

We shall hush this child, embrace
this moment, place
it in an hour glass
sift it to and fro
Watch each infinitesimal grain
fall dismally between cells
as if the final sand
was the hand clenching your collar
demanding you hold on
for another go round

Joy Gaines-Friedler
Morning

A flower

The color of dawn

In the shade of a hosta leaf

A sigh

A minor chord

Forgiveness

In the first bit of glow

When the edge of

Pine trees take shape

A renewal

A faith in light

The hosta

Gold againt its own shade

Like a friend

Or lover

Like a word

Such as, *thinking*

And, *you.*

Tricia Crawford Coscia

The Dog Knows

Wasn't it just yesterday?
We were laughing at the shoes,
found when we tilled that place
under the trees where the Indian
Paint Brush keeps taking over.
Dog-buried boots and sandals,
muddied, missing halves of pairs.

Now you are still, with folded hands.
Someone in the line says,
"At least they didn't give him
a fake smile." If the dog were here,
he'd be licking your face.

Your friends gather in the usual place,
outside your garage, without you.
Only your motorcycle, your tool bench
organized and shining with chrome
and clean peg-board, not even one
cigarette ash.

The dog won't go outside,
won't come barking to the fence
to beg a beer or a bite of steak.
Everyone is wearing suits
and dresses, and you are gone.

In dog years, he is older than you
ever became, snoring deep dog
dreams. A motorcycle roars past
and he lifts his head, hoping,
for something big
thrown over the fence—
a trash can lid, the old baby pool,
or just a glimpse of you.

No one else quite knows
how to play.

I remember you, at the fence,
snapping these pictures:
Sam, pissing in the hydrangeas,
naked except for his rain boots.
(You said, "I hope I taught him that.")
Ella, with her Sharpie tattoos,
the cowering dog,
cornered by a groundhog.

We were laughing.

Ronald Aden Alexander
I'm Not Going to Clean My Room Anymore

I'm not going to clean my room anymore.
I'm not going to clean the house.
It's a waste of time
to wash clothes and dishes
when tomorrow they'll just be soiled again.
I have better things to do.
I have appointments to miss
and people to flee.
I have worries to ruminate over and over and
over and a computer to keep
on life support.
I have an overgrown garden that demands ignoring,
a faithful lover who requires avoiding,
petulant gods that must be denied
and two demanding
calicos that tolerate none of the above.

To procrastinate, to do it well
takes effort and commitment.
To put off the essential,
to focus on the inconsequential
Is an art not lost on me.
But I will excel.
I will decide not to decide,
and pursue the life I was born to live.

I will spare my heirs the burden of a long
obituary, too many accomplishments to list.
I will leave this life undone, unnoticed,
unaccomplished at the meanest
tasks and enter eternity peacefully,
blissfully laid out in my sleek
stainless steel coffin.

Mourners will ask, "Did he ever finish
anything? that novel?
that poem?
that sentence?"
Devotees will find inspiration in the works
I never produced,
the autobiography unwritten
and I will pass into oblivion except, perhaps,
in the heartless ruminations
of those damned cats.

Raymond Luczak

Two Decades and then Some

No one writes about the dead anymore.
The fear of infection and loss isn't so dramatic now.
Pills are today's answer to everything.
Each month brings us new findings,
often conflicting with each other. No matter.
Progress, progress is being steadily made!
The last person I know who died of it went five years ago.
Nowadays men advertise condom-free encounters.
Death's now a punch line to a joke that no one gets.

Two decades ago I stared, trying not to vomit
when far too many patients lined up,
the purple splotches tattooing their stick arms
reaching out for God, Allah, Zeus—anything!
Their craggy faces cried surrender
to the rivulets of toxins slithering like snakes
inside their skins swelling pus by the hour.
But I was no Florence Nightingale.
I was too scared of quarantine with them.

Back then, no one could figure out anything.
These dying men became a circus of experiments,
one toxic drug trial after another. Nurses wouldn't
enter their rooms with their trays of food. I saw
friends wither away like bitter rosebushes in winter.
I fought nights not to masturbate. Mornings
I found my body outlined in sweaty salts
on my black futon sheets, scenes of a crime.
Long acquitted, I find the dead still sleeping in my bed.

Jeni Booker Senter

Scent of a Woman

For days I touched you,
your moist feverish skin,
rubbed your swollen saffron
limbs with almond-scented oil.
I breathed prayers rhythmically
to the hypnotic sound
of the machines tethering you
to my world.
Family members whispered—
making plans
at the foot of your bed
while "What a Wonderful World" played
faintly in the background.
As you calmly gave up
your last breath
I cried silently
and took my leave from your side.
Selfish as I am
I took that bottle of almond-scented oil.
And sometimes I slowly remove
the stopper
and breathe in
what is left of you.

Jim Nawrocki

Shades

> Inspired by the filming of Gus Van Sant's film
> *Milk*, in San Francisco's Castro district, January,
> 2008

They brought back facades from thirty years ago:
the camera shop and Toad Hall. They parked old Chevys,
old VWs and old Fords, up and down the hill.
Each morning, each evening, I walked through the 1970s.

The past can be as present as a light you switch on,
or walk into. One night I watched Sean Penn climb atop a wall
to rally a crowd the way Harvey did. I stood in the chill
beside the machinery of illusion—a line of police dividing us.

This was a season of the walking dead, and I wondered
if any of those, gone now twenty years, might be there too,
staring out through bar glass and walking within
that remade river of candlelight. Or maybe only waiting,

like those men I passed every morning each one
with a black jacket marked, SECURITY, each one
bored, lounging, and dozing beside the big white trucks,
guarding the apertures of memory.

c m mclamb

a small victory

It is three weeks
after being told of
his newly risen counts,
two weeks
after my official
undetectable diagnosis,
and the first time
we've returned to making
truly passionate love.

We are once again
full of each other
as we lay down to rest,
coiled around curves,
nestled into folds,
fingers entwined,
caramel skin pressed
against soft, wooly hair;
safe for the moment
from the fire fighting
to spawn within.

Patricia McFarland

Golden Gate Operator Services—1983

When the first one came, I knew there would be more.
Some looking at the ground, some with plaintive eyes.
Some couldn't ask, but when I took their hands
They felt the baby move and were so close to life.

Gifts and gladiolas, baby shower laughter.
A celebration of life.

Most were young, some beautiful, some funny, some kind.
Not the artists, not the famous, but the boys Foucault killed.
Some went home. Some stayed. And one went off the roof.
But one by one they were gone too far from life.

"Mom, what's up with gays? It's like they sniff me out."
"And years ago they breathed you in and filled their lungs with life."

Timmothy J. Holt

Crying

"You cry but harm nothing in yourself."
Tony Kushner, *Angels in American Part Two: Perestroika*

Those tears aren't real
they're not from your well
only borrowed and now returned
like rain on a sunny day
noticed but soon gone
not even sufficient to nourish growth.
Go ahead though, cry
return what's not yours
we can use the water.

Don't pretend its grief
don't think you really know
don't tell me of sorrow
don't mention a word
look elsewhere
with your lamenting eyes
only look at me again
only talk to me again
when the waters come from your well
only when you thirst to drink.

Chuck Willman

Making Stephen's Panel
in Memory of Stephen Allen Love, 3/19/53–4/9/99

Stephen was my husband's ex-lover, his first real relationship in the glory days of the 1970s when being queer was no longer an illness, and the celebration lasted a few years.

They met and lived together in college, but, after several years, parted ways, though always remaining close friends. When I met my husband I had never had a *relationship* with a man,

only short-term affairs, and many forgettable one-night stands. I was so jealous and threatened of *their* bond, believing a break-up was *final* like the divorces I knew in my family—permanent,

bitter, dead—and I wasn't sure *how* to love someone with the ghost of his past hovering over so closely. But Stephen accepted me, gently teaching me *how* to be gay; what *gay love* was really

about: a band of brothers bound together by bigotry, breaking boundaries with equal parts of respect, and a determination to *become equal*; loving each other always, a steadfast rule.

I got used to his phone calls, trips to see him, his trips to visit us, and I grew to love him. He became part of *our* family—my gay big brother—even traveling with us in 1993

for the March On Washington, where my husband and I joined thousands in a protest wedding that turned out to be more important to us than we expected. Stephen, wrapped in an American

flag and wearing a white cowboy hat, marched proudly, and wished us many years of happiness together, like any family member would. When we returned home we held a reception to

celebrate, though members of our *real* families wouldn't attend. And we faced death threats from local bigots after we allowed a news channel and newspapers to document our nuptials.

When Stephen started getting sick, he had friends and help around, and we visited each other as often as we could. He told me once, while visiting us in Las Vegas—he loved the glitz, camp,

and a good drag show—that I would need outside support when *I* got sick; that while my husband was a compassionate, gentle soul, he could never handle *the dying*. Stephen wasn't

being mean, just honest, like a big brother, making sure I was prepared. When he died, I knew what he meant. We decided to remember him with a panel for the AIDS Memorial Quilt, that

needles and thread tombstone growing each day. We used his favorite jeans, lots of beads and sequins, and the photograph of him standing proudly, wrapped in the American flag,

as well as other photos proving he had been on this earth. Then we made the difficult, but necessary trip to deliver the panel, releasing it—and Stephen—to the world the last year

the entire Quilt was displayed on the National Mall in Washington, D.C. We've since seen that special panel at AIDS Walks, in calendars, and other places in complete surprise, as if

Stephen's following us; still our brother cheering us on, helping us to march proudly forward. That's how he lived. How he loved. We miss him, and wish he were still here. *I* wish Stephen

could help me navigate the illness that will take me, too, someday. And I wish he could be here to help my husband make my panel.

Rob Zukowski
Test Run

It was the summer of 1987 and I was newly out. Like any 20 year old having just thrust open the closet doors, I was looking for experiences and adventures. I'd spent my young life nestled in suburbia, living between the northern-most Bronx and southern-most Westchester. In the early days of my gay life, I frequented an assortment of bars and dance clubs in North Jersey, Westchester, Rockland and Connecticut. I was bored with the white crunch socks, pastel colored shirts, piano bars, penny loafers and fruity drinks that were the gay 80s. I wanted something different—something with an edge and darker than I was accustomed to; just a little bit dangerous.

There was one bar in particular that I'd read about in the local fag rags; a very popular cruise bar along the West Side Highway. It was rumored, at least among the suburban gays, to be the wildest of the wild. I remember hearing one, very dramatic and detailed description of the establishment from a drag performer I knew. "It's a bar where men collect; wild, easy men; limitless and erotic." she told me. "If you are looking for fantasy after fantasy, with only enough time in between experiences for another cold beer and a quick clean up with a moist towelette, it's the place to be." She told me that the weekends were mostly leather and Levi's: rough sex, fetish, bondage and discipline. It was extreme for my tastes at the time but I was intrigued. She regaled me with stories of impromptu invitations to casual sex romps featuring a plethora of lust, flesh, fetish and kink. She spoke of men meeting men at the bar, leaving for sexual encounters and then coming back for more. There were rendezvous in dark alleys and groping on dimly lit side streets surrounding the bar. "If you can't find in the back room of this establishment," she said, "you won't find it anywhere." I couldn't help but fantasize, which lead to a plan.

I was excited. This would be a new experience for me. I lied to my friends that night and told them that I was staying home. The possibilities presented by a night like this at a place such as that were something I needed to explore alone. With the smell of the Hudson River seeping through my windows, I drove down the West Side Highway en route to the sin I craved. Upon arrival, I made my way through a maze of men to the chipped, wooden bar and ordered a cheap beer. I took every advantage of my slim and youthful station in life groping my way through the myriad of men in my path; stopping occasionally to hold a glance, consider a suggestion, and enjoy an inappropriate touch.

It was all that I heard it was and more. I was prompted to do things I'd never even heard of. Ideas were exchanged and possibilities presented that were completely unknown to me. Yet, I considered them all. After numerous drinks, ample experimentation and even more invitations I weighed further options. I smirked on my way the restroom. I was satisfied with myself. In spite of the goings-on around me I was cool and unaffected. Not bad for a newbie. Not bad at all. As I stood in the dimly lit rest room relieving myself, I glanced up for a moment noticing a photo hanging on the wall over the urinal. It was an ad of some sort in a tarnished, faux metallic frame. I leaned slightly forward and squinted to read the content. I moved my head to the side to see past the glow of the bathrooms bare light bulb reflecting on the dirty plastic cover over the image.

It was a picture of two men having anal sex. Both men were well built, smooth, pretty and young; very much exciting examples of the stereotypes each of their sexual roles suggested. There were text bubbles over each of their heads. Over the bottom's head it said "He must be negative too, he didn't wear a condom." And, in the bubble over the top's head, it said "He must be positive too, he didn't ask me to use a condom." I was stunned. Almost, I'd go so far as to say, distraught.

There are moments in life when everything changes. These are the moments you'll always remember with distinct clarity and razor sharp detail. Even years later, these are the memories that evoke that same swell of emotion they did the very first time. You'll stop to catch your breath. Call these moments realizations if you will. Call them an awakening or an epiphany. Or, simply call it the moment you woke up. But, I can assure you, whatever you call it, you have no other choice but to acknowledge it because that moment becomes a part of you, like it or not.

I've spent a lot of time, and a good number of therapy sessions trying to figure out what happened that night. What demons did that image awaken inside me? My best guess is what I call "cigarette commercial syndrome." We've all seen those quit smoking television commercials; the really explicit ones. There's the one with the man with the hole in his throat as a result of cancer, who misses swimming and talks about almost drowning in the shower. Or the one with the lady with her fingers and toes cut off, whose children are embarrassed by her appearance. I think that night in the bar produced the same effect; that recipe of explicit factors and obvious details that fall into place and drive a point home.

I stood there in the restroom for a moment, lost in thought and gripped with fear. Someone came from behind me, reached around, and grabbed me. He lifted my shirt with one hand and pulled my body back against his with the other. That was, after all, what I was there for. But I panicked. I thrust backward and pushed him away. I ran through the crowd past the men I'd played with and promised more. I ran through the leather-padded doors and went home. Welcome to the birth of a phobia. There's cake. Did you bring a gift?

In the years that followed, even more than a decade, my life and the way I lived it had been altered. These are years that I can never have back. I was stricken with a fear of HIV and AIDS so debilitating that it seeped into every aspect of my life. Everything suffered. Not only was my relationship with myself an exercise in self-inflicted emotional abuse, but my outer relationships and intimate encounters were only shadows of what they could have been. I didn't have sex, at least not in any traditional or common form. When I was intimate I was never really present for the encounter as my mind was inundated with worry. I refused anything beyond mutual masturbation. Even then, I agonized over every hangnail and paper cut. When I did go so far as to indulge in anything even slightly more than mutual masturbation, I was thrown into a state of anxiety and panic so severe that it would last for weeks or sometimes months. Penetrative sex was physically impossible for me due to emotional turmoil it accompanied. On the rare occasions that I tried, I became so petrified that I would lose my erection and flee the situation. As you might imagine, this made dating impossible. Not only due to my unwillingness to partake in most sexual activity, but to my refusal to be tested. I was afraid to know.

Perpetually single and sexually unsatisfied I immersed myself into a subculture of fetish and alternative sexuality. It seemed only logical to me to explore the world of kink in an attempt to add back to my sex life what fear and my abstinence had taken away. Often times, the focal point of fetish isn't about oral or anal gratification, it's about the bondage, the uniform, or the foot fetish, to name a few. It was a comfort to me to be able to experience some form of intimacy and sexuality, knowing that I couldn't be infected by the rope, police baton, or someone sucking on my toes. Make no mistake, I enjoyed the exploration. I was thrilled with new experiences and even found an assortment of kinks I that I truly enjoyed. In the end however, they only masked the greater problem.

Every birthmark and blemish that appeared on my flesh, in my mind, was a skin cancer caused by HIV. One occurrence stands out above the rest. I noticed a small brown patch of skin on my chest that I'd either never seen before, or that I hadn't recalled seeing. It was my focal point for weeks. I looked at it every day, watching for growth or change. Fear and panic will make you do crazy things. One day, so deeply depressed and frightened, I took a pair of scissors and cut it from my own body. I cut so deeply, that I required stitches.

Every sneeze, cold, and cough was a signal that the end was near. If I lost a pound or two, I'd binge on food only to prove to myself that I could gain weight. I avoided seeing doctors whenever I could, based upon the fear that whatever was wrong was HIV or AIDS related. I suffered through many an untreated infection, cold, flu and illness. I held a daily, constant fear of death and dying and sank into a very deep, constant depression.

More than a decade after that night in the bar I'd come to live with my emotional turmoil. There's a line in the movie *Torch Song Trilogy* where Anne Bancroft tells Harvey Fierstein, after losing his partner to a hate crime, that losing someone is like learning to wear a pair of eyeglasses or a ring. You get used to it. And this, no matter how tortured, no matter how phobic, was my ring. I stopped dating. I avoided those who pursued me and never set my sights on anyone whose needs, physically or emotionally, would upset my delicate balance fear and self-preservation. I was accustomed to sexual rejections and failed relationships. I resigned myself to being single and to living in the shadows of fetish and kink. Fear, anxiety and depression were my normal emotions. No matter how tortured my life was, it was my life to live.

It had been more than a decade since I'd seen a doctor and one day something went wrong. I have mild heart condition, in the sense that with treatment and medication, it can be controlled. Yet, I shied away from medical attention due to the belief that if they just looked, they'd find something. My doctor scheduled an appointment for me to have comprehensive blood work. As the nurse drew my blood I asked what they would be testing for. She ran through the battery of tests the doctor had ordered which included an HIV test. I lied and told the nurse that I'd recently been tested and refused the HIV test. He made the necessary notes on my chart and assured me that he'd tell the doctor that I'd opted out of the test. A week later I returned for my results. The doctor went through my report with me; blood sugar, cholesterol, etc. He continued with all negative results for assorted STIs and concluded his report with the proclamation of HIV-negative. The nurse had made a mistake and ordered the test. I started to shake. I could barely breathe. For the very first time I told someone my story. Through tears and gasps for breath I told the doctor everything. I was calm by the time I finished. He listened, between his profuse apologies for the error, to every word I said and offered me the kind of comfort and support I wished I'd sought more than a decade ago.

I can't help but think back to the life I didn't lead. I can't help but regret the experiences and the relationships I didn't have. There are, unquestionably, things that I missed. The days, weeks, months and years I spent consumed by worry and fear is time that I could have been living or loving. It's time that I can never have back. I'll always wonder who and what passed me by when I was living so deeply in my fear that I couldn't escape, or let anyone in for that matter.

All these years later I am still HIV-negative. I still see that very same doctor and every six months I am tested for HIV. Rest assured, I'm still scared, old habits die hard. But I recall what the doctor said to me after I told him how very much of my life I'd lost to my phobia. "No matter what the results may have been, maybe this is the universe telling you that it's time, and it's OK, to live your life."

BIOGRAPHIES

Moved to discontinue his practice in psychology by an AIDS diagnosis, **Ronald Aden Alexander** returned to his first love, poetry, which he abandoned years earlier after a tepid critique by a composition professor. After a couple of years back in the saddle, his award-winning work has been published in *A&U, ASKEW*, and the anthology, *A Bird as Black as the Sun: California Poets on Crows & Ravens* (Green Poet Press). He reads at venues on California's central coast and created and organizes the annual Whitman-Stein Poetry Fest in Santa Barbara. Ron lives with his very accommodating lover of over two decades and their calico cats, Sofie and Maxine.

Aldo Alvarez is the author of *Interesting Monsters: fictions*. He teaches English full time at Wilbur Wright College and, on occasion, creative writing in Northwestern University's MFA program. He has a PhD in English from SUNY Binghamton and an MFA in Creative Writing from Columbia University.

Poet and playwright **Rane Arroyo** was born in Chicago in 1954 and began his career as a performance artist. His eleven poetry collections include *The Singing Shark* (1997), which won the Carl Sandburg Poetry Prize, and *The Portable Famine* (2004), which won the John Ciardi Poetry Prize. Widely published, Arroyo was also honored with a Pushcart Prize and received a fellowship from the Ohio State Arts Council. His other works include numerous plays and a book of short stories, *How to Name a Hurricane* (2005). Receiving his PhD from the University of Pittsburgh, Arroyo taught at the University of Toledo. He died in 2010.

David-Matthew Barnes is the bestselling author of twelve novels and several collections of stage plays, poetry, short stories, and monologues. Two of his young adult novels have been recognized by the American Library Association for their diversity. His first feature film, the coming-of-age drama *Frozen Stars*, received worldwide distribution. He has written over forty stage plays that have been performed in three languages in eight countries. His literary work has been featured in over one hundred publications. He was selected by Kent State University as the national winner of the Hart Crane Memorial Poetry Award. He earned a Master of Fine Arts degree in Creative Writing at Queens University of Charlotte in North Carolina. He is a member of the Dramatists Guild of America, the Horror Writers Association, International Thriller Writers, Romance Writers of America, and the Society of Children's Book Writers and Illustrators. He has been a teacher for nearly a decade, instructing college courses in writing, literature, and the arts.

Patrick Barnes has been a composer with The 52nd Street Project since 1998. He wrote the book, music and lyrics for the musicals *Scarlet Street, The Zoltan Oberammergau Songbook,* and *Frankly Anne* (the musical of *The Diary of Anne Frank* as done by Walt Disney). He composed the score for *The Ha Ha Club* (NY Fringe Festival), and has written many songs for revues and cabarets. Other collaborations with Craig Lucas include The Conversion and Al Fresco.

David Bergman is the author of *Heroic Measures* and *Cracking the Code*, winner of the George Elliston Poetry Prize. He has also edited John Ashbery's *Reported Sightings* and Edmund White's *The Burning Library*. He teaches at Towson University in Maryland.

Mark Bibbins is the author of *They Don't Kill You Because They're Hungry, They Kill You Because They're Full* (Copper Canyon Press, 2014), *The Dance of No Hard Feelings* (Copper Canyon Press, 2009) and the Lambda Award–winning *Sky Lounge*. He lives in New York City and teaches at Columbia University and at The New School, where he co-founded *LIT* magazine. He edits the poetry section of *The Awl*.

Jeni Booker Senter is a poet, essayist, teacher, and journalist devoted to the advancement of women. She is a member of NOW and AAUW. Her writing has earned awards in the Duque Wilson Essay Contest and the LaRoche Memorial Poetry Contest, and she is a contributor to *NW Florida Business Climate, Blackwater Review Literary Journal, Journal of South Texas Studies, Socialist Women Magazine: International Women's Day Edition, A&U,* and *Troubadour*. In addition, she recently presented papers at the third Annual

High School Articulation Conference and the Pop-Culture Conference at Austin, Texas. Jeni has a first cousin with AIDS, a situation which greatly influences her writing.

From Savannah, GA, poet, novelist, playwright, and activist **Perry Brass** has published 16 books, winning awards for his poetry, plays, and fiction, and has been involved in the LGBT movement since 1969, when he co-edited *Come Out!*, the world's first gay liberation newspaper. In 1972, he co-founded the Gay Men's Health Project Clinic, the first clinic for gay men on the East Coast, still operating as New York's Callen-Lourde Community Health Center. Brass's work often deals with that intersection of sexuality, spirituality and personal politics that came directly out of his involvement with the radical queer consciousness of the late 1960s and early 1970s. His latest book is *King of Angels*, a Southern-gay-Jewish coming-of-age novel set in Savannah in 1963. He is currently a coordinator of the Rainbow Book Fair, the oldest LGBT book fair in the U.S. Visit www.perrybrass.com.

Brent Calderwood's poems have appeared in *American Poetry Journal*, *The Gay & Lesbian Review Worldwide*, and in the anthologies *Poets Eleven, Solace in So Many Words*, and *Divining Divas*. He is the Literary Editor for *A&U*, Associate Editor at LambdaLiterary.org and Bay Area Editor for the journal *Locuspoint*. Visit www.brentcalderwood.com.

Alex Cigale's poems have appeared in *Colorado Review*, *The Common Online*, *Green Mountains Review*, *McSweeney's*, *The Literary Review*, and *32 Poems*. His translations from the Russian can be found in *Cardinal Points*, *Cimarron Review*, *Literary Imagination*, *Modern Poetry in Translation*, *New England Review*, and *PEN America*. He is a 2014–2015 NEA Translation Fellow. Ted Rifkin was the Chair of the English Department at the Bronx High School of Science. An early casualty of AIDS (d. 1984), he is the reason Cigale became a poet.

Tricia Crawford Coscia has worked for non-profit arts and human services organizations as an educator, event and program coordinator, and grant writer. She lives with her husband and three children, and currently works for her spiritual community, Philadelphia Meeting of the Religious Society of Friends (Quakers). Coscia writes on the train while commuting to and from work and in the early hours of the morning. Much of her work experience involved working with people with physical, cognitive and emotional challenges and their stories and spirits influence her writing. One of her earliest professional jobs was working on the Art Against AIDS campaign in the late 1980s.

Louie Clay (né Crew), an Alabama native, is an emeritus professor at Rutgers. He lives in East Orange, NJ, with Ernest Clay, his husband of over three decades. Crew has edited special issues of *College English* and *Margins*. He has written four poetry volumes *Sunspots* (Lotus Press), *Midnight Lessons* (Samisdat), *Lutibelle's Pew* (Dragon Disk), and *Queers! for Christ's Sake!* (Dragon Disks). Visit http://rci.rutgers/edu/~lcrews/pubs.html.

Migdalia Cruz is an award-winning playwright who has written more than forty plays, operas, screenplays, translations and musicals including: *El Grito Del Bronx, TWO ROBERTS: a Pirate-Blues Project, Fur, Miriam's Flowers, Another Part of the House*, and *Cigarettes & Moby-Dick*, produced in NY venues as diverse as BAM, Classic Stage Company & Mabou Mines, also, National Theater of Greece/Athens, Old Red Lion/London, Houston Grand Opera, Ateneo Puertorriqueño, & Latino Chicago Theater Company where she was writer-in-residence from 1991 to 1998. She was nurtured by Sundance, the Lark and Teatro Vista, is an alumna of New Dramatists, and was mentored by Maria Irene Fornés at INTAR where she is currently at work on *Satyricoño 21*. Migdalia was born and raised in the Bronx.

Jameson Currier is the author of five novels, including *Where the Rainbow Ends, The Wolf at the Door*, and *The Third Buddha*; and four collections of short fiction: *Dancing on the Moon: Short Stories about AIDS; Desire, Lust, Passion, Sex; Still Dancing: New and Selected Stories*; and *The Haunted Heart and Other Tales*. His AIDS-themed short stories have been translated into French by Anne-Laure Hubert and published as *Les Fantômes* and he is the author of the documentary, *Living Proof: HIV and the Pursuit of Happiness*, based on the photography project by Carolyn Jones. His reviews, essays, interviews, and articles on AIDS and gay culture have been published in many national and local publications, including *The Washington Post, The Los Angeles Times, Newsday, The Washington Blade, Bay Area Reporter, A&U,* and *Body Positive.* In 2010 he founded Chelsea Station Editions, an independent press devoted to gay literature. In 2013 the press brought out two anthologies of original work that he edited: *With: New Gay Fiction* and *Between: New Gay Poetry.*

Born in 1950, **Tim Dlugos** was involved in the Mass Transit poetry scene in Washington, D.C., and later, in New York City, in the downtown literary scene. His books include *Entre Nous, Strong Place,* and *Powerless.* His collection of poems, *A Fast Life,* was edited by David Trinidad. Dlugos died of AIDS at the age of forty. *A Fast Life: The Collected Poems of Tim Dlugos* was published by Nightboat Books in Spring 2011 and is available at amazon.com and in many fine bookstores. The collection won the Lambda Literary Award for Gay Poetry for 2011 (in 2012).

An eight-time Pushcart Prize nominee, **Jéanpaul Ferro**'s work has appeared on National Public Radio, in *Contemporary American Voices, Columbia Review, Emerson Review, Connecticut Review, Sierra Nevada Review,* and others. He is the author of *All The Good Promises* (Plowman Press); *Becoming X* (BlazeVox Books); *You Know Too Much About Flying Saucers* (Thumbscrew Press); *Hemispheres* (Maverick Duck Press); *Essendo Morti—Being Dead* (Goldfish Press), nominated for the 2010 Griffin Prize in Poetry; and the recently released *Jazz* (Honest Publishing). He has been nominated for a Pushcart Prize nine times. Visit www.jeanpaulferro.com.

Charneice Fox Richardson is an award-winning screenwriter, producer, and director of film and theater. She is the Chief Creative Director of the multi-media organization, Straight, No Chaser Productions. Her work has been featured on CNN, The BBC, NBC, NPR, CBS and BET. She is the director of the highly anticipated documentary *The MLK Streets Project.* Her poetry has been published in several anthologies and magazines, including the critically acclaimed *Growing Up Girl.* In 2010 Charneice directed Ntzoke

Shange's classic *For Colored Girls Who Have Considered Suicide When the Rainbow is Enuf* for the inaugural D.C. Black Theatre Festival, to wonderful reviews. She wrote and directed the one act stage play *Rose Bushes and Machetes* which won Best Ensemble at the 2011 Maryland State One-Act Competition. *Rose Bushes* was invited to travel internationally by the American Academy of Community Theaters. Her biggest artistic accomplishment is being a mom to Noah and Nigel and step-mom to Kaya and Mathias.

Lisa Freedman writes and teaches in New York City. Her work has appeared in *The New York Times*, *A&U* and *POZ*. She has also written for and performed with the AIDS Theatre Project. She is currently at work on a memoir called *Culebra Means Snake*.

Samuel R. Friedman is Director of the Institute for Infectious Disease Research at National Development and Research Institutes, Inc. and the Director of the Interdisciplinary Theoretical Synthesis Core in the Center for Drug Use and HIV Research, New York City. He has worked in HIV epidemiology and prevention research since 1983. He has published many poems in a variety of publications. He is the author of three poetry chapbooks, *Murders most foul: Poems against war by a World Trade Center survivor* and *A Turnpike Utopia: Poems to resist environmental destruction for profit and war* (both Central Jersey Coalition against Endless War) and *Needles, drugs, and defiance: Poems to organize by* (North American Syringe Exchange Network). He has also published the full-length collection *Seeking to make the world anew: Poems of the Living Dialectic* (Hamilton Books).

For over twenty years **Joy Gaines-Friedler** earned her living as a photographer in the Detroit area. For her, the distance between camera lens and page is slim. Her poetry is widely published and has won numerous awards including First Place in the 2006 *Litchfield Review* contest for a series of poems based on the journal of her friend Jim who died from AIDS. Additionally, her work has been published in *The Driftwood Review*, *Margie*, *The Pebble Lake Review*, *RATTLE*, *The New York Quarterly*, and other literary journals. Joy teaches poetry for InsideOut Literary Arts Project, which puts poets into Detroit Public Schools and for Springfed Arts, which provides creative writing workshops for adults. She also works with young adults "at risk" at The Common Ground Sanctuary for Families in Crisis. Her first book of poetry *Like Vapor* was published by Mayapple Press. Visit www.joygainesfriedler.com

Diane Goettel is the Executive Editor of Black Lawrence Press. Diane studied fiction writing at Sarah Lawrence College and has a Masters in English from Brooklyn College. She lives in Hong Kong with her husband and a Doberman named Spoon.

Craig G. Harris was a journalist, fiction writer, and poet whose work has been anthologized in *Freedom in This Village: Twenty-Five Years of Black Gay Men's Writing, 1979 to the Present; In the Life: A Black Gay Anthology; Lyric: Poems Along a Broken Road; Taking Liberties: Gay Men's Essays on Politics, Culture, and Sex; Brother to Brother: New Writings by Black Gay Men; Gay Life, New Men, New Minds,* and *Tongues Untied.* He was also a community health educator, AIDS conference coordinator, and staff member of Gay Men's Health Crisis. Harris died of AIDS-related complications in 1991.

A native of Worcestershire, **Christopher Hewitt** emigrated from England to the United States in 1974. He received an undergraduate degree from University of Birmingham in England in 1971 and went on to earn master's degrees in English and Creative Writing from UC Davis and the Iowa Writer's Workshop at University of Iowa. Over the course of his career as a writer, he published poems and translations in *The New Yorker, American Poetry Review, The Advocate, The James White Review,* and *BENT,* among others. His work has been anthologized in *Queer Crips: Disabled Gay Men Tell Their Stories.* At the time of his death, he was working on a memoir titled *Brittle Bones,* in part about living with osteogenesis imperfecta. He taught writing at University of San Francisco, Fordham University and John Jay College of Criminal Justice, among others. Hewitt helped inaugurate *A&U*'s premiere issue and filled several editorial posts at the magazine, including Literary Editor, until his death in 2004 at the age of fifty-eight.

Marc Elihu Hofstadter has a B.A. from Swarthmore College, a Ph.D. from the University of California at Santa Cruz, and an

M.L.S. from the University of California at Berkeley. He has taught at Santa Cruz, the Université d'Orléans, and Tel Aviv University. He has published five volumes of poetry and one of essays. He lives with his partner David Zurlin in Walnut Creek, California.

William M. Hoffman is the author of *As Is*, which earned him a Drama Desk Award in 1986, an Obie, as well as Tony and Pulitzer nominations for best play. He also wrote the libretto to *The Ghosts of Versailles* (music by John Corigliano), which premiered at the Metropolitan Opera in 1991. Hoffman received a Guggenheim Fellowship, three National Endowment Awards, ASCAP and Fund for New American Plays awards, and two grants from the New York Foundation for the Arts. In 1992 his television work brought him an Emmy nomination and he received a Writers Guild award. In 2001 he premiered *The Cows of Apollo*, with composer Chris Theofanidis, at the Brooklyn Academy of Music; in 2002 he wrote *Morning Star* with Ricky Ian Gordon for the Lyric Opera of Chicago. January 2009 saw the world premiere of *Cornbury*. He is the host and Artistic Director of Conversations With William M. Hoffman, seen on CUNY-TV. He is Professor of Theatre at Lehman College.

A retired physician, **Timmothy J. Holt** is interested in the intersection of science and art, particularly healing and spirituality. He is active in the New Orleans gay HIV community, having served on the NO-AIDS task force and the board of the New Orleans Alliance of Pride. With Trinity Episcopal Church, Holt works in community outreach and is a member of Trinity Counseling and Training Center board. His creative work is forthcoming in *A&U, Diverse Voices Quarterly, Grey Sparrow*, and *RiverSedge*. Professional writings have appeared in numerous medical journals; he co-authored a book on integrated care for the Catholic Health Association. As a playwright, three of his plays, *Obsession, Teddy's Nightmare* and *Aurora Borealis*, have been produced at the Marigny Theatre in New Orleans.

At the time she wrote "Still," **Janet Howey** was working in an AIDS hospice in Portland, Oregon. Today she divides her time between Todos Santos and San Miguel de Allende, Mexico, and writes occasionally.

Joe Jiménez lives in San Antonio, Texas. His work has appeared in *Mariposas: New Queer Latino Poetry, Borderlands Texas Poetry Review, elimae, Saltwater Quarterly* and is forthcoming in *Caper Literary Journal*. The short film *El Abuelo [1983]*, commissioned as part of London's 2008 Fashion in Film Festival, is based on Jiménez's affinity for ironing. Jiménez was recently graduated from Antioch University-Los Angeles's MFA in Creative Writing program.

Arnold Johnston lives in Kalamazoo, MI. His plays, and others written with his wife, Deborah Ann Percy, have won awards, production, and publication across the country. His poetry, fiction, nonfiction, and translations appear widely in literary journals and anthologies. His books include *Sonnets: Signs and Portents, What the Earth Taught Us, The Witching Voice: A Play About Robert Burns, Of Earth and Darkness: The Novels of William Golding,* and *The Witching Voice: A Novel from the Life of Robert Burns*. His Jacques Brel translations have appeared in musical revues nationwide (including the acclaimed *Jacques Brel's Lonesome Losers of the Night*), and on his CD, *Jacques Brel: I'm Here!* His singable translation of Schubert's *Winterreise* premiered in 2010, and his lyrics for songs by Gabriel Fauré appear on the CD *By the Riverbank*. Johnston is a member of the Dramatists Guild, the Playwrights' Center, and the American Literary Translators Association.

Since 1978, **George Koschel** has had short stories, poetry, and essays published in a number of small independent literary journals, college affiliated, journals, and on-line magazines. Some of these include *A&U, Coe Review, Ellipsis, glbtq online encyclopedia, Nebo, New Laurel Review,* and *RFD*. Currently he also works as an assistant editor for *New Laurel Review*. Since 1992, he has been a volunteer at NOAIDS, doing HIV test counseling.

Dean Kostos's collection *This Is Not a Skyscraper* won the Benjamin Saltman Poetry Award, selected by Mark Doty. Kostos's other books include: *Rivering, Last Supper of the Senses, The Sentence That Ends with a Comma,* and *Celestial Rust*. He coedited *Mama's Boy: Gay Men Write about Their Mothers* and edited *Pomegranate Seeds: An Anthology of Greek-American Poetry*. His work has appeared in *Barrow Street, Boulevard, Chelsea, The Cincinnati Re-*

view, Southwest Review, Stand Magazine, Western Humanities Review, on Oprah Winfrey's website Oxygen.com, and elsewhere. His literary criticism has appeared on the Harvard UP website. He has taught at The City University of New York and The Gallatin School of New York University.

Lambda Literary Award-winning poet **Michael Lassell** is the author of several volumes of poetry, including *Poems for Lost and Unlost Boys, Decade Dance,* and *A Flame for the Touch That Matters.* He has also written several books on interior design and four about the making of Disney's Broadway shows. In addition, he has edited several volumes of LGBT poetry, fiction, and nonfiction. He lives in New York City.

Chip Livingston is the author of the short story and essay collection, *Naming Ceremony* (Lethe Press); two poetry collections, *Crow-Blue, Crow-Black* (NYQ Books) and *Museum of False Starts* (Gival Press); and the chapbook, *Alarum* (Other Rooms Press). Recent poems, essays, and stories appear in *Court Green, Potomac Review, Cimarron Review, The Florida Review, Ploughshares, Hinchas de Poesia,* and on the Poetry Foundation website. Chip lives in Denver, Colorado, and teaches in the low-res MFA program at Institute of American Indian Arts. Visit www.chiplivingston.com.

Craig Lucas is author of the plays *Missing Persons, Reckless, Blue Window, Prelude to a Kiss, God's Heart, The Dying Gaul, Stranger, Small Tragedy, The Singing Forest, Prayer for My Enemy* and *The Lying Lesson.* Screenplays include *Blue Window, Longtime Companion, Prelude to a Kiss, Reckless, The Secret Lives of Dentists* and *The Dying Gaul.* His musical works include *Three Postcards* (music & lyrics by Craig Carnelia); *The Light in the Piazza* (music & lyrics by Adam Guettel); the opera *Orpheus in Love* (music by Gerald Busby); *King Kong* (the musical premiering in Melbourne, Australia in June of this year); the opera *Two Boys* (music by Nico Muhly, premiering at the Met in December of this year); and the scenario for Prokofiev's ballet *Cinderella,* choreographed by Christopher Wheeldon. He has provided new English-language adaptations of Strindberg's *Miss Julie,* Chekhov's *Three Sisters* and *Uncle Vanya* and Brecht's *Galileo.* His directorial work includes the movies *The*

Dying Gaul and *Birds of America*, the world premiere of *The Light in the Piazza*, the world premiere of Harry Kondoleon's final play, *Saved or Destroyed*, the New York premiere of Kondoleon's *Play Yourself* as well as his own play (co-authored with David Schulner) *This Thing of Darkness*. Lucas received the Excellence in Literature Award from the American Academy of Arts and Letters.

Raymond Luczak is the author and editor of 16 books, including five poetry collections such as *Mute* (A Midsummer Night's Press) and *How to Kill Poetry* (Sibling Rivalry Press). He is the editor of the literary fiction journal *Jonathan*. Even though he lives in Minneapolis, MN, you can find him online at www.raymondluczak.com.

Mary Jo Mahoney worked as registered nurse in New York City and Houston while a graduate student at Sarah Lawrence College (1991) and the University of Houston (1999). Her writing appears in many journals including *The Kenyon Review, Prairie Schooner, The Paris Review, DoubleTake, A&U, Northwest Review, Teachers & Writers Magazine, PoemMemoirStory* and *The Nation*. She is the recipient of numerous writing awards, including fellowships from the National Endowment of the Arts and the National Endowment of the Humanities. She is a reader of memoir submissions for the *American Journal of Nursing* and an associate professor of English in New York.

Paula Martinac is the author of three published novels, including the Lambda Literary Award-winning *Out of Time*. She has also published three nonfiction books on lesbian and gay culture and politics, and numerous articles, essays and short stories. Her plays have had productions with Pittsburgh Playwrights Theatre Company, Manhattan Theatre Source, Ganymede Arts Festival, the Pittsburgh New Works Festival, Rainbow Players Theater Company, No Name Players, and Womenscene. She works as a health writer and educator in Charlotte, NC.

Montgomery Maxton was born in 1980 in Cincinnati, Ohio where he began writing poetry at age sixteen. A noted photographer as well, his work appears repeatedly in *National Geographic Magazine*. His first collection, *This Beautiful Bizarre*, was published in

2010 by Moon Ice Press. His short novel, *The Manhattan Man*, and his second poetry collection, *Champage Requiem*, are forthcoming. He lives in Philadelphia with his partner where he is working on his first novel.

Tobias Maxwell is the author of two novels, *The Sex and Dope Show Saga* and *Thomas*; two memoirs, *1983: The Unknown Season*, and *1977, The Year of Leaving Monsieur*; and a poetry collection, *Homogium*. His articles have appeared in *Balita* and *Mom Guess What* newspapers, *LA Edge*, *New Century* and the *California Therapist* magazines

Gary R. McClain, PhD, is a therapist and educator in New York City. He specializes in working with clients who are facing chronic health conditions and maintains the website, JustGotDiagnosed. com. He has published short stories, as well as non-fiction articles and books with a body-mind-spirit approach, and writes a column on mental health issues in *HIV Plus* Magazine. "Key West in the Last Days" is adapted from a chapter in an unpublished novel.

Patricia McFarland was a manager in a San Francisco telephone company operator services office during 1982 and 1983. Her daughter Emily is 31 years old.

Arlene McKanic is a freelance writer who lives in Queens, New York and Blair, South Carolina. She has been published in *The Root*, *Obsidian III*, *The Maryland Review*, the *MacGuffin*, *American Theater*, *ArtNews*, *Poets & Writers*, *Caribbean Life*, *South Carolina Magazine*, *Belletrista*, *The Rumpus*, *Ms.*, and others.

c m mclamb is a performing and literary artist residing in NYC. He received his Bachelor of the Arts degree from Susquehanna University, which is where he began his formal artistic and literary training. McLamb's poems have appeared in *A&U*, *Pyrta Journal* and *The Fine Line*. He is an active member of GMHC, God's Love We Deliver, and other charitable volunteer organizations.

John Medeiros is a writer living in Minneapolis, Minnesota. His latest book is the poetry collection *couplets for a shrinking world*.

His work has appeared in publications, including *Collective Brightness; Sport Literate, Water~Stone Review; Gulf Coast; Talking Stick; Willow Springs; other words: a writer's reader; Gents, Badboys and Barbarians; Evergreen Chronicles; Hot Metal Press; Big Toe Review; Swell* and *Christopher Street*. He is the recipient of two Minnesota State Arts Board grants; a Jerome Foundation Grant for Emerging Writers; Gulf Coast's First Place Nonfiction Award; and the AWP Intro Journals Project Award. He received an MFA from Hamline University, in St. Paul, Minnesota, and his work has been nominated for a Pushcart Prize, and as a Notable Essay in Best American Essays of 2006. He is the co-curator of *Queer Voices: An LGBT Reading Series*, a reading series for queer writers sponsored by Intermedia Arts. Visit www.jmedeiros.net.

David Messineo is the Publisher of *Sensations Magazine* (www.sensationsmag.com), a rare three-consecutive-year winner in the national American Literary Magazine Awards, and an independent literary magazine operating without government grant funding or university affiliation for 28 years. He is the author of eight published poetry collections, copies of which sometimes come up for purchase at www.bookfinder.com. His eighth collection, *Historiopticon*, was published in 2014.

Ron Mohring lives in Lewisburg, Pennsylvania, where he runs Seven Kitchens Press. His book, *Survivable World,* won the Washington Prize and was a finalist for the Publishing Triangle's Thom Gunn Award in Poetry.

Michael Montlack is the author of the poetry collection *Cool Limbo* (New York Quarterly Books) and the editor of the Lambda-nominated essay anthology *My Diva: 65 Gay Men on the Women Who Inspire Them* (University of Wisconsin). He won the 2013 Gival Press Oscar Wilde Award. He splits his time between San Francisco, where he teaches at Berkeley College, and New York City. Currently he is at work on his first novel.

Mark Inglis Moody was born September 22nd, 1953 in Los Angeles, California. He received his Bachelor of Arts in English and Philosophy in 1975 from California Lutheran University and a Master of Social Work in 1992 from San Francisco State University. Early in the 1990s, Mark was diagnosed with Hodgkin's lymphoma and AIDS. To cope with his diseases he began to write. While preparing to undergo a stem cell transplant, he met his partner Dennis Puccini. Mark retired on disability in 1999 and in 2001 they relocated to Baltimore. In 2004 Mark returned to work. Sadly, Dennis succumbed to AIDS in 2006. Mark was again forced to retire on disability in 2010 when his lymphoma returned. Mark passed away September 9th, 2011. His amazing sense of humor and wit endeared him to all who crossed his path in life. He was loved dearly and will be missed greatly.

In 2011, RAW ArT PRESS published **Janell Moon**'s memoir, *Salt and Paper: Sixty Five Candles*, as winner of their 2010 Experimental Poetry Prize. She was appointed poet laureate of her San Francisco bayside city, Emeryville, CA, for 2011–2012. She is the author of eleven books including four poetry volumes. She works as a writing coach and counselor. Visit www.janellmoon.com.

Jim Nawrocki's poetry recently appeared in the anthology, *The Place That Inhabits Us: Poems of the San Francisco Bay Watershed* (Sixteen Rivers Press). It has also appeared in *Kyoto Journal*, *Poetry*, *Chroma Journal*, *modern words*, and the website poetry daily. com. He writes regularly for *the Gay & Lesbian Review Worldwide*.

Chael Needle is Managing Editor of *A&U*. He holds an MFA in Writing, Literature and Publishing from Emerson College in Boston, Massachusetts, and a PhD in Writing, Teaching and Criticism from the University at Albany, State University of New York. His poetry has been published in *Owen Wister Review*, *bottle rockets*, *Lilliput Review*, and *The Adirondack Review*, and his fiction has appeared in *Blue Fifth Review: Blue Five Notebook Series*. He is currently Adjunct Assistant Professor in the English department at Medgar Evers College, the City University of New York, where he helps organize the school's AIDS Awareness Week every year. He lives with his partner, Timothy, and their dog, Titus, in Queens, New York.

Arthur Nersesian is author of ten books including his first novel, *The Fuck Up*, and his last book, *Mesopotamia*. Visit www.ArthurNersesian.com

Lesléa Newman is the author of over sixty books for readers of all ages including the poetry collections, *Still Life with Buddy, Nobody's Mother*, and *Signs of Love*; the novel, *The Reluctant Daughter*; and the children's book, *Heather Has Two Mommies*. Her literary awards include poetry fellowships from the National Endowment for the Arts and the Massachusetts Artists Fellowship Foundation. A past poet laureate of Northampton, MA, she is currently a faculty member of Spalding University's brief-residency MFA in Writing program. Her newest poetry collections are *October Mourning: A Song for Matthew Shepard* (novel-in-verse) and *I Carry My Mother*.

Mark O'Donnell received the 2003 Tony Award for *Hairspray* and received a 2008 Tony nomination for *Cry-Baby*. His plays include *That's It, Folks!; Fables for Friends; The Nice and the Nasty; Strangers on Earth; Vertigo Park* and the musical *Tots in Tinseltown*. He collaborated with Bill Irwin on an adaptation of Moliere's *Scapin* and co-authored a translation of Feydeau's *A Flea in Her Ear*. He also adapted Feydeau's *Private Fittings* for the La Jolla Playhouse and a symphonic version of *Pyramus and Thisbe* for the Kennedy Center. He published two collections of comic stories *Elementary Education* and *Vertigo Park and Other Tales* (both from Knopf) as well as two novels, *Getting Over Homer* and *Let Nothing You Dismay* (both in Vintage paperback). His humor, cartoons and poetry appeared in *The New Yorker, The New York Times, The Atlantic* and *Esquire*. He received a Guggenheim Fellowship and the George S. Kaufman Award. He died in 2012.

Tom O'Leary is an award-winning playwright, screenwriter and humor writer. O'Leary wrote the screenplay for the short film *Where We Began*, which won a 2007 PlanetOut Short Movie Award and tied for the PlanetOut Audience Choice Award. *Nourishment*, another short film written by O'Leary, has played around the world at over 30 film festivals. With writer Cathy Crimmins, O'Leary co-authored the best-selling humor book *The Gay Man's Guide to Heterosexuality*. His play *David* won the Provincetown Theater Company Best New Play of 1998. David received its world premiere at the Theater on the Square in Indianapolis where it played to sold out houses. *Breath*, an evening of one-acts by O'Leary, was performed in both New York City and Los Angeles. His play *The Negative*

Room won the Best New Play Award at the Towngate Theater in 1994 and played to sold out audiences in Provincetown, MA.

Robert Vazquez-Pacheco is a native Nuyorican gay writer, poet and visual artist currently residing in Brooklyn. His work has been published in various anthologies. Currently he is working on a book of short stories.

Since 1964, **Robert Patrick** has had thousands of productions of dozens of plays on six continents from the first Off-Off Broadway theatre, the Caffe Cino, to the West End and Broadway. He traveled for ten years to over a thousand high schools and high school festivals for The International Thespians Society. Two consecutive Manhattan Borough presidents declared weekends honoring his *Blue Is for Boys*, the first play about gay teenagers. He has published plays, poems, columns, a novel, *Temple Slave*, and an autobiography, *Film Moi or Narcissus in the Dark*.

Deborah Ann Percy's short fiction collections are *Cool Front: Stories from Lake Michigan* (2010) and *Invisible Traffic* (2014). Her plays, and those written with her husband, Arnold Johnston, have won awards, publication, and production nationwide. Their books include the plays *Beyond Sex, Rasputin in New York,* and (with Dona Roşu) translations of Romanian playwright Hristache Popescu's *Epilogue, Night of the Passions,* and *Sons of Cain.* Their edited anthology *The Art of the One-Act* appeared in 2007 from New Issues Press, and a collection of their own one-acts, *Duets: Love Is Strange,* appeared in 2008. Many of their half-hour radio dramas have been broadcast on Kalamazoo's NPR-affiliate WMUK-FM as part of All Ears Theatre. For several years they served as Arts and Entertainment columnists for the national journal Phi Kappa Phi Forum. Percy is a member of the Dramatists Guild, the Playwrights' Center, and the American Literary Translators Association.

Virginia Pye's debut novel, *River of Dust,* now out in paperback, was chosen as an Indie Next Pick and is a current Finalist for the 2014 Virginia Literary Award in Fiction. Annie Dillard called it "a strong, beautiful, deep book," and Robert Olen Bulter said it is "a strong work by a splendid writer." Her short stories have appeared in literary magazines, including *The North American Review*, *The Tampa Review*, *The Baltimore Review*, *Failbetter*, and online at She-books. Her essays and interviews can be found at *The New York Times* Opinionator blog, "The Rumpus," Huffington Post, The Nervous Breakdown and elsewhere. For a complete list of her publications, please visit her website: www.virginiapye.com.

A Mississippi native, **Treasure Shields Redmond** is a St. Louis based poet, performer and educator. She has published poetry in such notable anthologies as *Bum Rush the Page: A Def Poetry Jam, Breaking Ground: A Reader Celebrating Cave Canem's First Decade*; and in journals that include *Sou'wester* and *The African American Review*. Treasure has also served as a distinguished panelist at the Gwendolyn Brooks Writer's Conference on Black Literature and Creative Writing. She has received a fellowship to the Fine Arts Works Center, and has been an invited visiting scholar with the Educational Testing Service in Princeton, New Jersey. Treasure is a Cave Canem fellow and has received an MFA from the University of Memphis. Presently, she divides her time between being an assistant professor of English at Southwestern Illinois College, and doctoral studies at Indiana University of Pennsylvania.

Steven Riel is the author of three chapbooks of poetry: *How to Dream*, *The Spirit Can Crest*, and most recently, *Postcard from P-town*, which was selected as runner-up for the inaugural Robin Becker Chapbook Prize and published in 2009 by Seven Kitchens Press. His poetry collection, *Fellow Odd Fellow*, was published in 2014. In 2005, Christopher Bursk named him the Robert Fraser Distinguished Visiting Poet at Bucks County (PA) Community College. His poems have appeared in several anthologies and in numerous periodicals, including *The Minnesota Review, International Poetry Review*, and *Evening Street Review*. He served as poetry editor of *RFD* between 1987 and 1995. He received the MFA in Poetry in 2008 from New England College, where he was awarded a Joel Oppenheimer Scholarship. In 1992, he received a grant from the Massachusetts Cultural Council. One of his poems was selected by Denise Levertov as runner-up for the Grolier Poetry Peace Prize in 1987.

Jerry Rosco is a New Yorker and the author of *Glenway Wescott Personally*, the biography of the 20s expatriate novelist. The book of late journals, *A Heaven of Words*, won a 2014 Lambda Literary Award. He has also edited two volumes of Wescott journals. When this story first published, the well-known rock musician Tomata du Plenty, who would himself succumb to AIDS, sent a postcard with only one sentence: "Thank you for your love story."

Assotto Saint (born Yves Lubin) was a Haitian-born poet, playwright, and activist whose explicitly black themes made him one of the most important literary voices in the burgeoning gay literary movement of the late twentieth century. To his fellow Haitians, who had also directly experienced the ugliness of the François Duvalier era, he offered a spiritual sanctuary, as "a grand, tall queen" who could be both big brother and mother. In addition to his work as a writer, Saint was a passionate advocate for the writings of others in his community, creating his own Galiens Press, and editing *The Road Before Us: 100 Gay Black Poets*. During his lifetime, he was able to publish two collections of his own writing, *Stations* and *Wishing for Wings*. Honoring him for their annual literary award, Lambda Literary Foundation described Saint as "one of the fiercest spirits ever to grace the planet." He died at the age of thirty-six.

Wayne Scheer has been nominated for four Pushcart Prizes and a Best of the Net. He's published hundreds of short stories, essays and poems, including *Revealing Moments*, a collection of flash stories, published by Thumbscrews Press. He lives in Atlanta.

Peter Schmitt is the author of five collections of poems, including *Renewing the Vows* (David Robert Books). His work has appeared in many of the country's leading journals, such as *The Hudson Review*, *The Nation*, *The Paris Review*, *Poetry*, and *The Southern Review*. He teaches creative writing and literature in Miami, Florida.

Aaron Shurin is the author of eleven books of poetry and prose, including the essay collections *Unbound: A book of AIDS*, and *King of Shadows*, and a new poetry collection, *Citizen*.

Lester Strong is Special Projects Editor for *A&U*. He is a regular contributor to *The Gay & Lesbian Review*, and his writings on the visual, written, and performing arts, as well as on historical subjects, have appeared in publications across the country, including

Out magazine, the New Mexico Historical Review, South Dakota Review, International Journal of Sexuality and Gender Studies, and *the Journal of Homosexuality.* He lives in New York City with his husband Dave.

Jennifer Su is a writer residing in the San Francisco East Bay Area. She writes mostly at her desk, sometimes in bed. She is healthy, strong, and postive for nearly twenty years. She is married with one son and has big plans for the future.

Laurie Novick Sylla has been involved with HIV work since 1982. She was the Co-Founding Executive Director of the AIDS Council of Northeastern New York and a Co-Founding Board Member of the Community Research Initiative of New England. She has also served as the Advocacy Manager at the AIDS ACTION Committee of Massachusetts, Executive Director of the HIV Action Initiative in Hartford, CT, Director of the Connecticut AIDS Education and Training Center based at the Yale School of Nursing, and as Director of International and Community Research at the Yale AIDS Program at the Yale School of Medicine. She has been an outspoken advocate for microbicides, and volunteered as a Steering Committee Member and Site Coordinator for the Global Campaign for Microbicides and furthered research in this area as a Co-Principal Investigator on microbicide and female condom acceptability trials. Ms. Sylla is co-author of *HIV Care: A Handbook for Providers* (Sage Publications). She has won numerous awards for her work in the epidemic. She currently lives in Seattle, WA, where she serves on the community advisory boards of defeatHIV and the Martin Delaney Research Collaboratory.

Rachel S. Thomas-Medwid's fiction has been published in *10,000 Tons of Black Ink, Farmhouse Magazine, Freight Train Magazine, In Posse, Literal Latte,* and *A&U.* Along with receiving the Alice Brandt Deeds Prize for Excellence in Creative Writing, a few of her writing honors include placing in nine screenplay competitions, the Writer's Digest Competition, the Lorian Hemingway Short Story Competition, the Literal Latte Contest, and the National John Steinbeck Competition. As news editor of the American Meteorological

Society's monthly magazine, Rachel both edits and writes about the hot topic of global warming. She lives outside of Boston with her husband and three young children.

After ten years as a filmmaker, **Randi Triant** received her MFA in writing and literature from Bennington College. Her nonfiction and fiction have appeared in several magazines and literary journals. "The Memorial" appeared in the anthology *Fingernails Across the Chalkboard: Poetry and Prose on HIV/AIDS From the Black Diaspora*. Ms. Triant has taught creative writing at Emerson College and Boston College.

Angela Lam Turpin is the author of three novels: *Out of Balance, Legs,* and *Blood Moon Rising.* She lives and writes in Northern California with her family.

Mary Kathryn Vernon began writing when she was 35. Since then, she has taken writing courses at local colleges and universities and has published poetry, memoir, and non-fiction. In 2009 she moved from San Diego, CA, to Wichita, KS, where she lives in her 1921 bungalow with her cats and writes short stories, poems, and letters to the editor.

Bruce Ward's play *Lazarus Syndrome* opened the 2007/2008 season at Theater Alliance in Washington, D.C., and was the recipient of the 2007 2nd place VSA arts/Jean Kennedy Smith award, presented at the Kennedy Center. A four-page article on the play appeared in *A&U* in 2008. Bruce has performed his acclaimed solo show, *Decade: Life in the '80s* across the U.S., including at the NYC International Fringe Festival and in residence with the N.Y. Theater Festival at Dartmouth College. Other plays have been produced across the U.S. and *Paint By Numbers* was highlighted in the "Trends" column of *American Theatre* magazine. Three of his ten-minute plays have been produced by the Boston Theater Marathon, and two have been published in anthologies by Bakers Plays. Bruce has received an M.F.A. in Creative Writing from Boston University (playwriting) and The New School (nonfiction). He has thrice been a Fellow at the Virginia Center for Creative Arts.

Ezekiel Weaver is a former playwright who now writes murder mysteries. He lives in Chicago with his partner, three cats and a dog. His novels include *Dead Words* and *Heidi on the Half Shell*. Visit www.ezekielweaver.com.

Richard Willett is the author of the plays *Triptych, Random Harvest, The Flid Show,* and *9/10,* among others, which have been presented off-off-Broadway and at theaters across the country. Honors include an Edward F. Albee Foundation Fellowship and a Tennessee Williams Scholarship. In January of 2008, his play *Tiny Bubbles* was chosen Best New American Play at the Firehouse Theatre Festival in Richmond, Virginia; earlier it was twice short-listed for the Public Theater's New Work Now! festival, and it will be premiered off-off-Broadway in 2012. In 2010, his screenplay of *9/10* was a semifinalist in two categories at the Austin Film Festival Screenplay Competition, and in 2011 it was designated a semifinalist for the Academy of Motion Picture Arts and Sciences' Nicholl Fellowships. His plays *Triptych, 2B,* and *The Flid Show* have all been published by United Stages. *Boys Will Be Boys* has twice been produced off-off-Broadway.

Phillip Brian Williams is a Chicago, Illinois native. Recently, he won BLOOM'S inaugural chapbook competition in poetry for his manuscript *BRUISED GOSPELS.* His work has appeared or is forthcoming in *Callaloo, Sou'wester, Painted Bride Quarterly, Boxcar Poetry Review* and others. Phillip is currently poetry editor of *Vinyl Poetry* and has recently completed a year with AmeriCorps' AIDS United Program in Chicago, IL.

Chuck Willman is basically a self-taught writer/poet who has been fortunate to have poems published in *Assaracus* (Sibling Rivalry Press), the anthology *Nurturing Paws* (Whispering Angel Books), *A&U,* and *Christopher Street* magazine. Nearly a dozen of his erotic short stories have been published under the pseudonym Ethan Cox in *FirstHand, Guys,* and *Manscape* magazines. His essays about sex and living with HIV/AIDS have appeared in *FirstHand* magazine under his real name. Chuck is a "long-term PWA" living a quiet life with his partner of over two decades, Gerry, and their beloved dog, Buddy, in the Las Vegas area. Contact him at chuckpoz2@gmail.com.

Ed Wolf's writing has appeared in numerous publications, including *Fray, Queer and Catholic, Beyond Definition: New Writing from Gay and Lesbian San Francisco, A&U, Rebel Yell: Gay Men of the South Short Story Anthology Series, Coracle Poetry Magazine, Poetry Motel, Crack Magazine, Prentice Hall's Discovering Literature, Christopher Street, The James White Review* and the forthcoming anthology, *Crooked Letter I: Coming Out in the South.* He has been nominated for the Pushcart Prize and was named Outstanding National HIV Prevention Educator of 2005 by thebody.com. He is also currently featured in the AIDS documentary, *We Were Here.* Visit www.EdWolf.net.

Emanuel Xavier is the author of the novel *Christ Like*, and the poetry collections, *If Jesus Were Gay & other poems* and *Nefarious*, among others. He was proclaimed a GLBT Icon by the Equality Forum in 2010 and is recipient of the Marsha A. Gomez Cultural Heritage Award, a New York City Council Citation, and a World Pride Award. He works for Random House and is the editor of *Me No Habla With Acento: Contemporary Latino Poetry* published by El Museo del Barrio in collaboration with Rebel Satori Press.

"Massage" is an excerpt of **Bonnie ZoBell**'s novel-in-progress, *Animal Voices*, which won the Capricorn Novel Award. Her linked collection, *What Happened Here*, was published by Press 53 in May 2014, and her fiction chapbook, *The Whack-Job Girls*, was published by Monkey Puzzle Press in March 2013. She received a NEA fellowship in fiction and a PEN Syndicated Fiction Award, has an MFA from Columbia University, and currently teaches at San Diego Mesa College. Visit her at www.bonniezobell.com.

Rob Zukowski is an activist, writer, licensed massage therapist, and photographer in New York City. He has worked professionally and personally in the LGBT community and in the arts since 1992.

A NOTE ON THE COVER ART

Kenny Scharf, *Darkness Bleeds*, 1990, oil, acrylic, and silkscreen ink on canvas, 91½ by 115½ inches

Along with his friend Keith Haring, Kenny Scharf was a key figure in the East Village art scene of the 1980s. Known for his self-described "pop surrealism," which often combines cartoon imagery and bright colors, Scharf works in a wide range of media, from painting and printmaking to sculpture and animation. He has exhibited widely, including the Salvador Dali Museum, St. Petersburg; Bienalle de Sao Paolo, Brazil; Tony Shafrazi Gallery and Queens Museum of Art, New York, Museum of Contemporary Art, Monterrey; Waddington Gallery, London; and the Fort. Lauderdale Museum of Art. He is represented by Paul Kasmin Gallery. Scharf currently resides in Los Angeles. Visit www.kennyscharf.com.